The Early Childhood & Kindergarten Calendar

(Monthly Teaching Resources From The Preschool/Kindergarten Papers)

by
Sherrill B. Flora

Publishers
T.S. Denison & Company, Inc.
Minneapolis, Minnesota 55431

Dedication
To my grandfather, Robert St. Clair – the writer!
To my other grandfather, Lawrence Brings – the publisher!

Standard Book Number: 513-02232-5
The Early Childhood & Kindergarten Calendar
Copyright © 1994 by T.S. Denison & Company, Inc.
9601 Newton Avenue South
Minneapolis, Minnesota 55431

Printed in the USA

INTRODUCTION

The Early Childhood & Kindergarten Calendar consists of the best material found in the monthly early childhood publication, *The Preschool & Kindergarten Papers.* The years included in this book are September 1989 through Summer 1993. All the material has been reorganized and bound into book form to provide early childhood and kindergarten teachers with a wealth of ideas to be used year after year.

The Early Childhood & Kindergarten Calendar offers teachers instructional units, organized by the month and subject areas. The practical activities and timeless teaching suggestions can be used to enrich or supplement a pre-existing curriculum program. The content has been tried, tested, validated as age-appropriate, and has been well-received by early childhood educators. *The Early Childhood & Kindergarten Calendar* is a book that all early childhood and kindergarten programs will want in their libraries and teaching resource centers.

The Early Childhood & Kindergarten Calendar can provide teachers with creative ideas all year long. For each of the nine school months and a special summer section, you will find:

- Fine Motor/Art Activities
- Gross Motor/Movement Activities
- Language Activities
- Stories
- Bulletin Boards/Wall Displays
- Experiential Activities
- Music Activities
- Finger Plays/Poetry
- Reproducible Activities

CONTENTS

September

THE SHADOWY, SHADY TREE

From the book, Quiet Times, by Louise Binder Scott
Copyright by T.S. Denison & Co., Inc.
(This is a wonderful story to read before rest time.)

Once there was a sleepy, sleepy place under a shadowy, shady tree. In that sleepy, sleepy place lay a small brown puppy. The puppy stood up. *(The children stand up.)* She stretched and yawned and stretched and yawned some more. *(Children stretch and yawn.)* Then she went to look for something to nibble and gnaw. She took a dogbone to her doghouse, but she couldn't keep her eyes open. So she went back to the shadowy, shady tree and went to sleep. *(Children sit down and clasp their hands beside their head.)*

Once there was a furry, purry, little gray ball of a kitten. He said in a wee sleepy voice, "Oh, dear! I am so sleepy." So he yawned and yawned and yawned. *(Children yawn.)* He found a basket on the back porch and climbed inside, but he couldn't fall asleep. So he went to the shadowy, shady tree and under it he curled up like kittens do, and went to sleep. *(Children pretend to sleep.)*

There was a baby chick who looked for something to eat. The mother hen knew that her baby chick was hungry, so she found some yellow meal for him. She knew that her baby chick was also tired, so she led him to the shadowy, shady tree and spread out her warm feathers so that he could creep under them. And he went to sleep. *(Children pretend to sleep.)*

There was a duckling, quack, quack, quack.
She had soft feathers on her back.
She was tired of swimming and everything,
So she put her head beneath her wing.   *(Children put arm over head.)*
And there under the shadowy, shady tree,
She slept until it was half past three.

A butterfly, blue, green, and red,
Sat with her wings above her head,   *(Children raise arms over head.)*
On a branch of the shadowy, shady tree,
Oh, what a sleepy place to be!

The children in the neighborhood saw all those marvelous sleepy animals. The children decided to lay down on their backs under the shadowy, shady tree, just like you are lying now in your very own quiet, sleepy place. *(Children lie down.)* And what do think the boys and girls did under that shadowy, shady tree?

This story can be told in installments. The children may wish to add other animals.

BEST FRIENDS

From the book, Telling Stories Together, by Linda Haver
Copyright by T.S. Denison & Co., Inc.

When telling this story, pause each time you come to the **bold *italicized*** question, "Will you be my friend?" then point to the children and have them say their line.

Before you present the story, as a group, practice saying, "Will you be my friend?"

Benny Bear and Barbara Bear were best friends. They played together every day. When the other animal children in the woods would come around and want to play, Benny and Barbara would tell them, "bears that are best friends only play with each other and no one else."

Everything was fine until Barbara Bear got the flu and had to spend a whole week in bed. The first day Barbara was sick, Benny spent all day alone, playing with his toys. By the second day Benny was lonely and he wished he had another friend to play with.

Benny decided to go out and look for someone to be his friend.

Benny had not walked very far when he met Randy Raccoon. Benny smiled at Randy and said . . . *"will you be my friend?"* But Randy Raccoon kept right on walking.

A little farther down the road Benny saw Sandy Squirrel. Benny smiled at Sandy and said . . . *"will you be my friend?"* But Sandy just smiled back and shook her head.

Soon Benny ran into Danny Deer. Benny smiled at Danny and said . . . *"will you be my friend?"* Danny Deer just hurried by and went down the road.

Ricky Rabbit came hopping along. When Benny saw Ricky, he smiled and said . . . *"will you be my friend?"* But Ricky kept right on hopping.

Next Benny met Gary Groundhog along the road. Benny smiled at Gary and said . . . *"will you be my friend?"* Gary Groundhog looked at the ground and kept right on walking.

By this time Benny was tired of saying . . . *"will you be my friend?"* So he turned around and sadly started walking back home. As he walked, Benny started thinking about Randy Raccoon, Sandy Squirrel, Danny Deer, Ricky Rabbit and Gary Groundhog. At first Benny was mad that none of the animal children would be his friend, but then he remembered how he and Barbara would never let any of the animal children play with them. I guess I just got what I deserved thought Benny.

Just then Benny heard someone say . . . *"will you be my friend?"* He turned around and saw Randy Raccoon, Sandy Squirrel, Danny Deer, Ricky Rabbit and Gary Groundhog all standing by a tree. They all looked at Benny and said again . . . *"will you be my friend?"* Benny was so happy he shouted "yes!" And when Barbara gets well we can all be best friends!

Turn into a flannel board story with the patterns found on pages 9 & 10.

Patterns for the story "Best Friends," found on pages 7 & 8.

Barbara Bear

Benny Bear

Randy Raccoon

Sandy Squirrel

Patterns for the story "Best Friends," found on pages 7 & 8.

Ricky Rabbit

Danny Deer

Gary Groundhog

SEPTEMBER LITERATURE RESOURCES

LITERATURE RESOURCES FOR THE THEME OF FRIENDSHIP

Reading about friendships between children, between animals, and between animals and children will help develop an understanding of the importance of friendships and what it means to be a friend. These are wonderful stories for beginning the school year.

DO YOU WANT TO BE MY FRIEND? – Eric Carle (Crowell, 1971)

Story Summary – This wordless book holds a surprise at each turn of the page as a little mouse looks for a friend. He follows a tail and then another and another until he finally finds a (mouse) friend. Part of a long green snake's tail winds across the bottom of the page.

Pre-Reading Activity – Ask the children, "Do you think animals have friends?" Show animal pictures to the children one at a time and ask "Who might play with this animal?" Ask the children to explain their answers.

Post-Reading Activity – Using animal pictures or stuffed classroom animals, review the story with the children and then go on an animal hunt to see how many story animals they can find.

IRA SLEEPS OVER – Bernard Wabe (Houghton Mifflin, 1972)

Story Summary – After being invited to a friend's house, Ira has a unique overnight adventure. While packing, his sister asks him if he is going to take his teddy bear. Ira worries, should I? Can I sleep without my teddy bear? He and Reggie have a great time, but when they get ready for bed, Ira gets a happy surprise!

Pre-Reading Activity – Draw a picture of your favorite stuffed animal. Have the children share their pictures with the rest of the class and tell why their stuffed animal is so special.

Post-Reading Activity – Using the pattern on page 13, copy the pattern onto heavy brown construction paper (each child will need two). Staple the two edges together, leaving one side open. Tear newspaper into tiny strips and stuff the bear. Finish stapling.

MAY I BRING A FRIEND? – Beatrice Schenk De Regniers (Atheneum, 1974)

Story Summary – In this rhyming story that covers the days of the week, a little girl is invited to have tea with the King and Queen. Being told she can bring a friend sets off a chain of events that ends up with the tea party at the city zoo.

Pre-Reading Activity – Discuss and help the children learn the days of the week. Count together the days of the week, and then the days of the current month - 4 Sundays, 5 Mondays.

Post-Reading Activity – First have the children make crowns out of construction paper and glitter. Set up a tea party in your classroom. Have the children wear their crowns and bring an animal to the party.

PLAY WITH ME – Marie Hall Ets (Viking, 1955)

Story Summary – A little girl goes into the meadow looking for a playmate and chases after a grasshopper, a frog, a turtle, a chipmunk, a blue jay, a rabbit, and a snake, but they all run away. When she sits down by the pond, not making a sound, the animals slowly come back and join her.

Pre-Reading Activity – Make 3" x 5" cards with a picture of each animal from the story. Show the children the cards and ask the children to name the animals. Ask the children to demonstrate how they think each animal moves. Ask the children where they think each animal might live.

Post-Reading Activity – Using the cards that you have made from the pre-reading activity, punch a hole in each of the top corners. String yarn through the hole so that each card can be worn as a necklace. Let the children dramatize the story wearing the animal cards as story props.

FROG AND TOAD ARE FRIENDS – Arnold Lobel (Harper, 1971)

Story Summary – A collection of five short stories about the friendship of Frog and Toad. Toad likes the flowers that grow in Frog's garden. Frog likes the chocolate chip cookies Toad baked. They do things together, solve problems, share and have fun.

Pre-Reading Activity – Make a classroom chart of a frog and a toad. Ask the children to tell you the difference between a frog and a toad. (Frog: has smooth skin, lives in water or wet places, has long back legs and is a good jumper, has smaller eyes. Toad: usually has rough, warty skin, plump and broad, has larger eyes, lives on land, is slow and cannot jump as well as a frog.)

Post-Reading Activity – Make frog and toad puppets for retelling the stories. Have the children play leap frog. Plant seeds in your classroom. Sing songs to your seeds just like Toad did. Describe Toad from the book and have the children guess who it is. Describe Frog from the book and have the children guess who it is. Describe each child in class and have the children guess who it is. Start with "Frog and Toad have a friend who..."

WILL I HAVE A FRIEND? – Miriam Cohen (Macmillan, 1967)

Story Summary – When Jim goes to school for the first time, he worries if he will find a friend. At first he just watches. The other children ignore him and he is unhappy. Finally at nap time, he finds that he has a new friend.

Pre-Reading Activity – Make "We're all friends" bracelets by having each child decorate one bracelet. Put all the bracelet strips in a box. Children stand in a circle. The first child draws a bracelet from the box, puts it around the next child's wrist and tapes the ends together. Continue until each child has a bracelet.

Post-Reading Activity – Draw a picture, roll it up and tie it with a ribbon. Set up chairs in a circle, one for each child. Take children aside and let one at a time go inside and place their gift on a chair. Return to the classroom, open the gifts and call out together "thank you friend."

TEDDY BEAR PATTERN

From the post-reading activity, Ira Sleeps Over - page 11.

WHO RIDES THE BUS?

The teacher will need to preapre a large school bus for the background of the bulletin board. The teacher could draw the bus on white paper and let the children paint the bus. The bus should have enough windows so that each child in the class has a window. The children can draw pictures of themselves to put in the windows of the school bus. It is also fun to use photographs of the children in the windows of the bus.

I AM SPECIAL

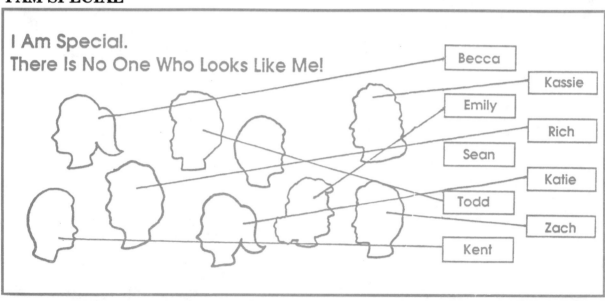

The teacher makes black silhouettes of the children. Use a film projector or slide projector as a light source. The children stand in front of the light, and his or her shadow will be cast on a piece of paper the teacher has taped on the wall. The teacher can quickly trace the outline and later cut it out. The children can then match their names to their silhouettes on the bulletin board.

SEPTEMBER BULLETIN BOARDS

FRIENDSHIP TREE

This is a bulletin board that can remain up all year long. It will change with the seasons and holidays. Cover the bulletin board with white paper. The teacher can draw the outline of a tree (no leaves). The children paint the trunk brown. Begin the year with hanging pictures of the children on the branches. Later in the year you can add pumpkins, ornaments, hearts, etc.

COLORS

COLORS — COLORS — COLORS				
RED	BLUE	YELLOW	GREEN	ORANGE
PINK	PURPLE	BROWN	BLACK	WHITE

Cover a bulletin board with white paper and divide the bulletin board into ten sections. Label each section with a different color word. Let the children finish the rest of the bulletin board. They can make or cut out colorful pictures. The children put the pictures in the corresponding color section of the bulletin board.

SEPTEMBER FINE MOTOR ACTIVITIES

NAME PLATES

You will need; one 9" x 4" strip of manila paper per child; scissors; pencil; ruler; crayons.

Show the children how to fold the paper in half *(as shown in the illustration)*. Children who are able to print their own names can do so in pencil on one side of the card. They can then write over it in crayon. The teacher should print the names for the children who are unable to print their names by themselves. Those children can trace their names in crayon also. The children could decorate their name plates with glitter, stickers or anything else that you might have on hand. Use the name plates for snack time, group time, circle time, etc. The children will enjoy finding their names and learning to recognize the names of their friends.

INDIVIDUAL CRAFT KITS

It is a lot of fun for children to keep their own art supplies in their very own box. Have each child bring a shoe box from home. Have the children paint the outside of their shoe boxes. The teacher should write the child's name in glue on the lid of the box. The children can press yarn into the glue. Let this dry thoroughly.Varnishthe boxes. The children now have their own place to keep glue, crayons, scissors and other materials needed for art projects.

HUMPTY DUMPTY

Have the children recite "Humpty Dumpty." Talk about the rhyme. Some of the children will decide that he was an egg. Have large sheets of paper *(newsprint 12 x 18 will do nicely.)* Some children will want to draw their own Humpty Dumpty. Don't structure the child's drawing by telling him what to draw. Write on the child's picture whatever he tells you about the picture.

LUNCH BAG PUPPETS

Have each child fill a lunch bag with crumbled newspaper. Tie the bags tight at the top. Turn the bags upside down, so that the tie is at the bottom. Provide the children with a multitude of materials that can be used for creating a face and hair on the lunch bag puppets. Using straight pins, these bags can be displayed nicely on a bulletin board for a three-dimensional effect.

LACING CARDS

Cut squares of medium weight cardboard. On each square draw a simple design. Punch hole at intervals along the outline of the design. *(Follow the example shown next to this activity.)* Lacing cards provide children with an excellent fine motor experience.

SEPTEMBER FINE MOTOR ACTIVITIES

SCHOOL BUS

That first bus ride to school is an exciting experience for children. As your class makes this bus, discuss with the children the shapes, colors, parts of the bus, the child's bus number and bus safety rules.

Have the large bus shape pre-cut out of white construction paper for those children who are unable to use scissors. Children who have mastered scissor skills will want to cut out their own bus shape. The children should paint the entire bus yellow (or orange). When the bus is dry, the doors and windows, cut from construction paper, may be glued on. The teacher adds the child's bus number with a marking pen. It is also fun to add sticker faces in the windows.

PORTRAITS

Ask the children to pick out a partner. Have the partners draw pictures of one another. Encourage the children to help each other by giving suggestions to one another. When the portraits are finished the children will enjoy playing "Guess Who" with the portraits that they have drawn.

CORNSTARCH FINGER PAINT

Finger painting is a tradition in all early childhood programs, and is often an activity that many children have never done before entering school. Here is a successful recipe for cornstarch finger paint:

You will need: Saucepan; mixing spoon; 8 parts water; 1 part cornstarch; food coloring.

What you do: Bring the water to a boil and dissolve the cornstarch in the water while stirring. Bring the water to a boil again. Add the food coloring until you have reached the color of your choice. *(Cooled paint will be slightly thicker; good for brush painting as well as finger painting.)*

ARTWORK DISPLAY

Find a space in your classroom where you can permanently mount clothesline string within the reach of the children. Have each of the children paint two wooden clothespins. Let the clothespins dry. Glue 2 small pictures of each child on the clothespins and attach to the line. Now when your little artists have completed a masterpiece they can go to their clothespins and hang up their creation with pride.

TEAR AND PASTE

Allow the children the fun of tearing colored paper and pasting it onto a large sheet of construction paper. Tearing the paper and learning how to use paste is a wonderful fine motor experience. Frame the pictures with a border of colored construction paper and put on display.

SEPTEMBER FINE MOTOR ACTIVITIES

BLACK BOARD PICTURES

Have your students create chalkboard pictures by gluing a piece of black construction paper onto an outline of a chalkboard frame. Let them draw a picture with chalk on the black paper to complete the project. Spray with hairspray to preserve.

BULLETIN BOARDS FOR KIDS

Make inexpensive bulletin boards using styrofoam sheets, fabric, thumb tacks, and ribbon or braid. Cover a thin piece of styrofoam with a piece of fabric large enough to cover the front and back of the styrofoam. Secure in the back with thumb tacks. Decorate the front by gluing ribbon or braid close to the edge. Each child will have his/her own bulletin board to take home.

STENCILS

The plastic lids from coffee cans or margarine containers make wonderful stencils. Cut common shapes, numbers, or letters in the plastic lids. The children can trace the shapes on white paper.

ALPHABET BLOCK PRINTS

Using alphabet blocks with raised letters, have the children dip the blocks into a pie pan filled with tempera paint. Press the block onto construction paper or butcher block paper.

MESSY PROJECT SHIRTS

Ask all the children to bring an old shirt from home which will stay at school to be used as the "messy project shirt." A t-shirt works the best for young children since there are no buttons to be fastened.

Make the shirts more interesting by allowing the children to decorate them. Here is a fun fabric paint recipe: Add 1 cup of powdered albumen to three cups of liquid tempera paint. Add a few drops of vinegar. After the paint has dried on the fabric, set the colors by placing the fabric between two pieces of paper and steam with an iron.

Here's a picture of me
For you to see,
That I'm going to school
As happy as can be!

SEPTEMBER MOVEMENT ACTIVITIES

FACE TO FACE

This is a very simple game that is wonderful for the first of the year. It helps children become acquainted with partner (cooperative) games and helps the children become more familiar with the other children in the class. All the children have to do is follow the directions of this simple verse:

Face to face,
Back to back,
Face to face,
Busy Bee! *(change partners)*

HOT POTATO

This "Hot Potato" game is somewhat different that the traditional version of "Hot Potato." A medium-sized ball is put in the center of the ring. "It" pushes the ball with his feet, trying to get it out of the circle. The children stop the ball with their feet. Once it is out, another "it" is chosen. The ball is called the "hot potato" and the children enjoy trying to keep it in the "oven" (circle).

ANIMAL MOVEMENTS

Have the children repeat with you and do what the following poem suggests:

We'll hop, hop, hop like a bunny.
We'll run, run, run like a dog.
We'll swim, swim, swim like a fish.
We'll jump, jump, jump like a frog.
We'll stretch, stretch, stretch like a giraffe.
We'll fly, fly, fly like a bird.
We'll walk, walk, walk like an elephant.
And not say another word.

Encourage the children to make up other verses.

BALLOONS

Blow up balloons and tie them with string. Divide the class into groups of 4 or 5 children. Let each group, in turn, wave the balloons in time to music. Choose a selection of music in which the tempo varies.

SMALL AND TALL

This is a fun action rhyme for children.

Here is a giant who is tall, tall, tall;	*(stand on tiptoes)*
Here is an elf who is small, small, small;	*(bend knees slowly)*
The elf who is small, small will try, try, try;	*(slowly stand erect)*
To reach the giant who is high, high, high	*(stretch tall on tiptoes)*

SEPTEMBER MOVEMENT ACTIVITIES

ROPE WALKING

Most young children who are beginning school have not had the experience of walking with a large group. Walking in a line and staying with the group is not always easy for a young child. Have your classroom of little wanderers practice walking around the school and schoolyard holding onto a long rope. The children will think holding the rope is fun and it will help instill the idea of "staying together."

Once you begin any field trips, your children will already know how to hold onto the rope and stay together. *But it does take some practice!*

FOLLOW THE LEADER

Follow the leader is a game that had been played for decades. Children always enjoy imitating the movements of others and of course, enjoy their turn at being the "leader."

Encourage a wide range of movements. Playing the game follow the leader to music can add to the fun!

THE BOUNCING BALL

Bouncing a ball can be a real challenge for a young child. Children often spend more time chasing the ball than they do bouncing it. Here is a fun song that can be sung when your children are practicing their "bouncing skills."

(Sung to the tune of "Row, Row, Row Your Boat)

Bounce, bounce, bounce my ball
Up and down the hall
Bumpity, bumpity, bumpity, bump
I can bounce my ball.

JUMPING

Have the children break into groups of three. They stand about a foot away from one another in a straight line side to side. The middle child of the three gives the command to "jump" and springs forward landing with feet together. As he/she jumps, the two outside children attempt to jump and land where the center child does. The children should be told to keep their eyes straight ahead, feet together. Alternate the middle child so each child gets a chance to be the first to jump.

STRAIGHT LINE

Use tape on the floor about 20' long. Have the children walk forward on the tape; walk backwards on the tape; hop on the tape; skip on the tape. Use any number of movements. The children will also enjoy tiptoeing, crawling etc.

SCHOOL BUS PATTERN

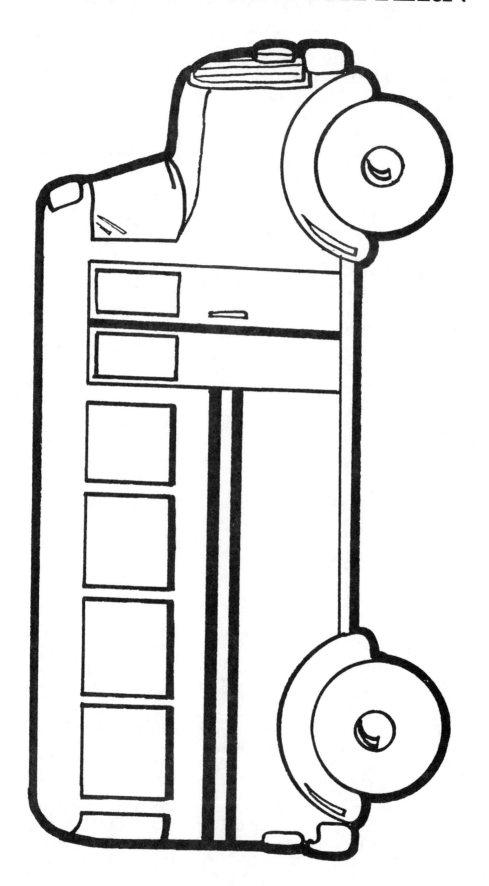

Enlarge this school bus pattern for each child. After the children color the picture, they can cut out pictures of children's faces from magazines or catalogs and glue in the windows.

SEPTEMBER LANGUAGE ACTIVITIES

SUITCASE DRAMATICS

Fill an old suitcase with an assortment of articles suitable for role-playing; such as an apron, old hats, shoes, caps, gloves, jacket, high-heels, scarf, spectacles, etc. The children will have a lot of fun play-acting and pretending to be different people with the props.

BRAINSTORM

Have the children "brainstorm" or together think of as many things in a category in a certain amount of time. You can use colors, children's names, foods, etc. Let all the children contribute. Write a list of all the words that the children were able to come up with.

PICTURES AND OBJECTS

Ask a child to choose an object and tell all that he can about the object. How is it used? How large is the object? What color is the object? Where would you find the object? Then ask him to choose another object and tell in which they are alike. Then ask him how they are different. It will probably be necessary for you to give examples so the children will understand. Try to develop the concepts of size, color, shape, use, and location.

(e.g. red car and a red pencil - they are alike because they are both red; they are different because one is small and one is large; one is used to ride in and one is used to write with.)

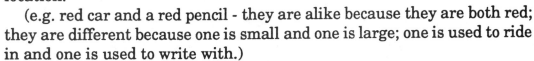

APPLE SALAD

Cooking experiences are also a wonderful language arts experience. While the children are cooking they are also learning a vast amount of new vocabulary and basic concepts such as "hot/cold, wet/dry, sweet/sour, full/empty, etc. The possiblities for enriching vocabulary while cooking are endless. Here is an easy and fun recipe. The recipe does call for chopping and coring apples. You will have to supervise closely and judge how able your children are in preforming these tasks.

6 or 7 large apples; 1 small can chunk pineapple; 1/2 pound grapes; 1/2 cup minature marshmallows; 1/4 cup mayonnaise; 1/4cup sugar.

Core apples and chop into 1/2 inch chunks. Drain pineapple. Add 1/4 cup pineapple juice and the sugar to the mayonnaise. Cut grapes in two. Add minature marshmallows. Mix all the ingredients together.

APPLE DUMPLINGS

You will need: 2 pie crust sticks; 8 unpeeled apples; 4 cups sugar; 4 tsp. cinnamon; 4 tsp. butter.

Roll out pie crust. Cut into squares (4 to each pie crust stick). Core the apples. Fill the hole with sugar, butter and cinnamon. Wrap the apple in dough. Pinch top edges together. Bake at 350 degrees for 45 minutes.

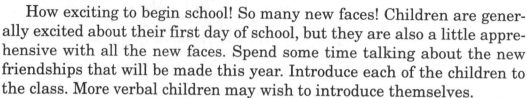

SEPTEMBER LANGUAGE ACTIVITIES

TALK ABOUT FRIENDSHIP

How exciting to begin school! So many new faces! Children are generally excited about their first day of school, but they are also a little apprehensive with all the new faces. Spend some time talking about the new friendships that will be made this year. Introduce each of the children to the class. More verbal children may wish to introduce themselves.

Take polaroid pictures of each of the children first thing in the morning. During "morning circle" pass the pictures around for all the children to see. Let each of the children say their name into a tape recorder and then play back the recording for all the children to listen to.

CLASSROOM BIG BOOK

Spend the next several weeks taking pictures of the children participating in everyday activities (playground time, art time, puzzle time, lunchtime, etc.). Mount the pictures on large pieces of construction paper and label the activity. Laminate each page and bind together in book form.

The children will enjoy "reading" their classroom big book, featuring all the activities that they are becoming familiar with.

As the year progresses be sure to add pages featuring special events and field trips. This book will become a classroom treasure.

SHOW TIME

Creative dramatics is a wonderful tool for enriching language development. Spend some time reviewing some of the classic nursery rhymes. (Although many children may never have heard nursery rhymes.) Assign roles to each of the children hand have the children pantomime the nursery rhymes. This activity is especially fun with "props" are added.

CLASSROOM OBJECTS

Fill a bag with everyday objects from your classroom (blocks, doll, pencil, crayon, marker, scissor, puzzle piece, brush, cup, paper, musical instrument, etc.). Ask each child to take something out of the bag and say what it is and explain what you do with that object.

LOOK IN THE MIRROR

Use a hand mirror, or a full-length mirror if you are lucky enough to have one in your classroom. Have the children look into the mirror and describe themselves. Encourage the children to use descriptive vocabulary such as curly brown hair; long black hair, pink and white striped shirt. etc.

Encourage the children to make positive statements about themselves.

SEPTEMBER LANGUAGE ACTIVITIES

CLASSROOM MASCOT

Before the school year begins, purchase or make a special puppet for your classroom. This puppet can be the classroom's special mascot.

Use the puppet during language development time. Puppets often put children at ease when speaking in front of a group.

Not only is the puppet a wonderful tool for language development, but your special mascot can be used to introduce new activities, run classroom meetings, and help to maintain order. When the classroom is too noisy, the classroom mascot can be the one to ask the children to try and be a little more quiet. The children will want to please and respond to their special friend.

I CAN DRAW A PICTURE OF ME

Talk about all the facial features: eyes, ears, nose, mouth, lips, cheeks, chin, eyebrows, eyelashes, etc. Discuss the features in detail. Can the children name all the facial features.

Give each child a sheet of white paper. Have the children draw a picture of their face. How much detail does the picture have?

Show the pictures to the class one at a time. Let the children have fun guessing who each picture belongs to. Save these pictures until the end of the year. During the last month of school repeat this activity. You will be surprised to see how much the drawings have matured from the first of the year.

WHAT DO YOU DO BEFORE SCHOOL?

Talk about all the daily activities that people do before they get ready for school or before they go to work. Make a list of all those activities. Have the children try to sequence how they begin their day. (Get out of bed, brush teeth, get dressed, brush hair, eat breakfast, etc.)

HOW MANY IN YOUR FAMILY?

Make a chart with the children showing how many people are in their families.

Ask the children to name all of the family members and then count how many people that makes. Remember to include a category for pets.

Look at the chart when it is finished. Who has the biggest family? Who has the smallest family? Who has the most pets? Who has a grandma or grandpa living with them? How many children are the oldest child in the family? How many children are the youngest member of the family? How many are an only child?

SEPTEMBER FINGER PLAYS/POETRY

INDOORS

I've just come in from playing
I'm tired as I can be.
I'll cross my legs and fold my hands.
And close my eyes, so I can't see.
(A nice rhyme for after playing outside.)

THE APPLE

I have a little apple, red and round	*(form circle with hands)*
In a tree it is found	*(make a tree with palms upraised from elbows)*
If you take a bite	*(take bite, nod head yes)*
You will see	*(point to eyes)*
Just how tasty it will be	*(rub stomach)*

AT SCHOOL

At school I learn to count	*(write with imaginary pencil)*
And also print my name.	*(imaginary crayon)*
I draw, I cut, and paste and paint	*(imaginary scissors)*
And also play some games.	
My teacher's name is _____	*(point to teacher)*
She's/he's as nice as she/he can be.	
I do my best in school,	
And (teacher's name) helps me.	*(point to teacher)*

WIGGLES

I wiggle my shoulders,
I wiggle my nose.
I wiggle my fingers,
I wiggle my toes.
Now there are no wiggles left in me.
And I am as quiet as can be.
(perform actions as indicated.)

THIS LITTLE CHILD

This little child is just going to bed.
Down on the pillow he lays his/her head,
   (palms together at side of face)
Wraps him/herself up in his blankets tight,
   (hands folded across chest)
And this is the way he/she sleeps all night.
Morning comes. He/she opens his/her eyes.
   (children sit up tall)
Back with a toss the covers fly.
   (spread arms apart quickly)
Soon he/she is up and dressed for play,
Ready for school and a bright new day.
   (big smiles!)

THIS IS ME

This is me, and this is you.
And these are all our friends.
Spread us out; this you can do.
Watch this one as he bends.

Some of us are tall and thin.
Some of us are shorter.
One of us might have a twin.
One might have a brother.

Now bring us all together.
Just see how nice we stand.
Oh, we'll be friends forever!
Like fingers on a hand.
(use as a finger play)

SEPTEMBER FINGER PLAYS/POETRY

CLEAN UP TIME
(Sung to the tune of "Jingle Bells")
Clean up time
Clean up time
Time to put away
We're all finished with our play, but
Don't you go away! Hea!
Come sit down
Come sit down
I have a special friend, he would like
To meet you all, *(puppet to a story)*
So lets be nice to him!
*(This is a good song to use for cleaning
up and then moving the children into
storytime.) Vicki Birditt - Head Start
Mommouth, IL*

FINGER PAINTING
Red, green, yellow, brown and blue,
Orange, purple and black too!
A bright color in each dish,
With your fingers - Dip and Swish!
*(Fingers dip down and make swishing
motions.)*

INDICATING BODY PARTS
Touch your left knee, then your right;
Touch your left thumb of small height.
Raise your right hand to the sky;
With your right hand, touch your eye.
Now, please shake hands with a friend;
Touch your left foot down at the end.
Touch your left ear, then your shoulder;
Show me left before you're older!
Touch your right leg, and left hip;
Touch your upper and lower lip.
*(Say the rhyme very slowly so the children
will have ample time to think in terms of
"left" and "right." If movements are too fast,
the children will have difficulty in following
the directions.)*

COLORS
Red, red. I see red.
   It's an apple growing overhead.
Yellow, yellow. I see yellow.
   A big banana, long and mellow.
Orange, orange. Can it be?
   An orange growing on a tree.
Blue, blue. I see blue.
   My kitten's eyes - she says, "Mew, mew."
Green, green. I see green.
   From my garden, one string bean.
Purple, purple. What do I see?
   Grapes on a vine, just for me!
White, white. I see white.
   Fluffy clouds, so soft and light.
*(Turn into a flannel board rhyme by making
a red apple, a yellow banana, an orange,
a kitten with blue eyes, a green bean, purple
grapes and a white cloud.)*

THERE WERE TEN IN BED
There were ten in bed,
And the little one said,
"Roll over, roll over."
And they all rolled over,
And one fell out!

There were nine in bed,
And the little one said,
"Roll over, roll over."
And they all rolled over,
And one fell out!

End the poem this way:
There were none in bed,
And nobody said,
"Roll over, roll over."
So no one rolled over,
And no one fell out!
       - An old English Rhyme
*(The children lie in a row on the rug.
Each one rolls over once, then one at a
time leaves the rug. A child may tap a
triangle when one falls out of the bed!)*

SEPTEMBER FINGER PLAYS/POETRY

WHAT THE ANIMALS DO

We'll hop, hop like a bunny,
And run, run like a dog;
We'll walk, walk like an elephant,
And jump, jump like a frog;
We'll swim, swim like a goldfish,
And fly, fly like a bird;
And sit right down and fold our hands,
And not say a single word!
(Children imitate animals as
they recite the rhyme.)

THIS IS MY EYE

This is my eye   *(cover one eye)*
This is my ear   *(cover one ear)*
This is to see   *(look)*
And this is to hear. *(listen)*

THE SQUIRREL

I have a little squirrel
        (nod "yes" with fist)
He lives in a tree.
        (look upward)
When the sun comes out
        (make circle with arms)
So does he.
        (make thumb pop straight up)

THIS LITTLE GIRL (or boy)

This little girl (boy) is ready for bed.   *(hold up thumb)*
Down on the pillow she (he) lays her (his) head.   *(put thumb across palm of other hand)*

Wraps herself (himself) in covers so tight,   *(close fingers over thumb)*
And this is the way she (he) sleeps all night.   *(put hands up to cheek and close eyes)*

MAGIC MIRROR

I couldn't learn to whistle.
I tried it every way.   *(pretend to whistle)*
But not a bit of sound came out
Until one magic day.
I stood before the mirror   *(pretend to look in mirror or use small mirror)*
My whistle came a-squeaking out
From somewhere down inside.   *(everyone really try to whistle)*
(Most young children will not be able to whistle, but let them chirp away if they can.)

AT SCHOOL

We play a lot of games,
And we learn each other's names.
We count to ten or more,
And make a grocery store.
We learn our ABC's.
We make sets of threes.
And a puppet from a bag.
And then we salute the flag.

SEPTEMBER

Autumn is near, and September is here.
What will boys and girls do
When the weather is cool?
They will get on a bus
Say goodbye to us
And they'll ride off to school
Yes, ride off to school!

SEPTEMBER MUSIC ACTIVITIES

It is fun for children to sing some familiar songs when they are beginning a new school experience. Here are some old, but classic songs for children!

THE ALPHABET SONG - *Old French Song*
ABCDEFG, HIJKLMNOP, QRS and TUV, WX and Y and Z
Now I've sung my ABC's. Tell me what you think of me.

WHERE IS THUMBKIN? - *French Song*
Where is thumbkin? Where is thumbkin? Here I am. Here I am.
How are you this morning? Very well, I thank you. Run away, run away.
(Repeat the song with each finger using the following names: Pointer, Tallman, Ringman, Pinky)

THE FARMER IN THE DELL
The farmer in the dell. The farmer in the dell.
Heigh-O the dairy-O, the farmer in the dell.
(other verses:The farmer takes a wife. The wife takes a child. The child takes a nurse. The nurse takes a dog. The dog takes a cat. The cat takes a rat. The rat takes the cheese. The cheese stand alone.

SEPTEMBER MUSIC ACTIVITIES

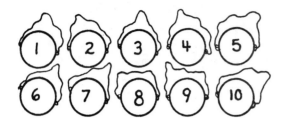

NECKLACES FOR MUSIC
 Make number necklaces for the children to wear while you sing, "One, Two, Buckle my Shoe," "This old Man," or any song which uses counting as a theme.

AT SCHOOL
(Melody: Old MacDonald Had A Farm)

Dip the paint brush in the jar – at my nursery school*
I paint a picture of a car – at my nursery school
With a swish, swish here and a swish, swish there
Here a swish, there a swish; everybody swish, swish
Painting, painting – oh what fun – at my nursery school.

Squeeze the playdough in my hand – at my nursery school
Roll it, pinch it once again – at my nursery school
With a squish, squish here and a squish, squish there
Here a squish, there a squish; everybody squish, squish
Squishing, squishing – oh what fun – at my nursery school.

Pounding big nails in the wood – at my nursery school
I hold the hammer like I should – at my nursery school
With a bang, bang here and a bang, bang there
Here a bang, there a bang; everybody bang, bang
Pounding, pounding – oh what fun – at my nursery school.

Playing with the little cars – at my nursery school
Riding big trucks very far – at my nursery school
With a vroom, vroom here and a vroom, vroom there
Here a vroom, there a vroom; everybody vroom, vroom
Driving, driving – oh what fun – at my nursery school.

Pour the water from a can – at my nursery school
Wash the dishes in a pan – at my nursery school
With a splash, splash here and a splash, splash there
Here a splash, there a splash; everybody splash, splash
Splashing, splashing – oh what fun – at my nursery school.

* (at any child care center, at my kindergarten)
Classification game that accompanies this song is found on pages 31 & 32.

AT SCHOOL (2 PAGE CLASSIFICATION GAME)

Song found on page 30.

The children group the pictures into six categories: painting, playing with playdough, woodworking, playing with trucks and cars, waterplay, and music time.

AT SCHOOL (2 PAGE CLASSIFICATION GAME)

Song found on page 30.

The children group the pictures into six categories: painting, playing with playdough, woodworking, playing with trucks and cars, waterplay, and music time.

LET'S LEARN ABOUT COLORS

Colors are something that every early childhood program provides activities for. Here are some ideas that can be used all year long as you introduce various colors.

COLOR WHEEL - Cut a cardboard circle so that the diameter is 10". Divide the circle into 8 equal wedges. Paint each wedge a different color. Cover with contact paper for durability. For every wedge paint a clothespin in a matching color. The children will enjoy selecting clothespins and attaching them to the same color on the color wheel.

COLOR GAME - Line up color sheets or color lollipops. One child who is "it" chooses a color and whispers it to the teacher. The other children try to guess which color was chosen. The one who guesses correctly will get to be the next "it."

LOLLIPOP GAME - Use lollipops made from colored construction paper and stapled to tongue depressors. A child skips around and stops before a friend who will choose a lollipop by color. *(The children may enjoy making their own set of lollipops to take home.)*

COLORFUL FISH - Cut out fish of the eight basic colors and put these on the flannel board. In a large box, place fish cut from colored construction paper. Each child reaches in the box and "goes fishing." As a fish is caught, the child must say the name of the color. It is then placed under the corresponding colored fish on the flannel board.

CLASSROOM ICE CREAM CONE - Tape a large cut-out of a cone on the bottom of a wall. Each day that you introduce a new color, add that color *(an ice cream circle)* on the cone. Before long you will have a giant ice cream cone on your classroom wall.

FELT BOX - You will need a shallow box and assorted colors of felt material. Cut two circles from every color. Glue one set of the colored circles inside the box. The other set of colored circles stores loosely in the box. The children can now use the loose set of circles and match them to the set of glued circles.

EVERYDAY IDEAS - • Point out objects in the room that are the color of the day. • Give out crayons of only that color. • Cut construction paper in different shapes and have the class help match the colors in piles. • Have the children wear "the color of the day" to school. • Try to think of objects not in the room that are the color of the day. • Review constantly from story books and other materials.

COLORS

Name

Date

MYSTERY BAG OF COLORS

Fill a bag or box with a multitude of various colored objects. Let the children take turns selecting an object and then telling the rest of the class the color of the object. The children will also enjoy sorting the objects by color.

A HELPING HAND

Cut a tagboard hand for each child in the class. Punch a hole in the top of the hand. String yarn through the top hole and tie a knot in the string. Glue a short snap clothespin on the back of each hand and reinforce with masking tape over the glued clothespin.

The "Helping Hand" necklaces can be worn around the neck to help carry home important notes and papers. The children should return the hands to school immediately for the next note.

COLOR CAPERS

The objective of this activity is for the children to have practice in classifying pictures according to color. Have the children work in small groups (3 to 5 in a group). Provide each group of children with a large paper with columns for the colors the students are to be classifying. Provide old magazines, catalogs, scissors and paste.

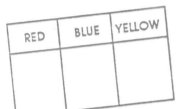

RED	BLUE	YELLOW

Instruct each group to cut out pictures and paste them under the correct color heading.

SHOELACE MATCHING GAME

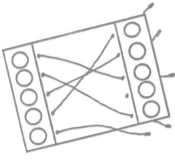

Use a large piece of tagboard or chipboard. Cut out two sets of circles of 7 or 8 colors. Glue one set of circles down one side of the board. Glue the other set of circles down the opposite side of the board in a different order. Punch a hole next to each circle on both sides of the board. Attach a shoelace next to each circle on the left side of the board. The children can then use the shoelaces to match the colored circles. *(See illustration)*

SIDEWALK OF COLORS

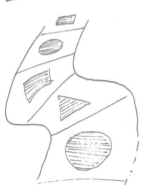

Make "sidewalks" from strips cut from the edges of discarded window shades. Tape the strips together to make the desired length. Divide the sidewalk into squares and glue on the colored geometric shapes. The children can walk along the sidewalk and name the shape and/or color.

You can also use the "sidewalk" like the game "Candyland." Make a spinner with the corresponding shapes. The child spins the spinner and then moves to the shape and color that appears on the spinner.

Discarded window shades can be used for many activities; numbers, alphabet, animals, words, etc.

SEPTEMBER EXPERIENTIAL ACTIVITIES

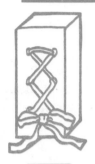

LEARNING TO LACE AND TIE
Punch holes in a shoe box lid and string a long shoe lace through the holes. Children can learn to lace and tie on this special and easy-to-make board.

HEIGHT CHART
Purchase or make a growth chart to hang on a wall in your classroom. Record the children's heights sometime during the first week of school. Record their height throughout the year. Children love to actually "see" how much they are growing.

STUDENT MAILBOXES
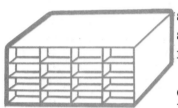
This type of organizational box can be purchased through office or school supply stores, or you can easily make one by stacking and taping together shoe boxes. (Many shoe stores will be happy to provide you with a large number of shoe boxes.)

Children enjoy having a special place to keep important papers and drawings. It is also a nice place to put notices that you want to send home. It becomes part of the children's daily routine to check their mailboxes for important mail.

SORTING REAL NUTS
Label small margarine containers or bowls with pictures of different kinds of nuts. Have the children sort the nuts into the correct bowls.

Talk about squirrels during this activity. Show the children pictures of squirrels. What do the squirrels do with the nuts they have found?

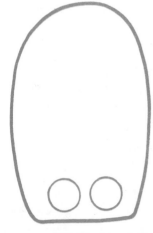

"ME" FINGERPUPPET
Enlarge the blank fingerpuppet illustration and make a copy and re-produce on tagboard or heavy construction paper for each child. Have the children draw an illustration of themselves on the fingerpuppet, leaving room for their fingers to be used as the legs on the puppet. The children will enjoy playing with the puppets and in using them to describe themselves.

October

HALLOWEEN SUBTRACTION

(Use as a flannel board rhyme.)

Three little ghosts on Halloween night,
    Saw a witch and shrieked in fright.
The witch just laughed and shouted "Boo!"
    One ghost ran home, and that left two.

Two little ghosts in two little sheets
    Went to a door to say, "Trick or treat."
But when the door swung open wide,
    A scary goblin stood inside.

One ghost gulped and said to the other,
    "I'm going home and stay with my mother."
Of the three little ghosts, there was now one alone,
    Too frightened to utter a groan or a moan.

One little ghost who shivered and shook
    With every single step he took,
A fraidy-cat ghost can't have much fun,
    So he cried, "Wait for me!" and
        then there was none.

ghost
(make 3)

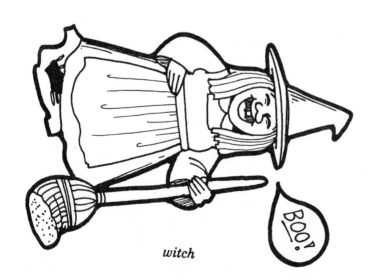

goblin

witch

GORDON THE GHOST

From the book, Telling Stories Together, by Linda Haver
Copyright by T.S. Denison & Co., Inc.

For this story, divide the children into three groups. The wind group should howl, the black cats meow, and the witches cackle. Allow time for each group to practice their part.

When you are telling the story, pause each time you come to a **bold, italicized** *instruction and point to the appropriate group and give them time to do their part,*

The wind **howled**. . ., the black cats **meowed**. . ., the witches **cackled**. . ., it was Halloween. But Gordon the Ghost did not feel much like celebrating. All of the other ghosts were busy practicing their Halloween tricks, but Gordon was feeling very sad and very sorry for himself.

"I wish I was not a Halloween ghost," said Gordon, "everything else about Halloween is so scary. The wind **howling**. . ., the black cats **meowing**. . ., the witches **cackling**. . . But I am just a little ghost and I am not at all important to Halloween. Maybe I could pretend to be something else this Halloween. I will go see Wise Old Owl, maybe he can help me."

As Gordon walked along to see Wise Old Owl it was getting dark. He could hear the wind **howling**. . ., the black cats **meowing**. . ., and the witches **cackling**. . ., he knew the time for Halloween tricking was getting close.

"Wise Old Owl," said Gordon when he came to the big oak tree where the owl lived, "please help me."

"What is the problem?" asked Wise Old Owl.

"I want to be something special this Halloween. The wind **howls**. . ., the black cats **meow**. . ., and the witches **cackle**. . ., but no one needs a little ghost like me at Halloween."

"I have an idea," said Wise Old Owl, "why don't you go visit the wind that **howls**. . ., the black cats that **meow**. . ., and the witches that **cackle**. . ., and see if you can join them this Halloween."

So Gordon the Ghost was off to visit the wind that **howled**. . . When he came to where the wind lived, Gordon started **howling**. . ., and yelling, "listen to me wind, can I howl with you this Halloween?"

"Sure," said the wind, "Halloween can always use more howling, come join us."

Well, Gordon *howled*. . . down the street, he *howled*. . . up another street, he *howled*. . . all over the town. But he discovered that he really did not like howling. So Gordon the Ghost said good-bye to the wind and went off to visit the black cats.

When he came to where the black cats lived, Gordon started *meowing*. . . and shouting, "black cats I want to be with you this Halloween, can I meow with you?"

"Of course you can," answered the black cats.

Gordon went *meowing*. . . down one street, *meowing*. . . up another street, *meowing*. . . all over town. But he found that he did not like meowing either, so Gordon the Ghost said good-bye to the black cats and went off to visit the witches.

When he came to the place where the witches lived, Gordon *cackled*. . . as loud as he could. "Listen to me witches, I want to cackle with you this Halloween."

The witches said, "we would love to have the company."

So Gordon *cackled*. . . down one street, he *cackled* . . . up another street, he *cackled*. . . all over town. But he learned that he did not like cackling, so Gordon the Ghost said good-bye to the witches and started on his way home.

As he walked along, Gordon was still feeling very sad and very sorry for himself. I tried being the wind that *howls*. . . I tried being a black cat that *meows*. . . I even tried being a witch that *cackles*. . ., but I am still not happy.

As Gordon walked farther he saw a little boy named Kevin going down the street with his mother. As Gordon got closer he could hear Kevin say to his mother, "Mom, I am so sad, this has been a terrible Halloween. We heard the wind *howling*. . . We heard the black cats *meowing*. . . We heard the witches *cackling*. . . but it just does not seem like Halloween because not one ghost played a Halloween trick on us."

When he heard what Kevin said, Gordon whished down over Kevin and his mother and knocked the hat right off Kevin's head.

Kevin shouted, "A ghost, a real ghost! It is a wonderful Halloween after all."

Well that made Gordon the ghost feel very important and very happy. Never again did Gordon want to be the wind *howling*. . ., the black cats *meowing*. . ., or the witches *cackling*. . . Gordon was happy just being himself!

(Flannel board patterns for "Gordon the Ghost" can be found on pages 41 & 42.)

STORY PATTERNS

(Flannel board patterns for "Gordon the Ghost." The story can be found on pages 39 & 40.)

Witches Cackling

Gordon

Kevin

Howling Wind

STORY PATTERNS

(Flannel board patterns for "Gordon the Ghost." The story can be found on pages 39 & 40.)

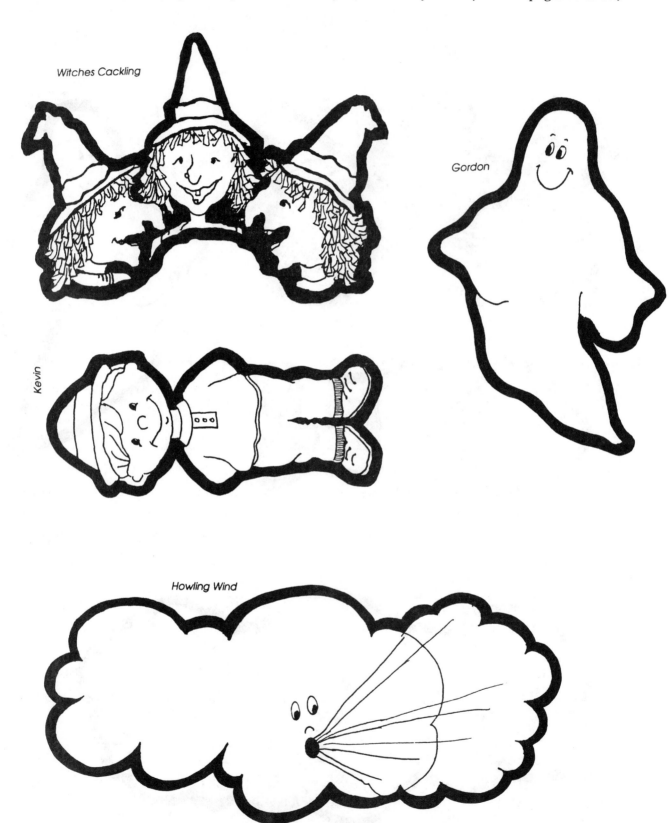

Witches Cackling

Gordon

Kevin

Howling Wind

COLORS OF FALL

From the book, Telling Stories Together, by Linda Haver.
Copyright by T.S. Denison & Co., Inc.

*When you are telling this story, pause each time you come to a **bold**, **italicized** color word. The children are to identify the appropriate color by holding up a crayon or a piece of paper that color. Each child should have the colors red, orange, brown, green, and yellow.*

For a variation, instead of holding up the appropriate color, you might try having the child raise their hand each time you mention a color they are wearing.

Kate and Barry loved the fall, it was their favorite season of the year. One day their teacher asked them to write a report about why they felt fall was the best season. "This will be an easy report," Barry told Kate, "Of course we like fall because of football and cooler weather."

"Wait a minute," said Kate, "the reason we like fall is because of soccer and the start of a new school year."

Barry thought a second and then said, "No, that is not the reason we like fall. The best thing about fall are all the pretty colors of the changing leaves."

"You are right," Kate agreed, "the colors are the very best part of fall, and **red** is the prettiest fall color. **Red** reminds me of fire trucks, candy apples, and Valentines."

"I think *orange* is the nicest color," Barry replied. "*Orange* is the color of pumpkins and goldfish."

"*Orange* is nice," said Kate, "but how about *brown*?" "*Brown* makes me think of bears, chocolate cake, and root beer."

"*Green*, we forgot about *green*," exclaimed Barry. "*Green* is the color of grass, frogs, and celery."

"Another color that I really like is *yellow*," said Kate. "*Yellow* always makes me think of sunshine, bananas, and corn."

"I have an idea for our report. We should gather some pretty fall leaves, press them between waxed paper and label what kind of tree they grew on!" exclaimed Barry.

On the way home from school Barry and Kate started looking for different colored leaves. Under the maple tree on the playground, they found several perfect *red* leaves. Next to the maple tree was an oak tree, there they found beautiful *yellow* leaves.

When they were done collecting on the playground Kate and Barry started down the street. In front of Kate's house they picked up a couple of *orange* leaves. They went into the backyard and found some more *red* leaves. "Let's get a snack then go to your house and to look for more leaves," said Kate.

At Barry's house they discovered a tree with *green* leaves. They picked up some pretty ones, then went searching for *brown* leaves. While they were looking they found more *orange* leaves. "I think we have enough leaves," said Barry. "Why don't we get started on our report?"

"Great," replied Kate, "we have leaves that are *red*, *green*, *orange*, *yellow*, and *brown*. All the colors of fall."

(Turn this story into a flannel board presentation, by using the patterns found on page 45.)

STORY PATTERNS

(Flannel board patterns for "Colors of Fall." The story can be found on pages 43 & 44.)

Kate

Red Maple Leaf

Orange Maple Leaf

Brown Oak Leaf

Barry

Green Oak Leaf

Yellow Oak Leaf

OCTOBER BULLETIN BOARDS

PUMPKIN FACES

The background is very attractive when it is covered in black paper with an orange border. Give each of the children a large piece of orange construction paper and let them cut out their own pumpkin shape. The bulletin board is the cutest when all the pumpkins are different shapes. With black construction paper the children can add the jack-o-lantern's facial features. A green construction paper stem can be glued on the top of the pumpkin. Black lines can be drawn on the pumpkins with a black crayon.

SCARECROW

Take two pieces of wood and glue, then tie them together to form a cross shape.

For the scarecrow's head, stuff cheesecloth with crushed newspaper. Wrap string around the neck part to hold the head securely together.

Use an old white shirt stuffed with crushed newspaper, and the the pants are done in the same way.

Cut construction paper (brown, yellow, orange, beige) in thin haylike shapes. Insert these in the arms, legs and around the neck. Top the figure with an old straw hat.

Put the scarecrow on the wood crossbar which is inserted in a box, as pictured. You might put stones or sand in the box to make it stand more firmly.

OCTOBER BULLETIN BOARDS

SPONGE-PAINTED GHOSTS

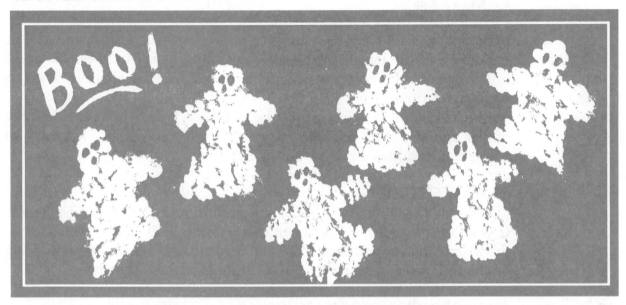

Cover the bulletin board with black paper. Lightly draw in the ghost shapes with white chalk. Let the children sponge paint the inside of the ghosts with white paint.

Orange sponge-painted pumpkins can be added at the bottom of the bulletin board and a large yellow moon in the upper corner of the bulletin board.

PUMPKIN NUMBERS

This bulletin board is designed for the children to play with. Put up ten large pumpkins. Each pumpkin should have dots on it (1 to 10 dots per pumpkin). Using self-stick velcro, place one side of the velcro on a pumpkin, the other side of the velcro on the back of a numeral card (numerals 1 to 10). The children can match the numeral card to the appropriate pumpkin.

OCTOBER FINE MOTOR ACTIVITIES

FALL TREE

In the fall, draw a large outline of a bare tree on brown paper. Provide little sponges and vivid paints of yellow, orange, and brown. Let the children add the leaves to the tree. Put animals in the tree. Make a big mural or individual pictures. Some four and five-year-olds can draw their own tree outline.

VARIATION: Sponge print a large brown tree. Children add cut-out apples and autumn leaves. In the winter Ivory Snow whipped thick with water can be added for snow on the branches.

SEED PICTURES

Provide the children with dried pumpkin and squash seeds, construction paper, glue, and chalk outlines of witches, bats, cats, pumpkins, etc., drawn on construction paper. The children glue the seeds inside the designs or the children can make thier own designs with the seeds.

HALLOWEEN NOISEMAKERS

It is fun to make Halloween noisemakers by stapling two small-size paper plates together, with a few beans inside. The children can paint them, or color them, or decorate them with Halloween stickers. These are a lot of fun to use a rhythm instruments during music time, or at your Halloween party.

PILLOWCASE COSTUMES

Ask each child to bring a pillowcase from home. The teacher should cut a hole for the child's head in the top seam of the pillow case, and cut out arm holes in the side seams of the pillowcase. The children can use paint or fabric crayons to decorate their pillowcases.

These make darling costumes that the children are able to manage easily. The pillowcase is large enough to cover a small child, and short enough that it will not be tripped on.

HALLOWEEN MASKS

I do not suggest or encourage small children to wear masks on Halloween. I personally think that they can be dangerous, not to mention that many small children really do find masks to be "too scary!"

But making a mask as an art project can help children see that masks are pretend. The teacher should mark where the eye hole should be cut. After that, just let the children enjoy creating some type of scary Halloween monster.

OCTOBER FINE MOTOR ACTIVITIES

SPONGE PAINTED TREES
You will need: Brown construction paper; white 12" x 18" paper for background; aluminum pie tins; sponges cut in 1" squares; clothespins; tempera paint in fall colors.

What you do: Pre-cut tree trunks from brown paper for those children who are not able to use scissors. Distribute one sponge with a clothespin attached for each child. Demonstrate how to dab the sponge on the paper. Trade sponges and paint tins until each child has used all the colors.

LEAF PRINTING
You will need: Paper; tempera paint; leaves; an ink roller (brayer) or paint brushes; pan for paint.

What you do: Apply an even coat of paint onto the side of the leaf in which the veins show. Paint may be applied with a roller or with brushes. Place a sheet of paper on top of the painted side of the leaf and rub gently with fingers. Remove the paper and allow time for the paint to dry.

PUMPKINS AT NIGHT
Have the children draw pictures of pumpkins and then color with orange crayons. When the color crayon pictures are finished, the children may paint over the entire picture with black water color. The water color will not cover the crayon drawing.

HALLOWEEN MURALS
Divide your classroom of children into groups of three to five. Provide each group with a very large sheet of paper, crayons, pencils, markers, paints, etc. Instruct each group to create a "spooky" Halloween picture after a discussion about Halloween. *(This activity may be adapted to any holiday!)*

GHOST BALLOONS
Ghosts made from balloons make wonderful Halloween party decorations. Blow up a white balloon and knot it. Cut a small hole in a large sheet of white tissue paper. Put the tissue paper over the balloon, making sure that the knot of the balloon is put through the hole in the tissue paper. (See illustration) Loosely tie a string around the base of the balloon and the tissue paper. This will separate the head of the ghost from it's body. Draw on the eyes with a black marker. Tie another piece of string around the knot of the balloon so the ghost can be hung from the ceiling.

OCTOBER FINE MOTOR ACTIVITIES

PAINT REAL PUMPKINS

Give each child their own small pumpkin to paint. Give the children three to four colors of paint. Some paints require the addition of glue for better adherence to the pumpkins. Thin the glue with water.

LEAF CREATURES

Glue real leaves or leaf cut-outs onto pieces of construction paper. The children can add faces, hands and feet to create their "leaf creatures."

SPIDERS

These darling spiders are easy-to-make. Spray paint (black) 4 inch styrofoam balls. The children can give their spiders legs by inserting eight pipe cleaners into the ball. Glue on construction paper eyes and a mouth. (Movable eyes are also a fun extra touch.)

NATURE PICTURES

Make nature pictures on poster board by gluing sticks around the edges to make a frame. Add leaves, small pebbles, and other "treasures" that the children have found outdoors.

PAINTING WITH PINE NEEDLES

The tips of pine needles are dipped in paint and stroked across construction paper. This is a fun autumn activity. Encourage the children to use "autumn" colors.

HALLOWEEN TRICK OR TREAT BAG

Fold down the top edge of a grocery bag. Put a piece of duct tape around the inside edge of the bag. Punch holes, about three inches apart, through the top edge of both the front and back sides of the bag. (4 holes total.) Cut two pieces of twine about 24 inches long and tie them through the holes in the bag to form handles. Draw a ghost on one side of the bag and a pumpkin on the other side. Sponge paint the ghost white and sponge paint the pumpkin orange.

INVISIBLE PICTURES

This is a fun Halloween art project that is very easy! Draw a picture with a white candle or white crayon on a white piece of paper. Cover the picture with a thin coat of black paint. The picture will magically appear.

PUMPKIN SEED MOSAIC

Draw designs on a piece of cardboard. Apply glue to the center of the design area. Sprinkle the seeds onto the glue and let dry.

BLACK PAPER BAT

Use this pattern to cut out a black construction paper bat. Mark lines with a pencil for the eyes and mouth. The children can put on their own glue and then add silver glitter. Hang from the ceiling to decorate your classroom.

OCTOBER MOVEMENT ACTIVITIES

JOHNNY JUMP UP

The children squat down quietly. The teacher or another child begins talking and saying things about the children in the room; such as, "Susie is wearing a red dress today. Tommy got a new hair cut." If the leader suddenly says "JUMP" or uses the word "JUMP" in a sentence, all the children must jump up. Varying the technique for using the word "jump" would necessitate more careful listening. This activity is not only fun for the gross motor movement of jumping, but it is also an excellent exercise for increasing listening skills and verbal expression.

CRAWL

Children, even when they are past the infancy stage, they still enjoy the skill of crawling. Here are some ideas for providing the children with crawling experiences:
1) crawl on a straight chalked line
2) crawl following the outline of a drawn or painted surface
3) in a circle
4) crawl around an obstacle course arranged using empty boxes, chairs, or other handy objects
5) crawl on three wide boards supported by low chairs or blocks to give a slight elevation
6) crawling fast and slow on tumbling mats

CATS AND MICE

The children choose to be either "cats" or "mice." When the teacher plays music in high tones the "mice" scamper about, but as soon as low tones are heard the "mice" stop scampering and the "cats" stealthily creep around. At intervals the teacher might surprise them by playing in both high and low tones and all the "cats" and all the "mice" become active. Children would enjoy variations of the animals (and of the music) for this game. Drums, bells, etc., might be used in indicate high, low, light, or heavy tones.

HALLOWEEN OBSTACLE COURSE

Arrange pillows in the form of a path. Let each children have a turn crawling through the dark Halloween forest. Use a pair of sunglasses, with the lens painted black as a blindfold. *(Many young children do not enjoy being blindfolded. Using sunglasses makes it less scary.)* Have the children crawl along the pillow path, finding their way by feeling where the pillows are.

OCTOBER MOVEMENT ACTIVITIES

BODY MOVEMENT SUGGESTIONS

Body movements are planned to help children move smoothly and safely through space and to effect the high levels of control necessary for fine coordination skills.

The following whole-body activities will be enjoyed by children at times throughout the day. They may be used with only fingers and hands or by encompassing the whole body.

balancing like a cat walking along a fence
bending like a tree branch in a brisk wind
hopping like birds looking for worms
fluttering gracefully like butterflies
chasing your tail like a puppy
crawling like a mouse into a hole; *crawling* to steal cheese
creeping like a caterpillar and making a bumpy motion
climbing up a tree; up a ladder; over a wall
dancing on tiptoes like a wound-up doll or clown
dancing like elves on the lawn
flopping in the wind like a scarecrow
falling leaves in autumn
hopping like a toad or rabbit
jumping like a grasshopper or cricket
curling up like a sleepy kitten
scampering like mice
putting presents under a tree like Santa
rocking on a rocking horse or back and forth
running like a beetle
skating on the sidewalk or on ice
snowing softly; *making* a snowman or snowwoman
hiding nuts like a squirrel
striding like a giant taking long heavy steps
throwing a ball and catching it
bouncing a ball
turning like a slow wheel
twirling like a top
waddling like ducks going to a lake for a swim
walking in the mud; up a hill; fast; slow
wiggling like a worm

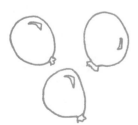

CHASING BALLOONS

Balloons provide so many opportunities for a variety of movements. Blow up many balloons and have the children move the balloons using only their feet. Working with a partner and kicking the balloon back and forth is a lot of fun!

HALLOWEEN GHOST
LACING CARD

Reproduce this ghost on tag-board. This is easily done on a ditto machine. The children can cut out the ghost, punch holes with a paper punch, and lace their ghost with yarn. For ease in lacing, wrap masking tape on one end of the yarn for a needle.

TOUCH THE OBJECTS

This activity will help increase memory skills. Choose one child to be the leader. He touches one object in the room and calls another child's name. This child must touch the leader's object and then touches another object. He calls on a third child who touches the two objects in sequence, adds a third, and call another child. This continues until someone cannot touch all the objects in the correct order. He then becomes the leader and the game starts over.

FILL IN THE BLANKS

The teacher will say a familiar poem, one which the children like very much, such as "Someone." As the teacher comes to certain words, she pauses and lets the children fill in the "blanks."

Here is an example:

"Someone came knocking on my *wee, small door.*
Someone came knocking, I'm *sure, sure, sure.*
I *listened,* I *opened,* I *looked from left to right,*
But naught there was a-stirring in the *still, dark night.*

LETS MAKE A HALLOWEEN STORY

Children love to hear stories that are made up by the teacher or with help from the children. Use the patterns found on page 29. Make several copies of each pattern. Mount the patterns with self-stick velcro or sandpaper.

Show all the Halloween patterns to the children. Have the children name each of the patterns and tell something about each pattern. Now (with your help) have the children make-up a Halloween story for the flannel board using the patterns.

This is a nice quiet time activity to be left available for children to use on their own.

REAL/PRETEND

The concepts of real and pretend or fictional are difficult for young children to understand. We often encourage children to believe in make-believe characters, such as Santa Claus, the Easter Bunny, the Tooth Fairy, etc. It is no wonder that children often believe that witches, ghosts, and goblins are also REAL! Discuss all the types of characters and costumes that the children may see on Halloween. Stress the fact that these are costumes and the characters are NOT real.

Show the children a variety of pictures and photographs. Choose good examples of pictures that depict things that are real and pictures of things that are pretend. Have the children talk about the difference between the two.

Use these patterns with the activity, Let's make A Halloween Story, found on page 55.

OCTOBER LANGUAGE ACTIVITIES

UP/DOWN CONCEPTS

Make a tree trunk from a piece of brown felt and a large variety of autumn colored felt leaves. Place the tree trunk on the flannel board and ask the children to take turns placing the leaves either "up" on the tree or "down" at the bottom of the tree.

The flannel board tree trunk and leaves are also wonderful for teaching the concepts "high," "low," "on," "off," and all the autumn colors.

WHERE IS THE COLORED LEAF?

This activity is really enjoyed by the children when it is done outside. Use a large leaf made from construction. *(You can use real leaves, but often a leaf made from construction paper is easier for the children to see.)*

Put the leaf in many different locations and have the children describe where they see the leaf. Ex: "On the slide," "under the swing," "next to the fence," "in the sandbox,"etc.

WHAT IS HAPPENING

Collect a wide variety of photographs and/or pictures from magazines and catalogs. For durability, mount the pictures on tagboard and laminate.

Show the children one picture at a time. Have the children describe to you "what is happening" in the picture. It is amazing how many different things children can see in the same picture. It is even more fascinating to observe how rapidly a young child's vocabulary development increases through the use of photographs and pictures. In September a child may tell you that they see "A boy sleeping" in a picture. By June the same child may tell you that ,"A boy is sleeping in a big bed with a yellow blanket. The boy has a teddy bear and a rocking horse."

It is well worth an early childhood teacher's time to collect pictures, mount them, laminate them and file them in an organized fashion. The uses of a picture file are endless!

HALLOWEEN GHOST FAMILY

Make a picture with three ghost family members. (see illustration) Show the picture to your class and ask the following questions:

How many people are in this family?

Who is the tallest?	How many people are in your family?
Who is the shortest?	Who is the tallest in your family?
Who is the thinnest?	Who is the smallest in your family?
Who wears glasses?	Who is the oldest?
Who is in the middle?	Who is the youngest?

OCTOBER LANGUAGE ACTIVITIES

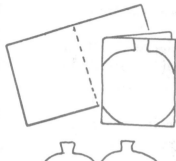

HALLOWEEN GREETING CARDS

Fold construction paper in half to form a card. Draw the outline of a pumpkin on the front of the card. Form the card into a pumpkin shape by cutting through both pages along the drawing. Keep the folded edge uncut. Tape a Halloween photo to the back of the front page so that it peeks through the opening. Write a Halloween message on the inside of the card.

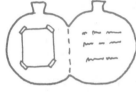

COLUMBUS' SHIPS

This is a fun project to do when you are talking about Columbus day. Make floating boats. Secure thick pieces of styrofoam (such as the type used in packing material) in a vice of a woodworking table. Supervise the children as they saw off pieces of styrofoam to use for their boats. Have each child put styrofoam packing noodles on colored toothpicks to stick in the styrofoam base. Provide the children with pans of water or a water table and let them float their boats.

THE MAGIC WHISPER

Tell this story: **"Once there was a Halloween ghost who lost her voice on Halloween. All she could do was whisper."** Whisper "happy Halloween" into a child's ear. He or she in turn whispers the same greeting into the next child's ear; this continues until all the children have participated. Then continue the story: **"The sun came out and warmed everything and the little ghost's voice came back. She didn't have to whisper anymore. She could talk in a voice just like you and me. What do you think the little ghost had to say about Halloween now that she could talk in a pleasant voice without whispering?"** The children respond.

LOUD AND SOFT

After reading the following poem to the group, ask, "Which quiet times do you enjoy the most? What noisy sounds make you happy? When is it important to have quiet times? Noisy times? Name the noisy sounds that don't belong in this room. Where should these sounds be? What are some good sounds we hear at school? At home?

I always like my quiet times;
When I can hear a word that rhymes;
When I hear a story read;
When I sleep in my bed;
When I give water to my plants;

When I watch the work of ants;
When I see a butterfly;
When I hear a lullaby;
I like my quiet times, do you?
But noisy times can be fun, too!

JACK-O-LANTERN MATCHING GAME

Make a matching game. Make two copies of the jack-o-lantern pictures.
Let the children experiment with matching identical faces.

OCTOBER FINGER PLAYS/POETRY

HALLOWEEN

This time of year we'll see scary things;
Ghosts, goblins, and witches and scary beings.

It's fun time for all to scare each other.
Let's put on some masks and go scare my brother.

You be a white ghost and I'll be a black witch.
You wait by the fence while I hide in the ditch.

My gracious, he's coming. You see what I see?
I think he's that black cat that's headed toward me!

FIVE LITTLE GOBLINS

Five little goblins on a Halloween night.
Made a very, very spooky sight.
The first one danced on his tippy-toes;   *(hold up first finger)*
The next one tumbled and bumped his nose;   *(hold up second finger)*
The next one jumped high up in the air;   *(hold up third finger)*
The next one walked like a fuzzy bear;   *(hold up fourth finger)*
The next one sang a Halloween song.   *(hold up thumb)*
Five little goblins played the whole night long!
(Use as a flannel board rhyme. Patterns found on page 60.)

JACK-O-LANTERN

I'm sometimes big,
    (large circle)
And sometimes small,
    (small circle)
But always round and yellow;
    (medium circle)
When children fix my famous grin,
    (show teeth)
Then I'm a scary fellow!
I'm called a jack-o-lantern
I like to stare at you;
Why don't you stare right back
And shout, "Hi, Mr. Boo!"

FIVE LITTLE GHOSTS

Five little ghosts dress all in white   *(hold hand upright)*
Were scaring each other on Halloween night.
"Boo," said the first one, "I'll catch you."   *(hold up thumb)*
"Boo," said the second, "I don't care if you do."   *(hold up index finger)*
The third ghost said, "I'll scare everyone I see."   *(hold up ring finger)*
The last one said, "it's time to disappear."   *(hold up little finger move behind back.)*
"See you at Halloween this time next year."
(Use as a flannel board rhyme. Patterns found on page 60.)

SQUIRREL

Whirlee, twirlee
Look at the squirrel,
Sitting in the tree.
Stuffing his cheeks,
1-2-3!
(pantomime actions.)

TWO LITTLE LEAVES

Here is a leaf it is yellow and brown.
    (hold up one pointer finger)
Here is a leaf that Johnnie found.
    (hold up other pointer finger)
Put them together . . . . . .
    (pull fingers together)
One for me and one for you.
    (point to self and someone else)

BOO OWL!

Say, wise old owl.
Up in that tree -
Why do you "oo!" -
To frighten me?

And if you're wise,
Just tell me, pray,
How come that "oo!"
Is all you say?

A PUMPKIN

I carved a pumpkin,
Orange and round.
I found it lying,
On the ground.
It is sitting on my doorstep,
And looking very bright.
To scare little ghosts,
On Halloween night.

OCTOBER RHYME PATTERNS

Pattern to be used with the rhyme "Boo Owl," found on page 60.

Pattern may be used for "Five Little Ghosts" and "Five Little Goblins," found on page 60.

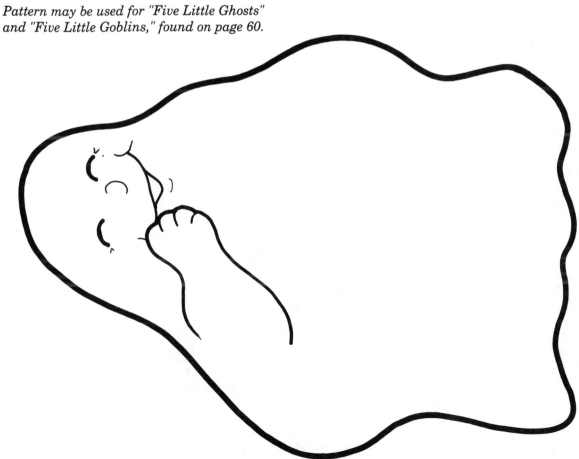

OCTOBER FINGER PLAYS/POETRY

HALLOWEEN WITCHES

One little, two little, three little witches
Fly over haystacks,
Fly over ditches,
Slide down moonbeans without any hitches.
Heigh-ho! Halloween's here.

(hold up one hand; nod fingers at each count)
(fly hand in up-down motion)

(glide hand downward)

COLUMBUS AND THE THREE SHIPS

Three ships sailed from the shores of Spain,
Over the seas and back again,
In the Nina, the Pinta and the Santa Maria.
Columbus was clever and very smart
To sail three ships with stars for a chart:
The Nina , the Pinta and Santa Maria.
Christopher Columbus and his band
Found their way to an unknown land
With the Nina, the Pinta and the Santa Maria.

THREE LITTLE PUMKINS

Three little pumpkins were sitting on a gate.
The first one said, "Oh, my! It's getting late."
The second one said, "I'm ready for some fun."
The third one said, "Let's run, run, run!"

Then Whoooooooo ... went the wind,
And out went the lights.
And the three little pumpkins rolled out of sight.

MAKING A JACK-O-LANTERN

Cut great big eyes all round and stare-y

If you would like to make me scary.
A crooked nose is useful too,

To let the light come shining through.
But if you carve a smile that's wide

I couldn't scare you if I tried.

(Pretend to cut eyes in pumpkin or circle own eyes with thumb and forefinger)

(pretend to cut a nose, or indicate one on own face)

(Carve a smile on own face with forefinger and smile a big smile)

DISAPPEARING WITCHES

Five little witches on Halloween night
Came out to play when the moon was bright
One took a broom and thumped on my door.
She flew away and then there were _____.
One did a witch's dance near the oak tree.
She flew away and then there were _____.

One swished her costume and made a loud
  BOO!
She flew away and then there were _____.
One scared a goblin and that was great fun.
She flew away and then there was _____.
The last little witch combed her long, thin hair.
She jumped on her broomstick and whizzed
  through the air.

(The children supply the number. They choose which witch they want to be and dramatize the rhyme. Each "witch" flies away and leaves the set.)

OCTOBER MUSIC ACTIVITIES

THE BLACK CATS COME

OCTOBER MUSIC ACTIVITIES

BE A COOL GHOUL

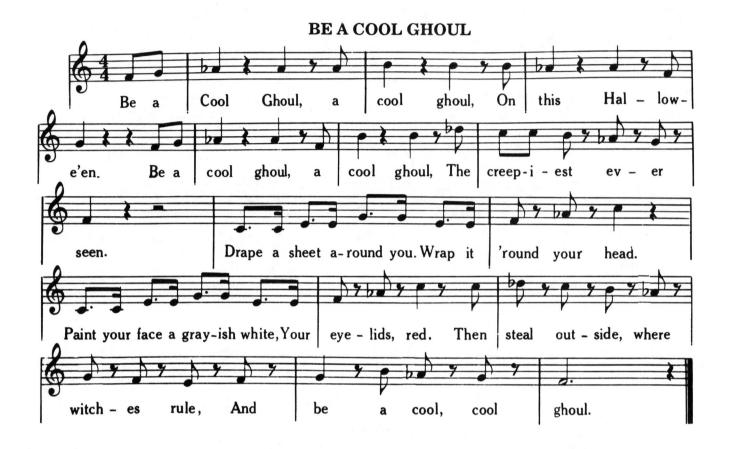

Be a Cool Ghoul, a cool ghoul, On this Hal-low-e'en. Be a cool ghoul, a cool ghoul, The creep-i-est ev-er seen. Drape a sheet a-round you. Wrap it 'round your head. Paint your face a gray-ish white, Your eye-lids, red. Then steal out-side, where witch-es rule, And be a cool, cool ghoul.

OCTOBER'S CLOUDS

VERY SMOOTHLY

Clouds of Oc-to-ber in skies___ of blue, Qui-et-ly, slow-ly you go. Mov-ing a-long___ like rest___ less lambs. Watch-ing, I stand be-low.

Color the AUTUMN leaves different colors.

OCTOBER EXPERIENTIAL ACTIVITIES

SCIENCE TABLE

Have the children collect various items that represent the season of autumn. These items can be displayed on a small table for the children to observe. It is fun to keep a looking glass on the table, so the children can more closely examine all the autumn items.

Here are some ideas for your autumn collection: various types of seeds, gourds, vegetables (squash and pumpkins) a multitude of colorful leaves, cacoon, pussywillows, and books and pictures about the autumn season.

VISIT A PUMPKIN PATCH

Many young children have never seen how pumkins grow. A pumpkin patch can be a most impressive sight. Many local florists or garden stores will know where you might find a pumpkin patch. If possible take your class to the pumpkin patch as a field trip.

While at the pumpkin patch you can usually inexpensivelypurchase a tiny pumpkin for each child in the class. (Sometimes the pumpkin patch will be willing to give away the very tiny pumpkins. It never hurts to ask!) Instead of carving the small pumpkins, let the children paint faces on their pumpkins. Painted pumpkins look adorable!

HALLOWEEN PARTY TREATS
Here are a few ideas of fun things to eat at a Halloween party:

CARAMEL APPLES

Slowly melt caramels in a pan. Push a popsicle stick into the bottom of the apple. Dip the apple into the caramel and place on wax paper. Allow the caramel to cool. (It is often a good idea to make these the day before the party.

PUMPKIN COOKIES

Use the prepared rolls of sugar cookie dough. Bake the sugar cookies following the directions on the package. Frost the cookies with orange frosting and add raisins for Jack-o-lantern facial features. A green gum-drop can be added for a stem.

WENDY WITCH'S MAGIC COOKIES

You will need; 1/2 cup honey, 1 cup powdered milk, 1 cup peanut butter, 1/2 cup chocolate chips, 1/2 cup coconut, and 1 cup bran flakes (crushed).

Mix the first five ingredients together. Roll into balls. Roll balls in crushed bran flakes. Refrigerate until firm. Makes about 3 dozen.

OCTOBER EXPERIENTIAL ACTIVITIES

GATHER THIS

The children will create a collage of natural items that they have gathered on a fall day. Once the children have finished collecting their fall items have the children work in groups of three to five. Provide each group with paper and paste.

The group members should work together to create a fall collage. Encourage the children to take turns and make suggestions to one another.

MATCH THE LEAVES

Find several leaves that are not dried or torn. Put them between self-stick laminate, clear contact paper, or press between wax paper and then cut out. Divide a square piece of cardboard into three rows with three sections in each row. (See illustration) Trace the outline of a leaf in each section. Match the pressed leaf to the outlined leaf.

FALL LEAF SORT

Have the children collect many fall leaves. These leaves can be used for a large variety of sorting activities; sort by color, sort by size, sort by shape. Provide the children with shoe boxes, so they have somewhere to put the leaves as they sort them.

PUMPKIN SIZE PUZZLE

This activity may be used for any holiday or with a variety of objects and shapes.

On a strip of tagboard, draw 5 shapes in a series of sizes. Laminate the tagboard. Make the corresponding shapes to fit in the shapes on the tagboard from felt, construction paper or any other material that would work nicely as a puzzle piece.

PUMPKIN SNACKS

This is a fun snack idea for your Halloween party. Pumpkin snacks are very healthy and are tons of fun for the children to make all by themselves.

What you need: Bread; spreadable cheese; spreading knives; raisins.

What you do: Give each of the children a slice of bread. Each bread slice should be cut into the shape of a circle. The children spread cheese all over the top surface of the bread. Raisins can be used to add facial features to the pumpkin.

JACK-O-LANTERN LACING CARD

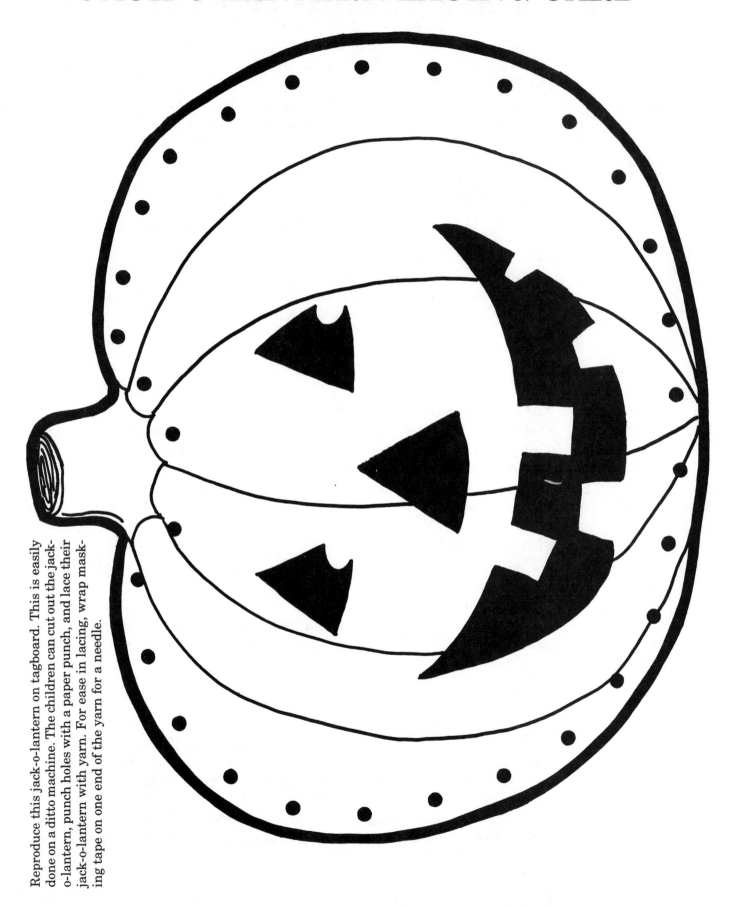

Reproduce this jack-o-lantern on tagboard. This is easily done on a ditto machine. The children can cut out the jack-o-lantern, punch holes with a paper punch, and lace their jack-o-lantern with yarn. For ease in lacing, wrap masking tape on one end of the yarn for a needle.

November

THE STORY OF THE PILGRIMS

A long time ago, the people of England were ruled by a cruel king named King James. He ordered all of the English people to go to his church. If they refused, he put them in jail.

One group of people did not like the king's church. They wanted to worship in their own way. One night it was very dark; they got on a big ship and sailed across the waters to find a new home.

This group of people were called "Pilgrims." A Pilgrim is one who travels from country to country.

They sailed to Holland, the land of the Dutch people. Holland is a land of windmills and canals. The windmills were used to pump the water off the land and into the canals.

In Holland, the Pilgrims were free to worship God the way they thought was right. The Dutch people were very kind to them. The boys and girls played like the Dutch children, and soon learned to wear wooden shoes like their Dutch friends.

The Pilgrim boys and girls also began to speak the Dutch language.

Although the Pilgrim mothers and fathers were very happy in Holland, they did not want their children to grow up to be Dutch people.

They began to talk about America. In America they could have their own church and their children would speak English and grow up to be English men and women. So they decided to leave Holland and sail to America. This time they sailed across the ocean in a ship called the "Mayflower."

It was wintertime when the Mayflower reached America. The Pilgrim fathers cut down trees in the forest and made log cabins for their families.

The Indian people showed them how to hunt and fish. In the spring they gave them corn and showed them how to plant it.

There were plenty of deer and wild turkeys in the forest. In the fall the Indians and the Pilgrims had a special celebration because of their good harvest. Everyone shared wild turkeys, deer meat, fish, pudding, baked bread, pumpkin pies, wild cranberries, nuts and maple sugar.

Everyone had such a good time that the celebration lasted for three days.

Today we celebrate "Thanksgiving" with a feast.

THE THANKSGIVING STORY PATTERNS

Tell the story of the first Thansgiving using the flannel board patterns found on pages 71-74.

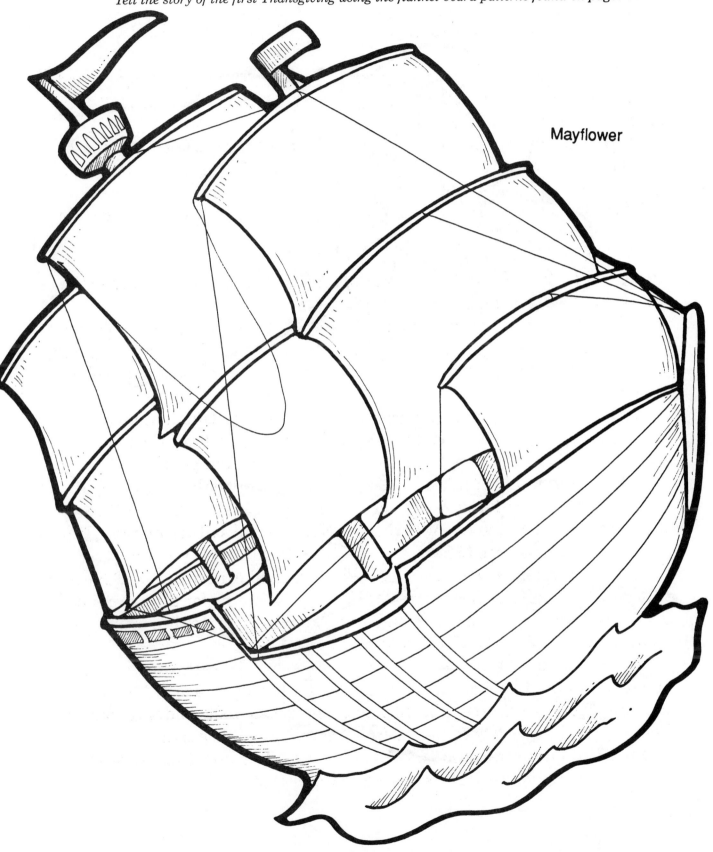

Mayflower

THE THANKSGIVING STORY PATTERNS

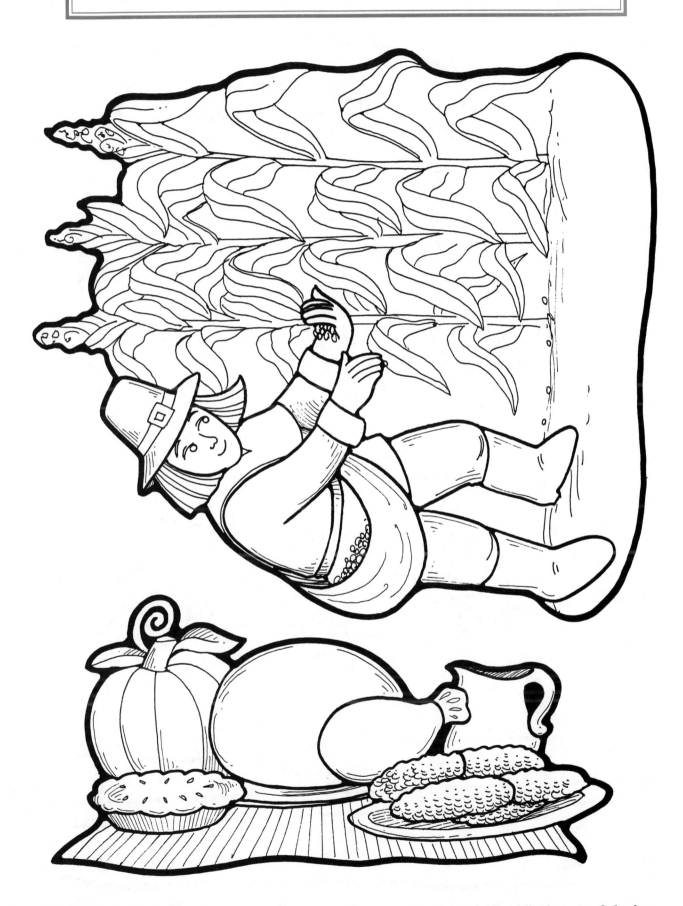

THE LITTLE GIRL AND HER THANKSGIVING DINNER

Written by Loretta Griffin, Monaca, PA

Divide the children into five groups. Give each group one part. Each time their character is named, they recite their part. **Little Girl** *(tee hee);* **Mother** *(tsk tsk);* **Father** *(hrumph hrumph);* **Big fuzzy Dog** *(bow wow);* **Turkey** *(gobble gobble)..*

Not so long ago, there lived a little girl *(tee hee)* who loved animals. She had a big fuzzy dog *(bow wow).*

She loved holidays and Thanksgiving was fast approaching. Her mother *(tsk tsk)* was a very good cook. The little girl *(tee hee)* could hardly wait for the pumpkin pies.

Several days before Thanksgiving, her father *(hrumph hrumph)* brought home a real, live turkey *(gobble gobble).*

The little girl *(tee hee)* was so excited. She never had a real, live turkey before *(gobble gobble).* The big fuzzy dog *(bow wow)* chased the turkey *(gobble gobble)* all around the yard. The little girl *(tee hee)* squealed with glee and joined in the fun. Mother *(tsk tsk)* and father *(hrumph hrumph)* watched thoughtfully from the kitchen window.

"Our little girl *(tee hee)* will be brokenhearted when Thanksgiving comes and I have to kill the turkey *(gobble gobble)* for our dinner," said father *(hrumph hrumph).*

"Oh dear, what shall we do?" said mother *(tsk tsk).*

The days passed and the turkey *(gobble gobble)* grew big and fat. The day before Thanksgiving, father *(hrumph hrumph)* got out his hatchet to sharpen it. As soon as the little girl *(tee hee)* saw it she started to cry. She ran to her room and shut the door. There she stayed until her mother *(tsk tsk)* called her for Thanksgiving dinner.

Reluctantly the little girl *(tee hee)* sat at the dining room table. Her mother *(tsk tsk)* appeared at the door holding the dinner, but it wasn't turkey *(gobble gobble).* It was a big plate of spaghetti.

The little girl *(tee hee)* was so happy. She jumped up from the table and ran out to the yard. Mother *(tsk tsk),* father *(hrumph hrumph)* and the big fuzzy dog *(bow wow)* followed.

Sure enough, there was the turkey *(gobble gobble).* The little girl *(tee hee)* hugged her mother *(tsk tsk)* and father *(hrumph hrumph).*

"This is the best Thanksgiving ever!" she squealed.

Mother *(tsk tsk)* and father *(hrumph hrumph)* smiled while the little girl *(tee hee),* the fuzzy dog *(bow wow)* and the turkey *(gobble gobble)* ran around and around the yard.

NOVEMBER BULLETIN BOARDS

CORNUCOPIA

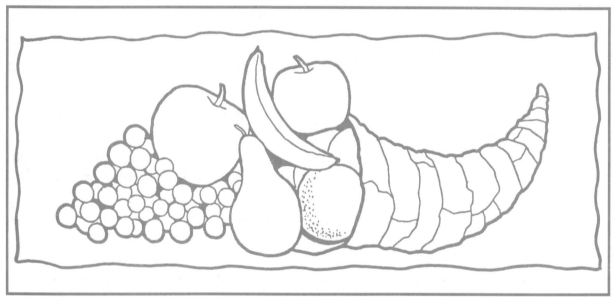

Explain to the children what a cornucopia is. Tell the children that they are going to make food to put in the bulletin board's cornucopia. Give each child the shape of a piece of food; apple, banana, grapes, etc. (patterns that you may enlarge of food and a cornucopia are included on pages 77 & 78). Have the children fill the food shape by gluing colored tissue paper on the shape. Place all the food in the cornucopia.

THIS IS WHAT WE WILL BE WHEN WE GROW UP!

Have the children cut out pictures from magazines of various occupations or the children may draw their own pictures. Each child's picture should represent what they would like to be when they grow up. Ask the children to dictate a sentence to you about "why" they would like to have this occupation. Post their sentence under the child's picture.

The patterns on pages 77 & 78 may be enlarged and used for the bulletin board activity found on page 76. The children may also use the patterns to create their own cornucopias to bring home.

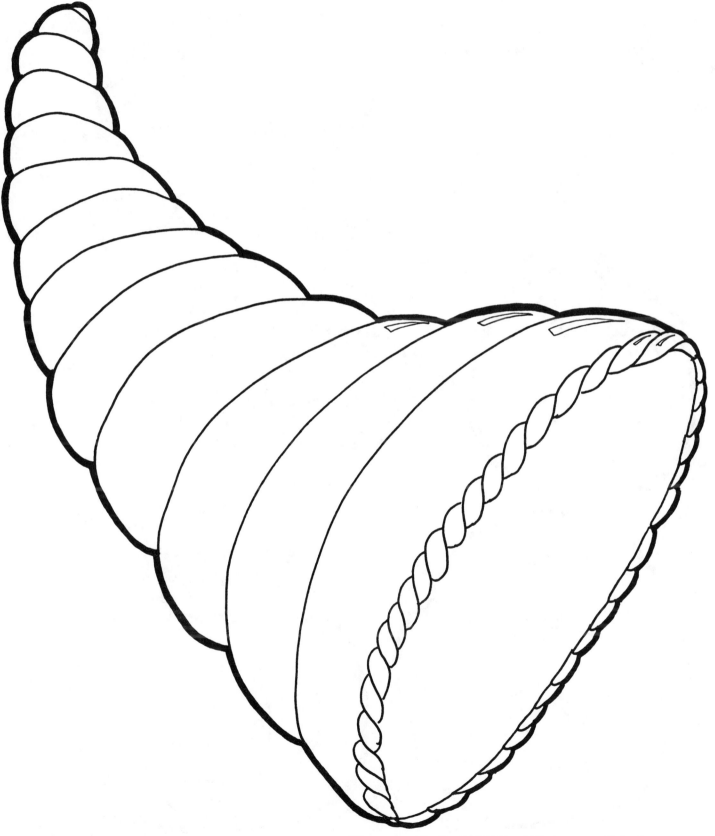

BULLETIN BOARD PATTERNS

The patterns on pages 77 & 78 may be enlarged and used for the bulletin board activity found on page 76. The children may also use the patterns to create their own cornucopias to bring home.

NOVEMBER BULLETIN BOARDS

LAND, SEA AND AIR

The background of this bulletin board should be organized so that part of the bulletin board is sky, part of it has roads and land, and part of it has a body of water. The children will enjoy creating the background or you may wish to make the background. When the background is complete, the children can make many types of transportation vehicles.

THE FIRST THANKSGIVING

This is a fun bulletin board to spend several days working on. The teacher will need to prepare a simple background. On day-one, the children can make Indians. On day-two, the children can make pilgrims. And on day-three food can be made for the Thanksgiving feast.

NOVEMBER COMMUNITY HELPERS

WHAT DO I WANT TO BE WHEN I GROW UP?

Make a list with the children of all the types of jobs that they can think of. After the group of children have come up with a large list, ask each child, one at a time, what they would like to be when they grow up? Request the child to give you a reason "why" they would like to have that particular job. Ask each child some questions about the type of job he/she chose. How does that job help people in a community? What would happen in a community where no one had that particular job? At the end of the class discussion, let each child draw a picture of him/herself doing the job that was chosen.

COMMUNITY HELPERS LIBRARY

If you do not have a school library, go to a public library and check out a wide variety of books showing pictures of various careers. Ask the children to bring books from home that relate to the topic of community helpers. Keep all the books on a table that is convenient for the children to use. The children will enjoy looking at all the pictures of different types of careers. It is also fun to ask some of the parents to come to class and tell the children about their jobs.

CLASSROOM CLINIC

All children have had some experience in a doctors office. Set up a classroom clinic by asking the children what they would see in a clinic. Ask them how they could set one up in their classroom. Encourage the parents to help you by requesting donations of cotton, band-aids, white t-shirts for doctor's coats, magazines for the waiting room, pads for perscriptions, etc. Let the children play in their clinic.

FIND MY CHILD

When discussing police officers with children, it is important to stress that a police officer's job in a community is to help the members of that community. Here is a fun game to play with the children:

The teacher (pretends) to lose a child and calls the police. The child who is the police officer asks, "What does the child look like?" The teacher describes the child. The police officer uses those clues and "finds" (identifies) the child. Another child is lost, and a new police officer is called and the game continues. After you play this game several times, the role of the teacher can be played by a child.

WHO WORKS IN AN OFFICE?

Children love discussing offices, because so many parents work in an office. Create a play office area in your classroom. Desks, calculators, typewriter , paper, pencils, telephone and a briefcase. The children will love role playing the jobs of their parents.

FIRE FIGHTERS HELP US

The job of a fire fighter is very exciting to most children. Many fire departments provide the service of coming to a school and letting the children climb on the fire truck and try on the fire fighter's clothing. If you have not called your local fire department to inquire about this service be sure to do so.

When you are discussing the role of the fire fighter it is also a good idea to discuss the danger of fire and matches. Every year it is amazing how many young children experiment with lighting matches or playing with a lighter and a serious fire occurs. Ask the children what they should do if they find a lighter or matches? What should they do if they see someone else playing with matches or a lighter?

Have a fire drill in your school. Send a note home to the parents reminding them that they should have a safety plan in case of a fire that the children practice.

CLASSROOM POST OFFICE

Ask each child to bring a box from home. *(Any type of box; shoe box, cereal box, tissue box, etc.)* The children should each make a mail box of their own. The teacher could even print the child's real address on the mail box.

Record the children's names on slips of paper. Put them in an envelope. Let each child pick a name. They must write a letter (or draw a picture to that person. The letters are then mailed in the mailboxes. Leave the mailboxes set up for a week in your classroom. During playtime the children can write other letters to their friends and mail them. Taping the children's pictures on the boxes will make it easier for the children to mail their letters independently.

SCHOOL LETTER CARRIER

Select a child who is charged with the responsibility of checking your school mail box periodically. Secure a letter carrier hat *(available through some school supply catalogs, or use a visor or make a hat)* and use a canvas totebag for the mail. When you send notes to other teachers or the office, let the child don the cap, take the totebag and experience the real role of the mail carrier. *(This is also a terrific behavior management incentive.)*

WHAT DO MOMS AND DADS DO?

Ask the children to describe the types of jobs that their parents perform. It is always fascinating to hear the descriptions. Have the children draw a picture of their parents at work. Have the children dictate a sentence describing their picture. Frame the pictures with colored construction paper. Chances are that many of these pictures will get real frames once they get home.

NOVEMBER FINE MOTOR ACTIVITIES

SAILBOATS

Ask the children to bring an empty and washed margarine tub and lid to school. Margarine tubs make wonderful sailboats. Have the children cut sails from vinyl and glue them onto a popsicle stick. Cut a small slit in the top of the lid. The popsicle stick can be pushed through the slit so the sail will stand up. These boats really float. The children will enjoy taking them home and playing with them in the bath tub.

PAPER VEHICLES

Give each of the children in your class a sheet of white construction paper and two black circles. Tell the children that the circles are wheels. Ask the children to draw any type of "transportation vehicle" that they would like. You may want to offer some suggestions: wagons, bike, bus , car, plane, boat, truck, van, etc. Once the children have drawn the vehicle of their choice, the children can then glue or paste the wheels on.

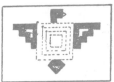

DRAWING GEOMETRIC SHAPES

These beginning drawing cards are wonderful to make for your class-room. The designs featured in this issue accompany our "Thanksgiving unit." You can make these cards for any holiday or with using any number of objects.

Make 9" x 12" cards. Using dots on each card draw graduated sizes of geometric shapes. For interest, use the lines of the shape as the base for a picture. Laminate the cards of make the cards on acetate folders. The children can use crayons on acetate and laminated surfaces which will wipe clean when they are finished.

INDIAN PENDANT

Cut a cardboard circle or any shape for each child in your class. Have the children glue assorted macaroni into a design on the cardboard. When the glue is dry, the macaroni can be sprayed with gold spray paint. Punch a hole in the top and put yarn through for a chain.

INDIAN BURLAP BLANKET

Show the children pictures of Indian writing, Indian designs, bead patterns and art. Give each of the children a small piece of burlap fabric. Let the children paint designs on the burlap. When the paint is dry fringe the burlap around all four sides.

SCRIBBLE TURKEYS

Follow the example next to this activity. The brown crayon goes around and around to make the body. The neck will stick out in a long shape; the head will be a round shape at the top of the neck. The wattle, mouth and eye are added. Where are his feet? Where shall we put tail feathers?

THANSGIVING NECKLACE

DIRECTIONS: *Reproduce the patterns for each of the children in your classroom. The children may color, cut out, punch a hole in the top of each, and string onto yarn for a necklace. Have the children use macaroni or pieces of cut straw as lacing pieces between each of the Thanksgiving patterns.*

PILGRIMS AND INDIANS

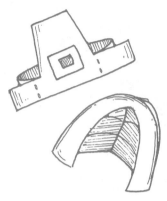

DRAMATIZATION OF THE PILGRIMS

Let the children re-enact the story of the Pilgrims. Let them make costumes and props. Provide the children with a wide variety of materials: construction paper, paper bags, crayons, scissors, glue, etc. Have plenty of reference pictures posted nearby.

A table turned on its side will work well as a ship. Ask if anyone has a pair of wooden shoes that you could borrow, so the children can have the experience of walking in wooden shoes.

It is amazing how much history young children are able to learn by role playing the characters they have heard about in stories.

MEET A FAMOUS NATIVE AMERICAN

Even teachers can have the fun of using educational theatrics in the classroom. Pick a famous Native American of your choice. Find out about this historical person. Dress as authentically (but not stereotypically) and adopt the personality of that individual. Greet your class as that character. Teach the children about the culture and traditions of Native Americans through the life of this person. Play related music in the background and have many props on hand. Many large school systems have a Native American Education Department that will be more than happy to assist you in locating materials.

Children enjoy learning words of another language so try to learn what you can. Uni means "hello." It is also a lot of fun to study the Native American tribe that inhabited your area.

CLASSROOM POW WOW

Explain that a Pow Wow is a gathering of people to discuss issues. Whenever anything comes up that requires a class meeting, use this as a chance to hold a pow wow to problem solve. Discuss the conditions of the meeting; one person speaks at a time, no interrupting the speaker, everyone gets a chance to speak.

NATIVE AMERICAN DAY

Combine all the history the children have learned about Native American people and their culture. Have a Native American Day and cook Native American foods; fish, squash, popcorn, pumpkin, fried bread, etc. Drink sassafras tea. Make necklaces by dying rigatoni with food coloring and rubbing alcohol. SUPERVISE CAREFULLY FOR SAFETY SAKE! Make noise makers from boxes, coffee cans, oatmeal boxes. Weave placemats. Younger children enjoying fringing placemats. Teach ceremonial dances and hold a pow wow.

TOOTHPICK TEEPEES

Provide each of the children with a small outline of a teepee (triangle). It will work the best if you draw the outline on a 3 x 5 index card. Give each of the children some glue and some wooden toothpicks. Show the children how to glue the toothpicks onto the index card. Once the toothpicks are dry the children can add stickers of stars or other types of stickers that could represent Indian symbol writing.

Be sure to tell the children that not all Indians lived in teepees. Show the children pictures of a variety of historical Indian homes.

PILGRIMS WORE BRIGHT COLORS TOO!

Explain to the children that the Pilgrims did not confine themselves to wearing black and white as commonly taught. The pilgrims also used pigments from plants to dye their fabrics different colors. If you ambitious you can use dandelion, onion skins and carrot tops to extract pigments to dye materials. You can also use fabric dye and let the children experiment with dying white cotton sheets. You can cut one sheet into many sections for the children. Use pinking shears.

NATIVE AMERICAN STORY TELLING

Storytellers were the "school teachers" of the tribe. The Indian people used the techniques of story telling to pass down history, to teach about nature, and human conditions and personality. In some tribes the storytellers wore "storytelling coats."

Go to the library or contact the Native American Education Department in your school system and ask for some Indian legends. Be a "Storyteller" and teach your children some of the magnificent Indian legends.

MY NAME IS ...

Read books and stories that contain Native American names. Discuss how these people selected their names (*after admired animal and bird traits, etc.*) Have the children select their Native American name. While you are learning about Native American names refer to the children as that name.

CLASSROOM FEAST

Divide your class into Pilgrims and Indians. Let each of them bring something to contribute to the feast. The menu can be as simple as Crock Pot Turkey Stew with each child bringing a carrot, onion, etc., For an added treat serve the stew with cornbread. If you forget that the Indain people taught the pilgrims about popcorn, I'm sure that the children will remind you.

INDIAN PICTURES

The children should draw in the missing parts.

NOVEMBER MOVEMENT ACTIVITIES

TRANSPORTATION TAG

This game is played in the same manner that children play any form of tag. One child is " it" and chases the other children until one is caught. The child who is caught is then the next player to be "it."

This version of tag has a little different twist to it. The children may stoop down and cannot be caught if, when they stoop down, they call out the name of some type of transportation vehicle. See how many types of transportation vehicles the children can come up with.

THE QUIET INDIAN GAME

Explain to the children how quietly the Indian people were when they went hunting. Indians were such good hunters because the animals could not hear them coming. Choose several children (3 or 4) to be the animals. Blindfold those children. Ask one child to be the Indian hunter. The Indian hunter must try very quietly to sneak up on one of the animals. If the animal hears the Indian the animal cannot be caught.

Play this game several times so all the children have an opportunity to participate.

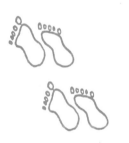

INDIAN FOOTSTEPS

Have the children draw around their own shoes. Cut out all the shoe prints and lay them in a pattern around your classroom or school yard. Let the children, one at at time, try to walk along the shoe path as quietly as they can. The other children sit with their eyes closed. Can anyone in the class walk the entire path without being heard? Who can walk the farthest down the path in silence? Who is the noisiestwalker? Can two people walk together and not be heard?

TURKEY HIDE AND SEEK

Most everyone eats turkey on Thanksgiving day. Let your classroom go on a turkey hunt. Divide half your class into turkeys and half your class into the hunters. Have all the turkeys hide. Each hunter is to catch one turkey.

After you have played the game once, have the turkeys and the hunters trade roles.

CARS, BOATS & PLANES GAME

In this game the children will be paired up according to transportation vehicles. Secretly, assign two children as planes, two children as race cars, two children as speed boats, two children as bikes, etc. On the teacher's command, the children must move about the room as if they were riding in or driving that vehicle. Each child must find the other child who is driving or riding in the same vehicle.

NOVEMBER LANGUAGE ACTIVITIES

BY WATER, BY AIR, ON LAND
Discuss different means of travel by water, by air and on land. You may wish to put up pictures on the blackboard, bulletin board or flannel board.

By water	By Air	On Land
raft	balloon	car
canoe	blimp	truck
sailing ship	glider	train
steamship	airplane	motorcyle
barge	jet	bus
freighter	helicopter	bicycle
speedboat	rocket	van
tugboat		ambulance

TRANSPORTATION PICTURES
Display pictures of the following means of transportation: truck, bus, car, train, plane, ship, rocket. Ask the following questions and let the children decide which vehicle answers the question.
1) Which one is used for going to the moon?
2) Which one travels on tracks?
3) Which one carries vegetables from the farm to the city?
4) Which one goes through the air?
5) Which one do we park in our garage?
6) Which one stops in many cities and carries many people?
7) Which one travels in the ocean?

PICTURE FILE
It is very important that children see pictures of Native American people today. Children, unfortunately often carry stereotypical ideas about Native Americans. Show children pictures (photographs are best) from books found in the library. Show current beautiful Native American art.

BOX CARS
Display many kinds of toy vehicles. Discuss each, allowing the children to contribute their thoughts. Let the children play with the toys. Get several large boxes from the grocery store. Let the children paint the boxes to represent different vehicles; car, boats, plane, etc. The children will enjoy driving the vehicles and role playing the drivers personality or career.

IMAGINE THAT
Introduce this activity by first providing sufficient information of Pilgrim life. Tell the children, "You are a Pilgrim! What did you do on the Mayflower?" Instruct the children to create a story or a picture to answer the question.

TRANSPORTATION PATTERNS

TRANSPORTATION PATTERNS

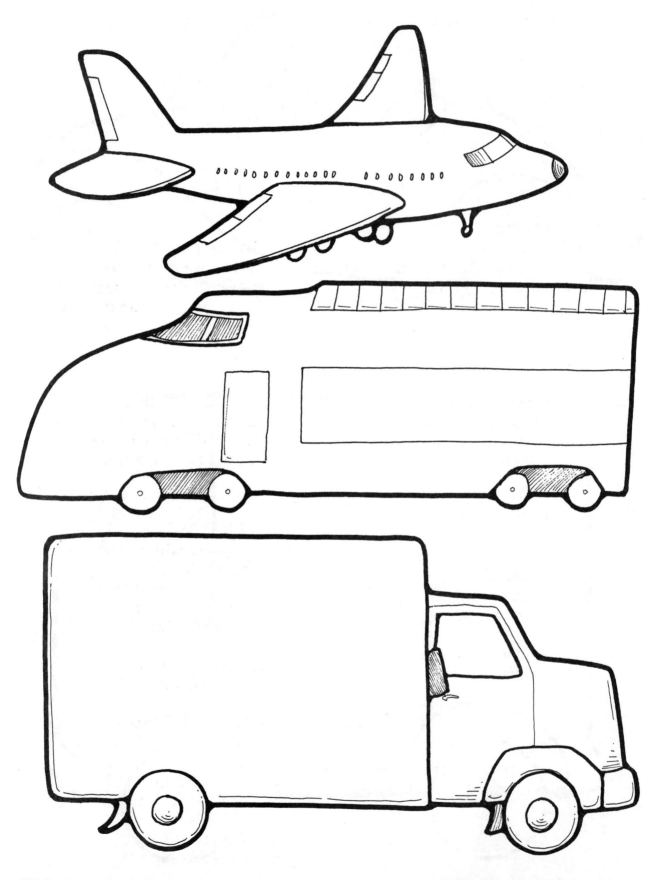

NOVEMBER FINGER PLAYS/POETRY

FIVE LITTLE INDIANS

Five little Indians	*(raise five fingers)*
On a nice fall day.	
Jumped on their ponies	*(put one finger on top of another finger*
And rode far away.	*and gallop off)*
They galloped in the meadow	*(move hands out from chest)*
They galloped up a hill.	*(make hands go up)*
They galloped so fast,	
They all took a spill.	*(tip hands over)*

FOUR LITTLE TURKEYS

Four little turkeys lived in a pen.	*(hold up four fingers)*
The little turkey's mother was a pretty fat hen.	*(form pen with fingers)*
They gobbled and gobbled all the day.	*(make hands into a beak and*
	move them in gobbling motion)
This turkey family is happy and gay.	

POLICE OFFICER

Who's your friend in the big blue car?
You see him almost every day.
He will always try to help you.
If you ever lose your way.

He checks home with a watchful eye.
He might help us cross the street.
We all may need him by and by.
In fact, he's quite nice to greet!
Who is he?

(Alternate the "he" with "she." It is important that children know that both boys and girls can be police officers.)

MAIL CARRIER

Drop your letter in the slot.
Where does it go?

Mail Carrier looks at the address.
I bet he'll/she'll know.

He/She sends it on to Grandma.
Happy she'll be.

To get a special letter.
That day from me!

FIRE FIGHTER

See all the firefighters,
Sliding down the pole.

When the firebell sounds,
Each fire fighter then bounds.

To the truck they run.
So fast it could stun.

Whee, whee, whee, whee, whee.
Now what do you see?

The fire fighters are here.
There's nothing to fear.

Water from their hose.
Makes sure the fire goes!

NOVEMBER FINGER PLAYS/POETRY

MY BICYCLE
One wheel, two wheels on the ground;
*(revolve hand in forward motion to form
each wheel)*
My feet make the pedals go round and round;
(move feet in pedaling motion)
Handle bars help me to steer so straight,
(pretend to be steering a bicycle)
Down the sidewalk, through the gate.

FIVE LITTLE PILGRIMS
There were five little Pilgrims on Thanksgiving Day:
The first one said, "I'll have cake if I may."
The second one said, "I'll have turkey roasted."
The third one said, "I'll have chestnuts toasted."
The fourth one said, "I will have pumpkin pie."
The fifth one said, "I'll have jam by and by."
But before they had any turkey and dressing,
The Pilgrims all said a Thanksgiving blessing.
*(Make a "Thankful Book." In the book each child
pastes a picture of something for which he/she is
thankful. Write the child's name under the picture.)*

TRAVELING
I walk on my legs. I ride my bicycle
(fingers walk up arm; hands hold handlebars)
I drive a small car. It's a fine vehicle.
(hands hold imaginary steering wheel)
We go for a ride in a great big long bus.
(hands spread to indicate length)
We wave at people and they wave at us.
(wave)
Please watch as I paddle in my birch canoe.
(pretend to paddle)
The water looks nice and the sky is blue.
(hold hand above eyes as to be looking)
These are just a few ways to get to a place.
Now lets try a train. We won't take up much space.
(pretend to get on the train)
So, good-bye and so long to Mother and Dad.
(wave good-bye)
We'll be back quite soon. There's no need to look sad!

I'M A PLANE
I'm a plane with wings so bright
(stoop and spread arms)
Waiting here to take a flight
(rise slowly)
Now I sail up straight and high.
(stand with arms at sides)
Now I sail around the sky.
(turn body around)
Now I land upon the ground,
(turn body around)
With a very quiet sound.
(sit)

HAPPY CHOO-CHOO
I'm a happy little choo-choo;
Hear my clicky clack.
Come see my red caboose
That's tagging in the back.
Oh, won't you come and catch me -
We'll chug so merrily;
Hurry, little children,
Come take a ride with me.
Whoo! Whoo! Whoo! Whoo!
A choo-choo ride with me!

I'm a friendly little choo-choo,
Chugging down the track.
I don't know where I'm going
Or when I'm coming back.
Oh, come along and catch me
And take a choo-choo ride;
Hurry, little children,
And find a chair inside.
Whoo! Whoo! Whoo! Whoo!
Come take a choo-choo ride.
*(Let the children create a train
with chairs. The children will enjoy
role playing various train workers
and the passengers.)*

PILGRIM FINGER PUPPETS

DIRECTIONS: Reproduce the finger puppets for each child in your classroom. Have the children color and cut out the puppets. (The teacher may have to help the children cut out the puppets.) Help the children to fold and tape the puppets to fit their fingers. Tell the children to have their puppets talk about their Thanksgiving dinner and the games they played after dinner. These puppets may also be used with the rhyme "Five Little Pilgrims" found on page 92.

NOVEMBER MUSIC ACTIVITIES

I HAVE A WAGON

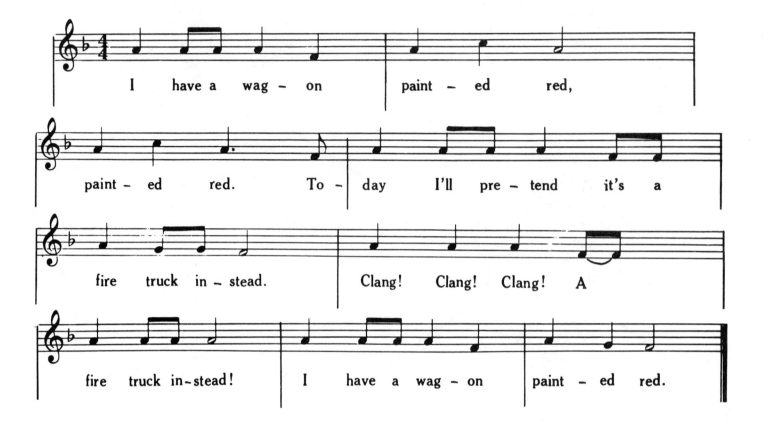

I have a wag — on paint — ed red,
paint — ed red. To — day I'll pre — tend it's a
fire truck in — stead. Clang! Clang! Clang! A
fire truck in-stead! I have a wag — on paint — ed red.

THE TRAIN
(Sung to the melody: This Old Man)

The engine is coming down the track.
It is very shiny and black.

The coach is next and it is brown.
The people in it are sitting down.

The pullman is rolling in between.
It has many berths and this car is green.

The refrigerator car is cold and white.
Its food will be good to eat tonight.

The stock car's animals are for the zoo.
They are in cages. This car is blue.

The tank car is loaded and it is yellow.
With gasoline for the service station fellow.

The mail car carries letters sad and gay.
It has packages and it is gray.

The caboose is always the last one, it is said.
We wave and wave. It is painted red.

(This is a wonderful song for the flannel board. Make each of the cars in the song and add them to the flannel board as you sing.)

NOVEMBER MUSIC ACTIVITIES

The following songs are from the book, Sing-A-Song All Year Long, by Connie Walters.
Copyright by T.S. Denison & Co., Inc.

I'M A LITTLE INDIAN
(Melody: I'm a Little Teapot)
I'm a little Indian on the go
Here is my arrow and here is my bow
When I go out hunting, hear me shout –
"Bear and buffalo – better watch out!"

I'M A LITTLE TURKEY
(Melody: I'm a Little teapot)
I'm a little turkey; I like to play
I'm very hungry; I eat all day
When I see the hunter with his gun
Then I know it's time to run.

THE TURKEY STRUT
(Melody" Shortnin' Bread)
See all the turkeys up in a tree
All the little turkeys like to hide from me
Please stand still, don't make a sound
You'll see all the turkeys as they strut around.

All the little turkeys go wobble, wobble,
All the little turkeys just like this. . .
All the little turkeys go gobble, gobble,
All the little turkeys just like this. . .

(Imitate the appropriate movements of
a turkey walking around as you sing the
second verse of the song, The Turkey Strut.
Dramatize the first verse.)

DRUM RHYTHMS
Have the children slap their thighs or pound their fists on the floor to different drum rhythms. have the children imitate sounds that you demonstrate first. Use different concepts such as loud, soft, fast, slow. Ask the children to take turns being the leader who decides what rhythm the other children should imitate.

THANKSGIVING TURKEY
Hobble goes the turkey,
　　(hands on hips, squat down and walk "turkey fashion")
See him strut along.
Gobble goes the turkey,
　　(rise up slightly, stretch neck)
He'll not be here long!
　　(run and hide)

Use tom-tom to beat the rhythm

Hobble goes the turkey

NOVEMBER EXPERIENTIAL ACTIVITIES

BEAD PATTERN

Use envelope-type folder, 6"x9" which is made of acetate and chipboard. Tape the top edge of the acetate. Tape sides and bottom of acetate to chipboard. Leave the top open.

Use acetate envelope-type folder. Punch holes at the left two sides and four inches from the top. Use a pair of 18-inch shoelaces. Knot the shoelaces and draw through the back. Make card with simple bead pattern on the top row. A child may continue the pattern as far as he/she can. The child may make his/her own pattern on the second row.

REAL TURKEYS

The turkey is the largest game bird in North America. Turkeys were a favorite of the pioneer hunters.

The adult male turkey can grow as big as four feet long and can weigh 36 pounds. Female turkeys are smaller than the male turkeys and weigh about 16 pounds. Male turkeys are called *toms,* female turkeys are called *hens* and a young turkey is called a *poult.*

Wild turkeys live together in small flocks in the forest. They like to eat insects, small nuts, berries and seeds. At night they rest in trees but they build their nests on the ground. Turkey eggs are about twice the size of chicken eggs. The eggs are creamy tan in color, speckled with brown.

PILGRIM PERILS

Talk about the pilgrims. How did they live? How did they get their food? Discuss the many conveniences that make our life easier than it was in the days of the Pilgrims. Divide the children into small groups of three to five children. As a group instruct the children to draw a picture showing modern conveniences that make our life easier. As a comparison, make bread with your class. Making bread from scratch is not easy. Then talk about when we need bread most of us just go to the store and buy bread.

BUTTER

You will need a 1/2 pint of heavy whipping cream. Use a small churn or shake the cream in a jar until it turns to butter. Drain the buttermilk from the butter and refrigerate both.

Use the butter on popcorn and on cornbread (two traditional foods of the Pilgrims and Indians). Add a little salt to the buttermilk and pour a small amount into paper cups for the children to taste.

PARACHUTES

Use scraps of thin fabric (square). Tie strings on each corner. Bring the strings together and tie around a weight (rock, etc.)

SWEET CORN

Buy ears of sweet corn, still in their husks, at the grocery store or produce stand. Let the children husk the corn and clean it themselves. Cook it for lunch and serve with melted butter (you might wish to use the butter recipe on page 96). Discuss the importance of the Indian people teaching the Pilgrims how to plant and grow corn.

PUMPKIN PIE

Pumpkin pie is always a treat during the month of November.

In a sauce pan combine: 1/3 cup brown sugar, 1 envelope Knox Gelatin, 1/4 teaspoon salt, 1 teaspoon cinnamon, 1/4 teaspoon nutmeg, 1/4 teaspoon ginger.

Into this mixture combine: 3 egg yolks and 1/2 cup milk.

Cook over a medium heat, stirring constantly until boiling. Remove from heat and stir in one cup of canned pumpkin pie filling. Chill one hour.

Beat 3 egg whites until soft peaks form. Gradually beat in 1/4 cup sugar to form stiff peaks. Fold pumpkin mixture into it. Turn into graham cracker crust and chill 2 to 3 hours before serving.

POTATOES

Give each student a jar which is 3/4 full of water, a potato and 3 to 4 plastic toothpicks. Put the potato in the top of the jar so that the bottom 1" or so is in the water. If the potato is small enough to fall through the jar, put the toothpicks in the sides to hold it up. Keep enough water in the jar to keep the end of the potato wet. Pretty soon roots will grow from the bottom and sprouts from the sides.

POPCORN

Pop popcorn in a pan on the stove. This is closer to the way the Indians did it than the modern popcorn poppers or microwave popcorn.

COMPARING BREADS

Provide each child with a plate containing small pieces of bread. The children decide which one they prefer. Here are some suggestions for the bread: banana bread, rye bread, pumpernickel, white, whole wheat, onion or onion rolls, cheese bread, sour dough bread, French bread, bagels, croissants.

FEATHERS

Bring in a variety of feathers for the children to examine. Discuss how feathers were once used as ink pens, and how they are used for pillows, and coat or quilt stuffing today.

THANKSGIVING WREATH

You will need: Orange, yellow, red, and brown construction paper; stapler and glue. Posterboard or construction paper circles that are approximately 10" in diameter and 2" in width.

What you do: Posterboard circles are cut out for each child. A turkey head-with-feet and colorful feathers are also cut out (See patterns.)

Each child is given a posterboard circle along with construction paper feathers. The feathers are glued on the circle. When finished, the teacher staples a turkey head-with-feet at the bottom of the wreath.

Multicolored feathers (available from craft stores) may be glued on the wreath along with the paper feathers.

The beak is cut of yellow construction paper, folded in half and one side stapled on the turkey's face.

brown head

red wattle

orange neck and feet

Finished wreath

PILGRIM HAT DOT-TO-DOT

December

THE JINGLE BELLS

Way up at the top of a church steeple, a man was pulling a rope to sound the bell. The bell went ding-dong, ding-dong. It was almost Christmas and time to call all the people in the town to come to church. Suddenly, the man saw two little bells lying in a corner next to the big church bell. He picked them up and shook them. Then he listened very hard.

"These don't ding-dong like my church bell," he said, "but I will take them to someone who needs them."

So the bellman put the little bells in his pocket and went to the firehouse. He showed them to the fireman, who took them and shook them and listened very hard.

"These don't clang-clang like the bell on my fire engine," said the fireman.

"They don't ding-dong like the church bell either," said the bellman, "but I will take them to someone who needs them."

So he took the bells home to his wife. She took them and shook them and listened very hard.

"These bells don't br-ring br-ring like my telephone bell," she said.

"And they don't ding-dong like the church bell or clang-clang like the fire engine bell," said the man, "but I will take them to someone who needs them."

So the bellman climbed into his car and drove to the farmhouse. He showed the bells to the farmer who took them and shook them and listened very hard.

"These don't clink-clink like my cowbell," said the farmer.

"They don't ding-dong like the church bell either," said the bellman. "They don't even clang-clang like the fire engine or br-ing br-ring like the telephone bell, but I will take them to someone who needs them."

So the bellman put the bells in his pocket and went down to the sea. He jumped into a small boat and sailed away. He sailed for many days and many nights. Every day it grew colder. Finally he came to an island and he sailed the boat right up to it. There he saw a big man with a long white beard. He was dressed all in red. The bellman showed the bells to the big man and said, "These little bells don't ding-dong like the church bell, or clang-clang like the fire engine bell, or br-ring br-ring like the telephone bell, or clink clink like the cowbell, and I want to give them to someone who needs them."

The big man took the bells and shook them and listened very hard. Then he laughed and laughed and said, "I have been looking all over the world for these bells. I need them to ride in my sleigh tonight and sing to all the children that Christmas is here. I am Santa Claus, and do you know what these bells are? They ... are ... the jingle bells!"

(Turn into a flannel board story with the patterns found on pages 102 & 103.)

STORY PATTERNS

Patterns for the story, "The Jungle Bells," found on page 101.

STORY PATTERNS

Patterns for the story, "The Jungle Bells," found on page 101.

THE LIFE OF SANTA CLAUS

Deep in the country of snows up and
  down,
Far in the northland - away from a town,
Santa's old house of remarkable charm
Lies in the snowdrifts that cover his farm.

All of the windows you see in the night,
Are bordered with snow and shining with
  light.
All through the evenings, all through the
  year,
The light you can see and the noise you
  can hear.

Busy old Santa is happy and wise,
Making new toys for a Christmas
  surprise,
Sawing and pounding and painting away,
Colorful things for the next Christmas
  Day.

Out of the chimney, the smoke rises high,
Straight through the air to the stars in
  the sky,
Up from the fireplace crackling and
  warm,
Out in the cold and the wind and the
  storm.

Dear Mrs. Santa is busy within,
Reading to Santa the letters to him,
Cooking and sewing and lending a hand,
Dressing new dolls for the girls of the
  land.

Knitting their sweaters and curling their
  hair,
Tying their bonnets and slippers to wear,
Rocking them softly to sleep with a song,
Thoughtfully sending their blankets
  along.

Just a short way from the big kitchen
  door,
Stands the old barn with a rough
  wooden floor,
Snuggled against a white hillside of snow,
Cozy and warm for the reindeer, you
  know.

Day after day, every morning and night,
Santa goes out with a lantern for light,
Pumping the water for all of the deer,
Feeding them hay from the loft that is
  near.

Patting them gently - each one in a stall,
Jingling the sleighbells that hang on the
  wall,
Calling their names; for they listen and
  know,
Santa will take them all out in the snow.

Then to the barn they will hurry once
  more,
Santa has finished his everyday chore;
Up to the house and right on with his
  work.
Never a moment would Santa Claus
  chirk.

All through the day and far into the
  night,
Year after year and with all of his might,
Santa is busy as busy can be,
Making good presents for you and for me.

Deep in the country of snows up and
  down,
Far in the northland, is Santa Claus
  town.

REINDEER TRAINING

From the book, "Fun with Action Stories" by Joan Daniels
Copyright by T.S. Denison

(This is a Christmas story in which the children pantomime they are reindeer, crawling on hands and knees, or they can simply pantomime the activities.)

It was a busy month before Christmas and as usual everyone at the North Pole was very busy. Even the reindeer were preparing by building their strength for the long hard ride delivering presents on Christmas Eve.

The reindeer **woke up** early, **stretching, shaking their heads, antlers** and **whole bodies**. Then they **swept** their stalls and **put down** fresh hay. Prancer was hungry so one of Santa's helpers gave the reindeer some oats and water for breakfast. They **chewed** their food slowly and carefully. Dancer decided to have some fun so he **pushed open the door with his head** and **motioned** for the others to join him.

They all **skipped** out of the barn into the heavy snow. The deer **ran** and **hopped first on one foot**, then **the other** and finally on **both feet**. They **skipped** from the pine trees to a brook which they **leaped across**. The snow was so soft and fluffy that the deer **sat down** and **rolled** in it. Then they **stood up** and **shook** the snow off. Vixen had an idea – he wanted to play hide and seek. The rest all agreed, **jumping up and down** with excitement. Blitzen was "IT" so the others scurried, **crouching down** behind snowdrifts or behind trees.

Suddenly, all the reindeer **stood still**. They heard a bell jingle so they **raced** back to the barn. Santa's helper **lined the reindeer up** for their flight exercises. While he counted, the reindeer **stood on the tips of their hooves** and **stretched** to the top of their antlers. They **sprang into the air** and **floated** back down. The reindeer **jumped forward** as far as possible, then **backwards**. They **hopped on one foot** and **then the other**. The reindeer **stood straight up** and **bending at their middle**, they **touched their hind hooves ten times**. The most important exercise was to practice **galloping in place** to build up their leg muscles. Last of all the reindeer **stood on their hind legs** and **squatted five times**.

The supper bell rang and the reindeer **herded** into their stalls for a special dessert of peanut butter and cheese which they **chewed slowly** and carefully. Tired from all their training and fun, Santa's reindeer **curled up** in the soft hay, **closed their eyes** and **went to sleep**.

DECEMBER BULLETIN BOARDS

GINGERBREAD COOKIES

The gingerbread man is a fun story to tell during the holiday season. Provide the children with a brown construction paper cut-out of a gingerbread man cookie. *(Pattern found on page 107.)* Let the children decorate the gingerbread man with sequins, buttons, yarn, scrap fabric, markers, or anything else you may have on hand. *(Additional decorating ideas are on page 107.)* Display on the bulletin board.

CLASSROOM CHRISTMAS TREE

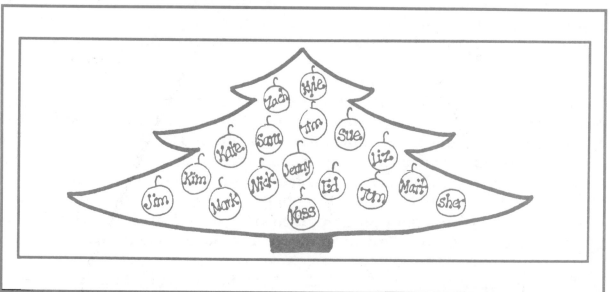

The teacher should make a large foil tree on the background of the bulletin board. The children can make round ornaments. Let the children print their name on the ornament in white glue and then sprinkle glitter over the glue. Let dry and display the ornaments on the classroom tree.

GINGERBREAD MAN PAPER DOLLS

You will need: brown construction paper, jelly beans, raisins, and glue.

What you do: a gingerbread man is cut out for each child (kindergarten children may wish to cut out their gingerbread man). Jelly beans and raisins are placed on a work table along with glue. The child glues on jelly beans for eyes and raisins for buttons.

DECEMBER BULLETIN BOARDS

CHILDREN ARE A SPECIAL GIFT

Children Are A Special Gift

Cover the bulletin board with white paper and trim the sides with ribbon, so the bulletin board looks like a giant package. Let each child draw a picture of him/herself on the package. Title your bulletin board, "Children are a special gift." This is a nice bulletin board for either the Christmas or Hanukkah celebration.

OUR CHRISTMAS TREE

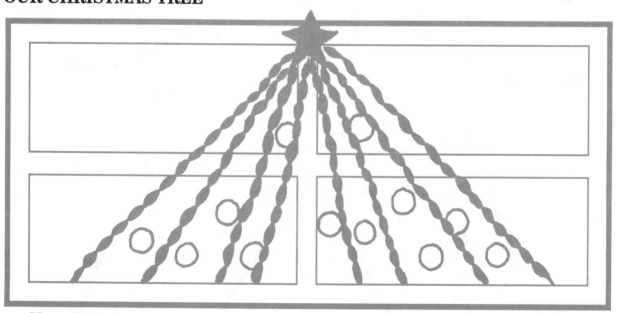

Use a bulletin board or a classroom window for this display. Twist crepe paper from the center of your display down to the bottom to form a Christmas tree shape. (Follow illustration.) Have the children make construction paper ornaments to decorate the tree. Add a star to the top of the tree.

DECEMBER FINE MOTOR ACTIVITIES

PAPER PLATE FAMILY PUPPETS

Make family members puppets using tagboard strips for handles and paper plates for faces. Faces can be drawn on or scrap materials can be used. The children can each make a set of puppets of their own or they can assist you in making several large families of puppets for use in the classroom. Children enjoy composing the "scripts" their puppets will use.

GRANDMA AND GRANDPA'S PORTRAITS

Let the children draw a portrait of their grandparents. If you are fortunate enough to have a laminating machine at your school, use it to laminate the portraits. Take the laminated portraits and make a construction paper frame. Grandparents will treasure these pictures for years to come. *(They also make a wonderful Hanukkah or Christmas gift.)*

MY ADDRESS IS ...

It is important that when our children begin kindergarten that they know their address and telephone number. Here is a fun idea for helping children learn where they live. Explain that each house or apartment has an address. An address tells where people live. Let each child use number stamps and index cards to stamp out their addresses using an address book which you compile. Then let them pair off to learn their address. When they know their address, staple in onto their house which is within a display or part of a bulletin board. *(Tape recorders and headphones are good devices for those children who learn auditorily.)*

HOME-A-RAMA

Using magazines, realty ads, etc., let the children make a collage of homes. Use National Geographics if you can bear to. This provides an excellent variety of homes around the globe. Travel magazines are useful here too.

CANDLEHOLDER *(Activity for Christmas or Hanukkah)*

You will need: Half-gallon plastic bottle (the type that has a handle); felt; Rickrack trim; glue; scissors.

What you do: Cut the top section from the bottle. Cut either Christmas or Hanukkah symbols from the felt. Glue these to the upper part of the holder. Glue two rows of rickrack around the bottom part of the holder.

COTTON BALL CHRISTMAS TREES

Give each of the children a tree in the shape of a triangle cut from green construction paper. Let the children glue small cotton balls on the tree. When the cotton balls are dry, the children may wish to add a red construction paper base to the tree and some ornaments. Small colorful buttons work nicely as ornaments.

SPONGE PAINTED ORNAMENT TREES

This art project works well as an individual project or it can be done as a large class project. The shape of a tree is drawn on a piece of white paper. *(A small tree 11" x 17" or a large tree drawn on newsprint and hung on the wall.)*

Cut sponges into shape of ornaments *(bells, circles, stars, etc.)*. Dip the sponges into tempera paint and dab onto the tree. Use a variety of colors.

STAR OF DAVID

Provide each of the children with six popsicle sticks. The popsicle sticks can be glued together to form the "Star of David." *(See illustration.)* When the glue is dry, the star can be painted with tempera paint or may be spray painted gold and hung from the ceiling of your classroom.

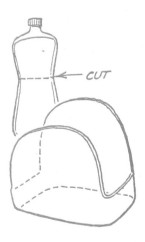

HOLIDAY CARD HOLDER

The "Holiday Card Holder" can make a wonderful Christmas or Hanukkah gift for the children's parents. Ask each of the children to bring a quart plastic bottle from home. *(Emphasize that the bottle needs to be washed well at home before it is brought to school.)* The Teacher uses a knife to cut the top section from each bottle and then cut down the sides of the bottle to 3/4 of an inch from the bottom. Cut out a section from each side. *(See illustration.)* Round the back portion of the holder. The children can glue rickrack braid around the front section and decorate the rest of the front by gluing on felt.

YARN WREATH

Give each of the children a small "cake-size" paper plate. Let the children glue green yarn around the edges of the paper plate. When the yarn is dry, the children may add red construction paper berries and a red bow at the bottom.

DECEMBER FINE MOTOR ACTIVITIES

TRACING HOLIDAY SHAPES

Give each child a large piece of lightly colored thin paper. The children trace Christmas or Hanukkah shapes onto the paper with cookie cutters and then color them. This paper can be used as wrapping paper for Christmas or Hanukkah gifts.

HOLLY WREATH

Give each child a paper plate with the inside circle already cut out. Children glue small torn pieces of green construction paper to cover the paper ring. Then add small paper berries or small red cinnamon candies and a real bow.

BAKING CLAY ORNAMENTS

Make baking clay by mixing together: 4 cups of flour, 1 cup of salt, 1 cup of water.

Roll the dough 1/4" thick with a rolling pin, then allow the children to cut out Christmas shapes with cookies cutters. Bake in a 400° oven for 45 minutes or until lightly browned. Let them cool completely and paint with tempera paints.

POTTED CHRISTMAS TREE

Go outside and get a nicely shaped tree branch. Place in a pot. Secure in a piece of styrofoam or bed of small rocks. Cut a piece of fabric large enough to cover the top of the branch. Cut a hole in the center and a slash to the outer edge. Use as a tree skirt. As the Christmas season progresses, decorate with ornaments that the children make.

GUMDROP TREE

You will need a styrofoam cone for each child in the class, gumdrops and toothpicks. Press a toothpick into each gumdrop. Press the toothpicks into the styrofoam cone. Cover completely. (Anytime that toothpicks are used with young children, very close supervision is needed!)

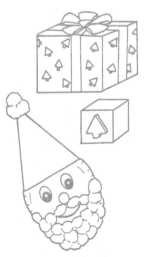

STAMPERS

Use Dr. Scholls adhesive foam. Cut the foam into shapes. Peel off the backing and stick to a wooden block. Pour paint over several layers of paper towels to form an ink pad. Dip the adhesive foam into the paint. Stamp onto paper. Use the paper as gift wrap or greeting cards. This is a good activity for Hanukkah or Christmas.

PAPER PLATE SANTA

Cut out a red triangle for Santa's hat. Glue a cotton ball to the tip of the hat. Glue the hat onto a paper plate. Draw a face on the paper plate and color. Glue cotton to the bottom of the paper plate for Santa's beard.

HANUKKAH MENORAH

Duplicate menorah for each child. The child colors the base of the menorah. Next the child dabs glue on each flame and sprinkles them with red, orange, or yellow glitter.

DECEMBER MOVEMENT ACTIVITIES

FAMILY FOLLOW THE LEADER

All children enjoy the game of "Follow The Leader." You can use this game to help teach the names of family members: grandma, grandpa, aunt, uncle, brother, sister, cousins. Choose one child to be the leader. That child begins walking around the room as a family member of his choice; skipping like a big sister. That child stops and chooses another child. That child gets to be the leader and begins a movement as another family member; such as crawling like a baby. The game continues until all the children have had the opportunity of leading the line and choosing a family member character.

MOTHER, MOTHER, WHERE IS YOU CHICK?

All the children sit in a circle. The "mother" or "father" sits in the middle covering her/his eyes. One chick *(child)* hides. The mother/father gets three chances to find the chick. The chick then becomes the mother/father and the game continues.

VARIATION: The mother/father must identify the chick by the sound of the chick's voice.

UNDER CONSTRUCTION

Provide the children with a large variety of building blocks; legos, duplo blocks, lincoln logs, kindergarten building blocks, coffee cans, assorted cereal boxs, etc. Let the children have the fun of constructing a house or building. The children may even wish to build an entire city.

GUESS WHAT I AM DOING?

In order to play this game, each of the children must think of some activity that they either would perform at school or at home. The children will take turns acting out their activity and the other children will try to guess what the performing child is doing.

If the children are having difficulty in thinking of something to do, make suggestions such as washing dishes, ironing clothes, playing tennis, baseball, football, riding a bicycle, fishing, swimming, mowing the lawn, painting, reading, cleaning the house, sewing, swinging, cooking, running, sleeping, eating, watching television, flying a kite, making a snowman, sweeping, hammering, coloring, etc.

DECEMBER MOVEMENT ACTIVITIES

BEAN BAG FUN

All children enjoy playing with bean bags. There are a variety of fun activities that can be done with bean bags that promote and help to increase better eye-hand coordination. Here are some fun bean bag activities that are great for indoors during these cold months:

1) *COFFEE CANS* - Have the children, one at a time, assume a standing position. From this position the child drops the bean bag from the waist into a coffee can.

2) *CARDBOARD BOX* - Cut a hole in a large cardboard box. The box will stand easily and not tip over. The children take turns tossing the bean bags into the hole.

3) *HOOLA HOOPS* - Place a hoola-hoop on the floor and have the children practice tossing the bean bags into the center of the hoola-hoop.

4) *PLAYING CATCH WITH A FRIEND* - The children play with a partner. The idea is to toss the bean bag gently to one another. Encourage the children to try and keep count of how many times they can catch the bean bag before it falls to the floor.

5) *CARPET SQUARES* - Have the children try to toss all the bean bags onto a carpet square. *(This is a very quiet gross motor activity.)*

DRIVING CAREFULLY

This is a delightful game for even the youngest preschoolers and is great fun when you are working on your transportation unit.

All the children get on their hands and knees in the middle of a circle. The circle should have a diameter of at least 30'. On a command from the teacher, the children race around inside the circle. THEY MAY NOT BUMP INTO ANOTHER CHILD or leave the circle area. As the children move about, they weave in and out of one another moving in all directions. On a second command, they come to a halt (freeze).

BUSY LITTLE ELVES

The children sit with their feet touching each other in a large circle. Each child has a ball (soft balls such as nerf balls work the best). On the signal of "go" all the children pass their balls to the person on the right. All the balls are moving around the circle.

The teacher can make this game more difficult by adding the second command of "switch." The children would then switch directions and begin to pass their ball to the person on their left.

To keep this game with our holiday theme. The children can pretend that they are elves helping Santa. All the balls are toys that must be passed through all the elves. At the end of the game all the balls can be loaded into Santa's bag.

DECEMBER MOVEMENT ACTIVITIES

RIBBON DANCING

You will need a two-inch roll of crepe paper cut into 18-inch lengths. Give each child a couple of strips of crepe paper to hold in each hand. Play a record, cassette tape, or the piano and let the children dance with their ribbons. Ribbons help the shy child become more involved and less inhibited.

RELAXING CAN BE FUN

The upcoming holiday season always seems to create some "extra active" moments in the classroom. Provide the children with some relaxing activities to help calm them from all the excitement.

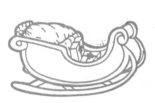

Have the children sit and hear a favorite story. This will help them relax. After the story, discuss how their arms and legs are relaxed. With music, do exercises to show tight muscles and relaxed muscles – jump, sit, stand, lie down, hop, skip, and discuss how it feels. Relax different parts of the body – arms, legs, head, eyes.

SANTA'S FLIGHT

Arrange the chairs so the children can pretend that they are flying in Santa's sleigh. Once everyone is in the sleigh begin playing music (piano, record, cassette tape). When the music stops, the children jump out of the sleigh, race to a designated corner of the room (pretend house) stack a pile of blocks (the pretend presents) and then race back to the sleigh. Once the children are all back in the sleigh, the game begins again.

Variation: Choose one child to be Santa and jump out of the sleigh and run to stack the presents.

JINGLE BELLS

The sounds of bells are often heard during the month of December. Here is a fun gross motor activity utilizing "bells."

Set up two chairs, about three feet apart. Tie a piece of yarn between the two chairs. Attach several bells to the yarn. Have the children crawl under the yarn without touching (or ringing) the bells.

When the children first begin this activity have the yarn up high enough so all the children are successful crawling under and not ringing the bells. As the children become more comfortable, lower the yarn to make the crawling activity more difficult.

MATCHING GIFTS

NAME _____

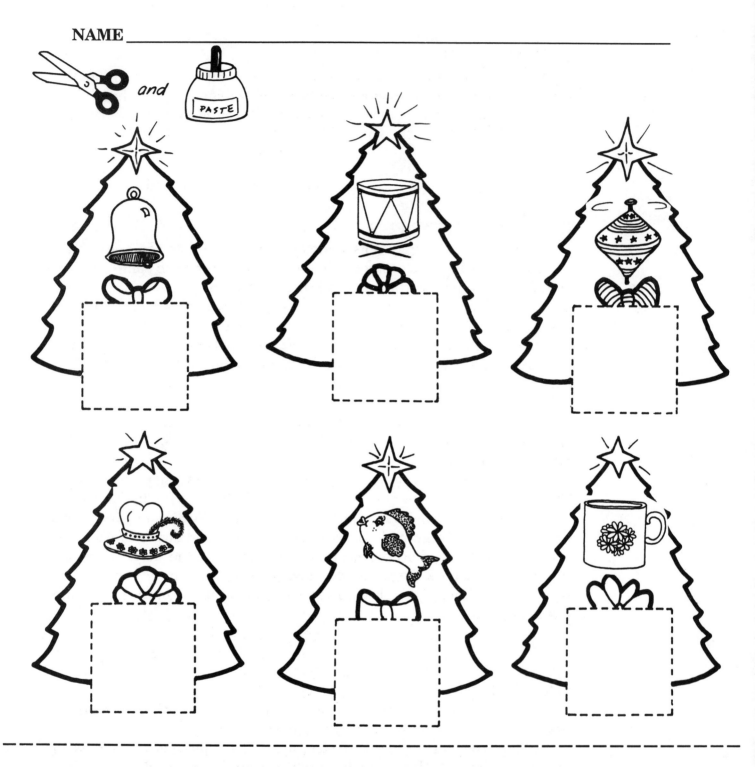

DECEMBER LANGUAGE ACTIVITIES

EMPTY/FULL

Children love experimenting with water play. Here is a fun activity that will also help children to understand the concepts of empty and full.

Provide the children with a multitude of containers that they can fill with water, sand, pebbles, salt, bean seeds, etc. The children will enjoy pouring and scooping these materials and will be able to visually see the concepts of empty and full.

This is also a good activity for working the fractional concept of one-half.

TASTE TEMPTERS

During this activity the children will be able to taste a variety of foods. Divide the children into small groups of three to five. At each group station provide a tray with a variety of foods with different tastes; sweet, sour, salty and bitter. Have an aide or parent at each station to assist with this activity. A blindfold will add to the fun.

Introduce the activity be reviewing the sense of taste and several words which might be used to describe different tastes. Instruct each group member to take turns describing and guessing the food sample offered by the helper at his/her station.

For easy serving, have the food samples bite-sized with a toothpick in each. The toothpicks should not pose any problems because there is an adult at each station.

TOY-MATCHING GAME

Make a background card from 12" x 12" chipboard. Draw a one inch border all around. Divide the board into sixteen 2½" squares. Glue *(or use stickers of toys)* a picture of a toy in each square. Make two corresponding sets of picture cards. *(You will need three identical pictures of each toy; one for the large chart and two for the sets of cards.)* Cover with clear contact paper or laminate.

Place one set of cards face down on the board. Divide the second set equally among the players and turn face up in front of them. The players take turns turning over a card from the board. If it matches one of his cards, he keeps it. If not, he returns it to the board, face down.

WHERE IS SANTA IN THE SUMMER?

The title of this activity is a fun story-starter for young children. We always think about Santa Claus during the late fall and early winter months living in the cold and snow and busy making toys! BUT ... Where is Santa in the summer? What is Santa doing? Does he go anywhere?

Chart the children's responses to these questions. Draw pictures of Santa in the summer.

DECEMBER LANGUAGE ACTIVITIES

HIDDEN SMELL JARS

Make "hidden smell" jars by poking holes in the lids of nontransparent jars. Fill each of the jars with scents that are familiar to this holiday season such as evergreen, ginger, mint, and candles. Let the children have fun guessing what the smells are and talking about what the smells remind them of.

PAPER CHAIN CALENDAR

At the beginning of December make a paper chain of 25 links and hang it from the ceiling. Each morning take one off and count how many links are left. The children will be able to see how fast the holiday season is approaching.

CHRISTMAS PLANTS

Keep different Christmas plants on your science table during the month of December for the children to examine. Examples would include holly, poinsettias, mistletoe, and Christmas cactus.

SANTA'S TOY SHOP

Reproduce the patterns found on pages 118 & 119 to make a toy lotto game for the children to play.

You can reproduce the pages as is for the game boards. Reproduce the same pages again and cut the pictures into the playing cards. Lotto is always a favorite game of young children!

GELT

Explain to the children the meaning of gelt: Hanukkah gelt in Yiddish means Hanukkah money. Each year in Israel the government issues a special commemorative coin for Hanukkah. Children are given a few coins as gifts. Chocolate coins wrapped in gold foil are also given. The chocolate coins are available in many gift and candy shops in the United States and Canada.

GREAT BOOKS FOR DECEMBER

The Night Before Christmas by Clement C. Moore
The Christmas Doll by Wendy Mathis Parker
Grandpa Bear's Christmas by Bonnie Pryor
My First Christmas Book by Colleen L. Reece
The Polar Express by Chris Van Allsburg
The Christmas Day Kitten by James Herriot

MATCHING MITTENS

Trace a mitten pattern and cut out matching mittens from wallpaper books or wrapping paper scraps. Place all the mittens in a basket and invite the children to match the pairs.

DECEMBER FINGER PLAYS/POETRY

HOW TO MAKE A HAPPY DAY

Two eyes to see nice things to do;
Two lips to smile the whole day through;
Two ears to hear what others say;
Two hands to put the toys away;
A tongue to speak sweet words each day;
A loving heart for work and play;
Two feet that errands gladly run;
Make happy days for everyone.
(Follow directions in verse.)

SANTA'S REINDEER

1, 2, 3, 4, 5 little reindeer
    (pop fingers up one by one)
Stand beside the gate;
"Hurry Santa," said the five,
"So we will not be late!"
    (make fist)
1, 2, 3, 4, 5 little reindeer;
    (pop fingers up one at a time)
Santa said, "Please wait!
Wait for three more little reindeer,
And then that will make eight."
    (hold up three more fingers)

CHRISTMAS CHORAL READING

Chorus: Christmas is a time of merriment.
    All things start to look magnificent
Small Group: But what is Christmas all about?
    What makes everyone sing and shout?
Chorus: Christmas is a time of great, great joy.
    Gifts will arrive for each girl and boy.
All Together: Let's celebrate Christmas with good cheer.
    Love those at home and those that are here.

SEE MY FAMILY

See my family! See them all!
    (hold up five fingers)
Some are short,
    (hold up thumb)
And some are tall.
    (hold up middle finger)
Let's shake hands, "How do you do?"
    (clasp hands and shake)
See them bow, "How are you?"
    (bend fingers)
Father,
    (hold up middle finger)
Mother,
    (hold up pointer finger)
Sister,
    (hold up ring finger)
Brother,
    (hold up thumb)
And me;
    (hold up little finger)
All polite to one another.

FIVE LITTLE ELVES

One, two, three, four, five little elves.
Putting toys on Santa Claus' shelves.
First little elf had something blue.
'Twas a small ballerina shoe.
The second little elf had something red.
It was a little girl's doll bed.
Third little elf had something white.
It was a truck shiny and white.
Fourth little elf had something brown.
It was a funny talking clown.
Fifth little elf had something black.
It was his very own knapsack.
(This is an excellent rhyme for teaching, colors and ordinal numbers. Use as a flannel board rhyme and make 5 elves and a blue ballerina, a red doll bed, a white truck, a brown clown and a black knapsack.)

DECEMBER FINGER PLAYS/POETRY

CHRISTMAS

My Christmas tree is nice and bright   *(make point with hands)*
With bells and balls and Christmas lights.   *(make circles with hands)*
I hope that Santa Claus will see   *(hand to eyes as if looking)*
The cake and cookies and remember me.   *(point to self)*

ONE LITTLE STAR

One little star was out last night.   *(cross one pointer finger over first two fingers on other hand)*

It was pretty as can be.
It was peeping through my window   *(hold hands up to face as if peeping)*
And looking right at me.   *(point to self)*

THE CHIMNEY

Here's the chimney   *(make a fist with right hand, thumb up, point to it)*
Here's it's top.   *(point to top of fist)*
Open the lid   *(use left hand to lift thumb)*
Out Santa pops!   *(raise thumb quickly)*
(Also use Rudolph, Christmas Carol, Frosty, etc., instead of Santa)

SANTA

What did Santa put under your tree?   *(stoop down and look around)*
Presents for you.   *(point)*
Presents for me!   *(point to self)*

CHRISTMAS TREE

Here is a great tall Christmas tree,   *(make large triangle shape with arms)*
That makes a pretty light.   *(wiggle fingers)*
Here are two little ornaments.   *(make two circles with thumb and forefinger)*
On top an angel bright.   *(point upward)*
Here are Santa's ten small elves   *(hold up ten fingers)*
That help in every way.
Here is Santa's jolly face,   *(make circle with fingers)*
And here is Santa's sleigh.   *(lock fingers and hold them downward)*

DREIDEL CHANT

Nun, gimmel, hay shin
Dreidel spin, dreidel spin.
Nun, gimmel, hay shin
Will I win? Will I win?
(Use with dreidel activity and patterns found on pages 128 & 129)

PHOTOGRAPH ORNAMENTS

Make copies of these patterns on heavy construction paper or posterboard. Decorate with glitter and add child's photograph. Wrap as a gift for parents.

DECEMBER MUSIC ACTIVITIES

NEW TOYS

(This song may be sung for Christmas or Hanukkah. The children can change the word "Santa" to a family member's name. The phrase "by the tree,' can be changed to "do you see.")

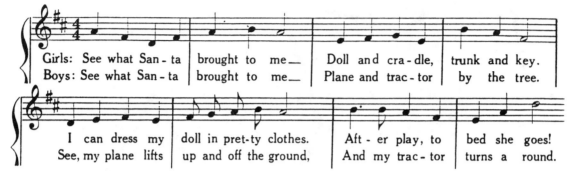

Girls: See what San-ta | brought to me— | Doll and cra-dle, | trunk and key.
Boys: See what San-ta | brought to me— | Plane and trac-tor | by the tree.

I can dress my | doll in pret-ty clothes. | Aft-er play, to | bed she goes!
See, my plane lifts | up and off the ground, | And my trac-tor | turns a round.

A CHRISTMAS HELPER

I will trim the Christ-mas tree

With the great-est care.

I can reach the ver-y top,

Stand-ing on a chair.

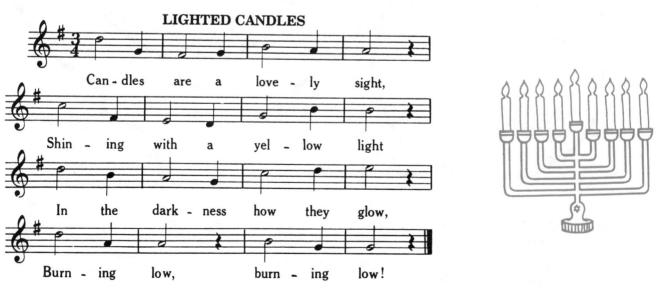

LIGHTED CANDLES

Can-dles are a love-ly sight,

Shin-ing with a yel-low light

In the dark-ness how they glow,

Burn-ing low, burn-ing low!

DECEMBER MUSIC ACTIVITIES

THE TREE FARM
(Melody: The Mulberry Bush)

Come, let's pick a Christmas tree
A Christmas tree, a Christmas tree
Come, let's pick a Christmas tree
So early in the morning.

Let's go find the tallest one
The tallest one, the tallest one
Let's go find the tallest one
So early in the morning.

We'll chop the tree so carefully
Carefully, carefully
We'll chop the tree so carefully
So early in the morning.

We'll drag the tree and take it home
Take it home, take it home
We'll drag the tree and take it home
So early in the morning.

Now, its time to decorate
Decorate, decorate
Now, its time to decorate
So early in the morning.

See the pretty Christmas tree
Christmas tree, Christmas tree
See the pretty Christmas tree
So early in the morning.

ON CHRISTMAS NIGHT

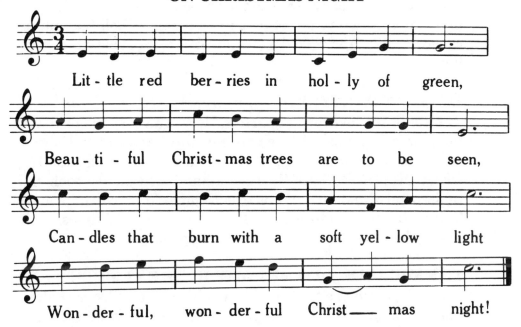

Lit-tle red ber-ries in hol-ly of green,

Beau-ti-ful Christ-mas trees are to be seen,

Can-dles that burn with a soft yel-low light

Won-der-ful, won-der-ful Christ___mas night!

NUTCRACKER SUITE

During the holdiay season play Tchaikovsky's "Nutcracker Suite" for the children. Let the children dance to the music, have rest time to the music or draw pictures as they listen to the music.

DECEMBER EXPERIENTIAL ACTIVITIES

SCHOOL SOCIAL

Invite the whole family to visit the classroom. Have nametags available for the families. Let the children host a guided tour through the classroom. Have the guests sign in on a roster. Ask parents to bring a favorite homebaked dish to share. This is an excellent event for parents to get to know one another better. Keep your camera ready. Put the photos in a class album or scrapbook. Hand mount children's drawings in your classroom Art Gallery for the parents to see.

FAMILIES EAT TOGETHER

Let the children prepare this easy snack that they can eat together while pretending that they are one large family. Here is the recipe for frozen bananas:

> 6 ripe bananas
> 1/2 cup lemon juice
> 1/2 cup water
> popsicle sticks
> Coverings; chopped nuts, melted chocolate chips, sesame seeds, or mixture of finely grated nuts, wheat germ and cinnamon.

Stick the popsicle stick into the banana. Mix lemon juice and water. Dip bananas in mixture to prevent color turning. Roll banana in any of the coverings. Place on waxed paper and freeze for at least one hour. Makes six bananas.

HOLIDAY PARTY (*Activity for Christmas or Hanukkah*)

All children love to have parties. Here is an easy recipe that can be made for your holiday party. The children will have as much fun making this recipe as they will eating it. Here is what you do for INDIVIDUAL CHOCOLATE PUDDING: Have a baby food jar for each child. Put one tablespoon of instant pudding in each jar. Add 1/4 cup milk and close the lid tightly. Let the children shake their jars at least 50 times. Wait 5 minutes. Top with Cool-Whip and/or chocolate sprinkles.

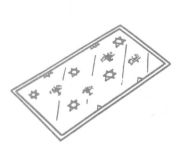

THE MIRACLE OF THE LAMP IN THE TEMPLE

Long ago, when a foreign king and his army took over Palestine and the temple there, the Jewish people fought their enemy for three years and at last they won. Lights were always kept burning inside the temple, but finally there was only enough oil left for one more day. Then the great miracle occurred. The light burned for eight days and nights, giving the Jewish people enough time to prepare more oil. Ever since then, Jewish people around the world celebrate Chanukah by lighting one candle each night of the eight nights until all are lit on the last day of the holiday.

DECEMBER EXPERIENTIAL ACTIVITIES

POPPY SEED CAKE

You will need: Measuring cups; bowl; mixer; rubber spatula; two bread pans; yellow cake mix; 1/4 cup poppy seeds; 1 package coconut pudding; 4 eggs; 1/2 cup oil.

What you do: Mix all the ingredients together and beat four minutes; pour into two greased and floured bread pans; bake at 350° for 50 minutes.

LATKES

Latkes are a traditional Hanukkah food. If the children in your class have never tasted latkes, that will enjoy sampling them.

What you need: 4 medium potatoes that are peeled and grated; 1 teaspoon grated onion; 2 teaspoons flour; 2 well beaten eggs; 1/2 teaspoon salt; vegetable oil; frying pan; spoon; spatula.

What you do: Mix all the ingredients together. The batter should be smooth but heavy. If the mixture seems too dry add another egg. Heat the oil in the frying pan and drop spoonfuls of the batter into the oil. Fry over medium heat until brown on the bottom. Turn and brown the other side. Drain on paper towels. Serve with applesauce.

ICE CREAM CAKE

This is a super treat to serve at your holiday party. It is to be made the day before the party.

What you need: 1 angel food cake; 1/2 gallon vanilla ice cream; 2 quarts of different sherbets *(lime and raspberry to keep with our holiday theme.)*

What you do: Grease tube pan. Break cake into small pieces. Alternately press cake, tablespoons of ice cream and sherbet into cake pan. Freeze overnight. Unmold and slice. Makes about 24 pieces.

CHRISTMAS PUNCH

During your holiday party serve this easy punch. Fill a large punch bowl with sugar-free 7-Up or sugar-free Sprite. Add grenadine syrup for color. Fill each child's cup with the punch and add a maraschino cherry and an orange slice. Children think that this drink looks very fancy and festive!

When I was a child this drink was often called a "kiddie cocktail." I am discouraging you from using the term "kiddie cocktail." I think it can send early messages to children that drinking a cocktail is fun, acceptable, and and something that people need to have at special ocassions. It is our job as educators NOT TO encourage or make drinking look exciting to children.

FABULOUS FINGER JELLO

Combine 4 envelopes unflavored gelatin, 3 three-ounce packages flavored gelatin and four cups boiling water. Pour into 13" x 9" pan. Chill until set. Cut into squares. Finger jello does not melt at room temperature after setting. Makes about 24 squares.

MAKING DREIDLES

Patterns on the following page.

DREIDEL #1

Make copies of Dreidel Pattern #1 on cardstock. Give one to each child. Instruct the children to color the four triangles that contain the symbols. Suggest that they use four different colors. This will make it easier for them to identify each symbol. Have them cut out the Dreidel. Make a hole in the center and insert a straw cut in thirds. Spin the Dreidel and it will rest on one of the four sides. This is the side which they must identify in order to play the game.

DREIDEL #2

Make copies of Dreidel Pattern #2 on cardstock. Give one to each child. Instruct the children to color the four squares that contain the symbols. They may use four different colors for easier identification of the symbols. They should cut out the pattern and punch holes in the center of the two X's. Fold on the lines to make a box, keeping the symbols on the outside. Tape the necessary edges. Put a sharpened pencil through the two X's. Spin the Dreidel and play accordingly.

SYMBOLS ON THE Dreidel

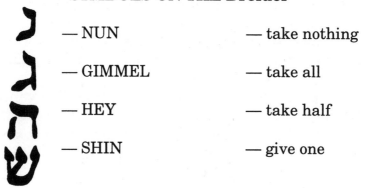

— NUN   — take nothing

— GIMMEL   — take all

— HEY   — take half

— SHIN   — give one

Picture Chart

If a child has two coins and the pot has 2 coins

Then:

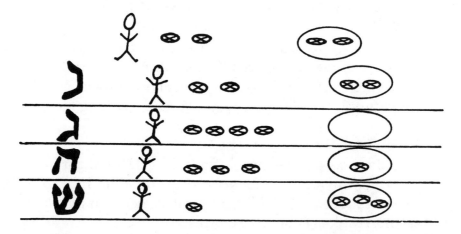

DREIDEL PATTERNS

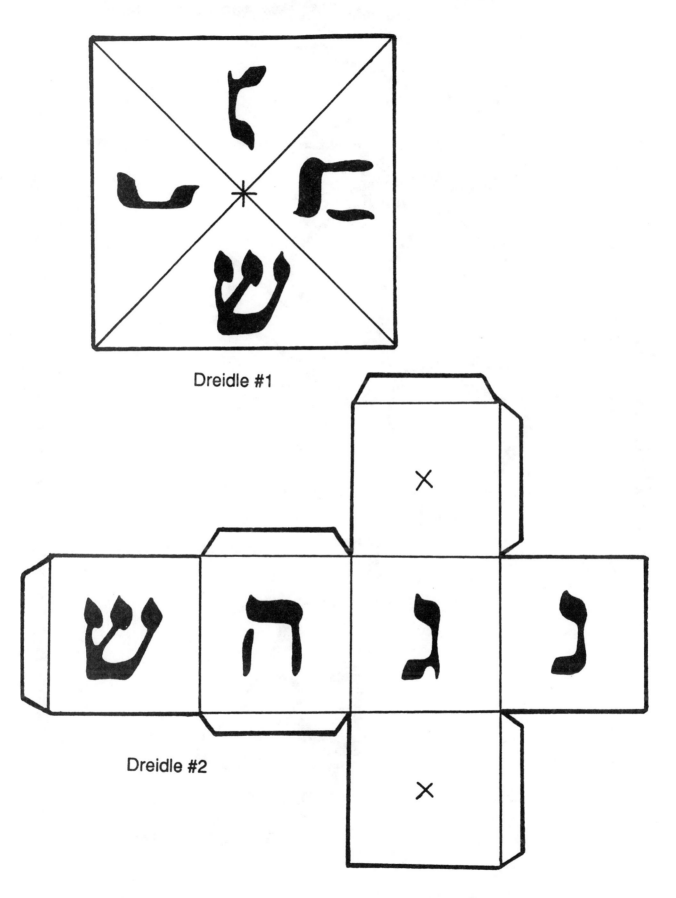

Dreidle #1

Dreidle #2

GIVING A GIFT

Draw a picture of a present that you would like to give to three different people.

January

THE WINTER PICNIC

Note to the teacher: As you read this story with your children, let them count the number of animals and objects mentioned in the story. (Use as a flannel board story. Patterns are found on pages 133 & 134.)

One winter day *5 rabbits* went hop-hop-hopping through the snow. They were going to visit the *4 squirrels* who lived in the *2 trees* down by the *lake.* Each rabbit carried a basket, and each basket had *5 nuts* and *2 carrots* in it.

On the way they met *3 chipmunks.* "Hello, *5 rabbits,*" said the *3 chipmunks.* "Where are you going?"

"Over to the *2 trees* by the *lake.* We're going to have a winter picnic with the *4 squirrels,*" they said. "Why don't you come too?"

The *3 chipmunks* hopped into their house. Then out they came with *3 bags.* In each bag they had *2 apples* and *5 nuts.*

"Now we'll have plenty to eat," said the *5 rabbits.* What a funny parade they made with *5 rabbits* hop-hop-hopping through the snow with *5 baskets,* and behind them *3 chipmunks* carrying *3 bags.* At last they reached the *2 trees* by the *lake.*

"How nice!" exclaimed the *4 squirrels* together. "You brought company!" Then *2 rabbits* spread a blanket on the ground, and *3 rabbits* unpacked the *5 baskets,* and *1 chipmunk* unpacked the *3 bags.* After everyone had eaten, the *3 chipmunks* and *4 squirrels* and *5 rabbits* played hide and seek in the snow. All too soon the sun began to set behind the *2 trees,* and it was time to go home.

"Come again," called the *4 squirrels* as the *3 chipmunks* and *5 rabbits* went off through the snow. What a lovely picnic!

STORY PATTERNS

Patterns for the story, "The Winter Picnic," found on page 132.

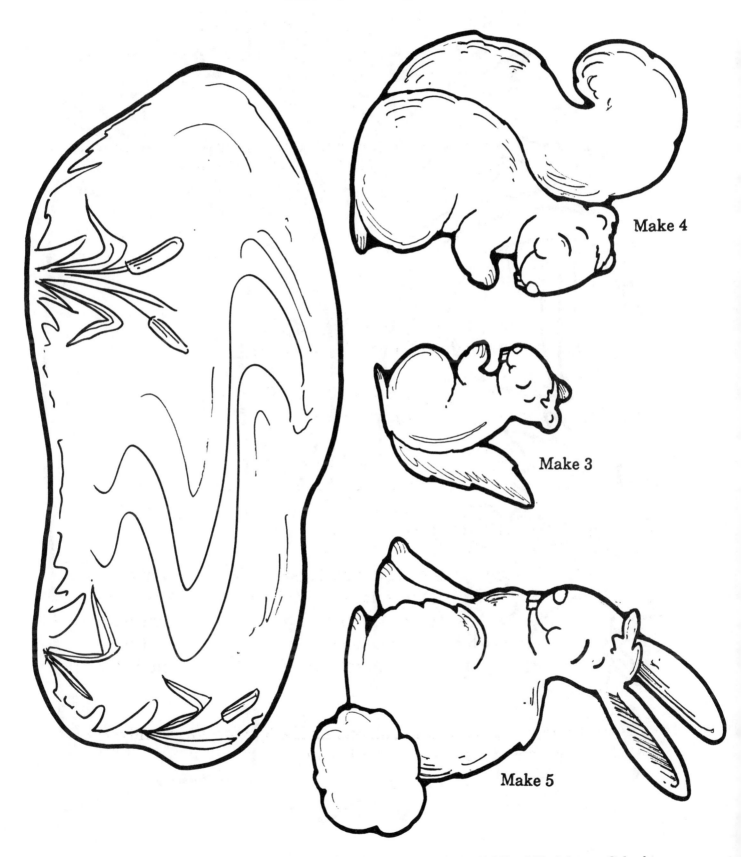

Make 4

Make 3

Make 5

STORY PATTERNS

Patterns for the story, "The Winter Picnic," found on page 132.

Make 2

Make 5

Make 6

Make 3

Make 8 groups

Make 10

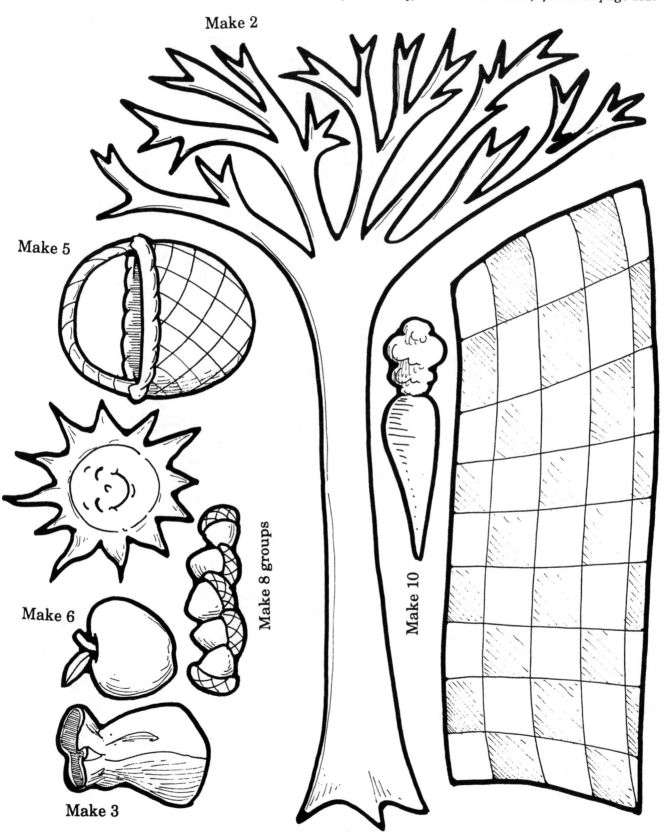

THE HOUSE THAT JACK BUILT

This is the house that Jack built.
This is the malt
That lay in the house that Jack built.

This is the rat,
That ate the malt
That lay in the house that Jack built.

This is the cat,
That killed the rat,
That ate the malt
That lay in the house that Jack built.

This is the dog,
That worried the cat,
That killed the rat
That ate the malt
That lay in the house that Jack built.

This is the cow with the crumpled horn,
That tossed the dog,
That worried the cat,
That killed the rat,
That ate the malt
That lay in the house that Jack built.

This is the maiden all forlorn,
That milked the cow with the crumpled
    horn,
That tossed the dog,
That worried the cat,
That killed the rat
That ate the malt
That lay in the house that Jack built.

This is the man all tattered and torn,
That kissed the maiden all forlorn,
That milked the cow with the crumpled
    horn,
That tossed the dog,
That worried the cat,
That killed the rat
That ate the malt
That lay in the house that Jack built.

This is the priest all shaven and shorn,
That married the man all tattered and torn,
That kissed the maiden all forlorn,
That milked the cow with the crumpled
    horn,
That tossed the dog,
That worried the cat,
That killed the rat,
That ate the malt
That lay in the house that Jack built.

This is the cock that crowed in the morn,
That waked the priest all shaven and shorn,
That married the man all tattered and torn,
That kissed the maiden all forlorn,
That milked the cow with the crumpled
    horn,
That tossed the dog,
That worried the cat,
That killed the rat,
That ate the malt
That lay in the house that Jack built.

This is the farmer sowing his corn,
That kept the cock that crowed in the morn,
That waked the priest all shaven and shorn,
That married the man all tattered and torn,
That kissed the maiden all forlorn,
That milked the cow with the crumpled
    horn,
That tossed the dog,
That worried the cat,
That killed the rat,
That ate the malt
That lay in the house that Jack built.

*(Turn into a flannel board story by using the
patterns found on pages 136 & 137.)*

Patterns for the story "The House That Jack Built," found on page 135.

This is the house that Jack built.

MALT

STORY PATTERNS

Patterns for the story "The House That Jack Built," found on page 135.

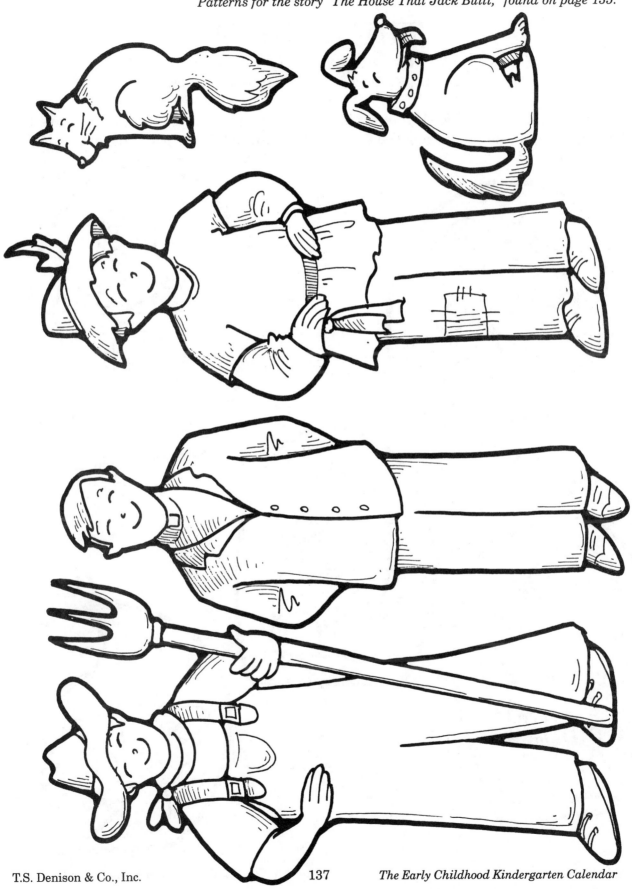

THE MITTEN

Retold and Illustrated by Jan Brett
A Ukrainian Folktale. G.P. Putnam's Sons, © 1989

Read the story of *The Mitten* by Jan Brett. After listening to the story, have the children retell the story using the finger puppets. Enlarge the patterns on the following pages.

STORY PATTERNS

"The Mitten" patterns continued from page 138.

Badger

Fox

Mole

Bear

Owl

Right Mitten

JANUARY BULLETIN BOARDS

THE ARTIST'S CORNER

	ZACH			STEVE	JOSH
KATIE		MIKE			
	BECCA	TODD		MATT	
KASSIE			SANDY		
EMILY		KENT			SARA
	ELISSA			MEAGAN	

This is a wonderful bulletin board to keep up all year long! Provide each of the children with a special space (on a wall or bulletin board) that is their very own. The children may decorate or hang whatever they would like to have in their special place. Some children will keep the same things up for weeks; other children will change their displays daily. Encourage the children to put a photograph of themselves on their display.

WINTER BIRDS

Research which birds are native to your part of the country during the winter months. Put a large green construction paper tree on the background. Glue cotton on the branches of the tree for snow. Have the children make birds and place them all over the tree. *(Bird patterns can be found on page 141.)*

BULLETIN BOARD PATTERNS

Patterns for the "Winter Birds" bulletin board found on page 140.

Blue Jay

Cardinal

JANUARY BULLETIN BOARDS

WINTER WINDOW SCENE

This bulletin board is very effective completed on a window. Tape some cut-out clouds and a sun at the top of the window and white paper or cotton batting at the bottom of the window to represent snow. Hang alternating strips of blue and white crepe paper streamers. Twist them from the top and pull them together at the center of each side. Spray a snow scene with canned snow.

COFFEE FILTER SNOWFLAKES

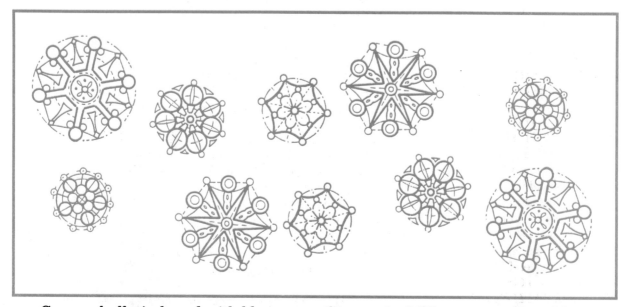

Cover a bulletin board with blue paper. Give each child a paper coffee filter. Fold the paper filter and let the child experiment with cutting out snowflakes. Display the snowflakes on the bulletin board. Before completing this bulletin board have the children look at snowflakes under a magnifying glass.

ENDANGERED ANIMALS

The concept of endangered animals is difficult for most preschoolers and kindergarteners. Nevertheless, the children will enjoy learning about these animals, because most of them are among our favorites.

I have chosen eight animals from the 1988 International Union for Conservation of Nature's List of Endangered Animals. The following eight animals represent the threat to animal life on a global basis and are animals that most children are familiar with.

When discussing with your class "why" these animals are in danger of becoming extinct, it is important to note that extinction in our time is usually due to two factors: 1) Man has over-hunted specific animals; and 2) Man has over-developed the land, thus causing a loss of habitiat for a variety of animals.

1) GIANT PANDA - This large black and white animal, who looks like a bear, is greatly loved and admired everywhere. The World Wildlife Fund, a society which is fighting to save all wildlife in danger of extinction has chosen the giant panda as its symbol. The giant panda once could be found roaming over most of southern China. Gradually the bamboo forests began being cut down to increase farmland. Bamboo is the main food in the giant panda's diet. When the giant panda began losing his main source of food, so began the possible extinction of this marvelous animal.

2) CALIFORNIA CONDOR - The condor is the largest bird in North America and one of the largest flying birds in the world. The condor has become a celebrity because of all the work that is going into saving these birds. Probably not more than 100 condors have survivied at any one time during this century. In 1988, a pair of condors in the San Diego Wild Life Park hatched an egg. This was the first hackling in captivity. With successful help from the conservation programs condors will be released back into the wild.

3) INDUS RIVER DOLPHIN - Dolphins are very intelligent mammals. Research has shown that dolphins are able to send messages to one another using a whole range of noises. It is possible that dolphins can actually "talk" to each other. Unfortunately thousands of dolphins are killed each year by tuna fishermen. It is estimated that in 1982, that possibily over 130,00 dolphins were killed. The dolphins get caught in the nets of tuna fishermen and die. Laws have been passed to protect dolphins, but new fishing techniques need to be developed to help save more dolphins.

4) MOUNTAIN GORILLA - In the mountains in Central Africa live the mountain gorillas. Each gorilla troop has a leader. The leader protects the group and decides where the group will travel to. Gorillas are in danger because they are losing their "habitat." The places where they need to live are being destroyed. Man is using the gorillas land for development. This development is causing a lack of food supply for the gorillas.

5) AMERICAN CROCODILE - This animal lives in the Florida Everglades. Although many of us do not think of crocodiles as beautiful, they are nonetheless a species of animal that needs protection. The Everglades has many plants that cannot be found anywhere else in the United States. The Everglades also provides crocodiles and alligators with the perfect environment. With all the housing developments and highways the crocodiles home is in jeopardy.

6) SNOW LEOPARD - The snow leopard is a beautiful animal only found in the high mountains of Central Asia. This large cat has thick white, gray and beige fur. Not much is known about the snow leopard. They usually live alone, but some have been seen in family groups. The snow leopard hunts by night and rests by day. Unfortunately the snow leopard is in danger for two resons. First, the animal has been hunted for its beautiful fur coat; and second, the snow leopard preys on domestic goats, so consequently the snow leopard has been considered a problem for some people in Asia.

7) TIGERS - Nearly all the different races of tigers are disappearing because of the destruction of the forests where they live. Tigers like to live in the forest and jungles. The color of their fur makes it easy for them to hide. Fifty years ago there were approximately 100,000 tigers in Asia, now there are approximately 5,000.

8) BLUE WHALE - The largest animal on earth is the whale. Whales may look like fish, but they are really mammals. A mammal is an animal who carries its babies inside its body for several months before giving birth. Whales are in danger because of all the years of whale hunting. In 1978, more than 20,000 whales were killed each year. There are still some countries who still hunt the whale. The World Wildlife Fund has helped set up sanctuaries for some whales in the hope to give them time to increase their numbers.

ENDANGERED ANIMAL PATTERNS

American Crocodile

Indus River Dolphin

Tiger

Snow Leopard

Giant Panda

Blue Whale

Mountain Gorilla

California Condor

PANDA PUZZLE

Cut out the pieces.
Paste them on the panda puzzle shape.

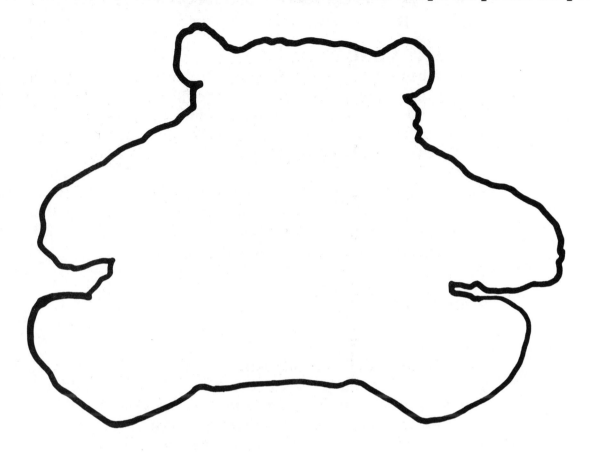

PUDDING MONO PRINT

As you overcome your initial reluctance to attempt this project you will discover an art project that young children love!

You will need: Instant chocolate pudding; bowl for mixing; large spoon; water; tin foil; 12" x 18" white construction paper.

What you do: Mix the pudding according to the directions. Place tin foil on table in front of each child. Spoon approximately 1/3 cup pudding onto the tin foil. Have the children smooth the pudding to cover the tin foil. Let the children draw patterns or pictures in the pudding using their fingers. Place white paper on top of the pudding and press gently. Lift the paper. Allow drying time. You now have a mono print!

SPONGE PRINT

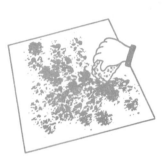

An array of mixed colors will result in simple understanding of mixing colors in this sponge print project.

You will need: 3" x 4" sponge (one for each child); food coloring (red, blue, yellow); 12" x 18" white construction paper; three bowls; three spoons.

What you do: Pour the food coloring into three bowls, one for each child. Stir in water *(Not too much water or you will dilute the color too much)*. Place one end of the sponge into the food coloring. (Don't dip the end of the sponge in too far!) Dab sponge onto paper. Using the same sponge to allow colors to mix. Change colors frequently.

SUGAR PAINTING

This project couples two strengths of young children, their love of abstract forms and their creative use of color.

You will need: White glue; colored sugar; 12" x 12" black construction paper; sugar dispenser *(a jar with holes in the lid)*; newspaper.

What you do: Fill dispenser with sugar; Pour glue onto paper in design or picture desired. Shake small amount of sugar on top of glue. Turn paper upside down and tap newspaper to remove excess sugar. Dry separately for one day.

COLLAGE

An assemblage of odds and ends can make an interesting collage.

You will need: 12" x 12" construction paper of any color; newspapers; construction paper scraps; tissue paper; yarn; wallpaper books; glue; scissors.

What you do: Tear or cut the newspaper, construction paper scraps, tissue paper and wallpaper into any shape and size. Glue on pieces of yarn and the paper that has been cut or torn. Overlap into interesting designs.

JANUARY FINE MOTOR ACTIVITIES

CHEERIO COLLAGE

This collage is fun and easy for both the teacher and the children. A few cheerios gobbled up will not hurt the art work.

You will need: A box of cheerios; white glue; 6"x9" poster board (red, blue, green, or violet).

What you do: Dab a multitude of small glue dots on poster board to form a design or picture. Do no more than 6 to 8 dots at a time or the glue will dry. Place the Cheerios on top of the glue.

FLOOR MURAL

Feel the freedom of working on the floor!

You will need: mural paper; masking tape; large crayons.

What you do: Roll mural paper out on the floor. Tape the ends to prevent paper from rolling up. Have the children remove their shoes. Sit or lie on the paper. Give each child a box of crayons and let them go to town creating whatever they would like.

CHALK FLOWERS

Soft pastel colors give a special feeling to this floral project.

You will need: 18" x 24" white construction paper; black markers; colored chalk.

What you do: Draw 2 or 3 large flowers, stems and leaves with markers. Use chalk to color in the flowers.

WOOD SCULPTURE

Block building is a part of every child's world. In this project we build a construction that will last!

You will need: Wood scraps of various sizes; glue; brushes; tempera paint.

What you do: Give the children time to play with the blocks. Glue the wood pieces together to make a real train, building or abstract sculpture. Allow glue to dry and then paint.

STRAW PAINTING

Children love to blow through straws and with this simple project, young children can create exciting explosions of color.

You will need: Drinking straws; food coloring (yellow, red, blue); 12" x 12" white construction paper.

What you do: Pour approximately one tablespoon of each color of food coloring onto paper. (Leave a few inches between each color). Place the straw at the edge of food coloring at a 45° degree angle and blow. Allow the food coloring to flow at random. Some of the food coloring should run into each other and blend to make new colors.

JANUARY FINE MOTOR ACTIVITIES

ZOO CAGE

Who doesn't love to go to the zoo! March these cages around your room or hall.

You will need: 4 - 1" x 18" black construction paper strips 2 - 6" x 6" black construction paper squares; 18" x 24" manila; tempera paints; brushes; water containers; white glue.

What you do: Discuss zoo animals and how they look. Select one animal and make a large painting of it on the manila paper. Allow the paint to dry (10 - 15 minutes). Glue on four cage bars. Round off corners of the two black construction paper squares to make wheels and glue the wheels at the bottom.

PAINT WITH WATER

Learn what it feels like to paint by using water on the blackboard.

You will need: Bucket of water; brush; blackboard.

What you do: Fill the bucket half full with water. Stand at the blackboard with the bucket beside you. Paint with water on the blackboard.

NATURE COLLAGE

This nature collage allows young children to express their love of collecting and the art of selecting.

You will need: 6" x 9" cardboard; white glue; small paper bag.

What you do: Walk around the school grounds and collect interesting pebbles, weeds, sticks and leaves and put them in your paper bag. Go back to the classroom with your "treasures" and glue them onto the cardboard to make an interesting arrangement.

SHAVING CREAM FINGER PAINT

Your children will love the feel of this!

You will need: Shaving cream (3 cans per class); tables (formica tops are best); tempera paint.

What you do: Spray generous amounts of shaving cream on the table. Sprinkle a few drops of tempera on the shaving cream to add color. Use your hands to mix and move around the shaving cream.

CLAY PAPER WEIGHT

You will need: Water-based clay (size of a tennis ball); glaze - several colors; felt (pre-glued peel-off circles); white glue.

What you do: The child should mold a smooth clay form that is flat on one side. Keep clay in one piece. Scratch name of child on the flat side. Allow to dry for three weeks. Fire clay then glaze clay. Glue felt to the flat bottom. This is a wonderful project. Call your local high school or art center to see if you can use their equipment to fire the clay projects.

ABSTRACT PAINTING

New color discoveries and experimenting with shapes are generated in this art project.

You will need: Tempera paint (yellow, red and blue); brushes; water containers; egg containers; 9" x 12" white construction paper (2 per child).

What you do: Demonstrate how secondary colors (orange, violet, green) are made by mixing two primary colors (red, blue, yellow) together. Let the children experiment by mixing paints on their paper. When they have finished let them show each other the colors they have made. Now give the children a second paper. This time they will mix colors again to see what interesting shapes they can create.

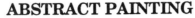

STABILE

A colorful 3-D creation. This project looks very complicated, but it can be a very successful project for 4 and 5 year olds.

You will need: 1" x 18" construction paper strips of all colors; 6" x 9" poster board (different colors - one per child); white glue; scissors.

What you do: Fold each strip in the following manner. *Each strip fold is about one inch from the end.* Strips may be cut into varying lengths. Put glue on the ends that were folded up. Glue to the poster board. Overlap and glue one on top of the other as illustrated.

BODY TRANSFORMER

Who can deny the allure of this body transforming project!

You will need: Mural paper 36" wide; pencils; markers; crayons; scissors.

What you do: You are going to need a lot of room so go out in the hall. Roll out long sheets of mural paper and tape the edges to the floor to prevent rolling up. Have children lie down on paper in any position but do not overlap arms and legs. Teacher traces around each child with pencil. The children then take crayons and markers and transforms the outline into any character - monster, superman, princess,etc.

TAMBOURINES

When you have finished these tambourines - have a parade!

You will need: Two paper plates; tissue paper (bright colors); tempera paint; brushes; water containers; a dozen pebbles; scissors.

What you do: Paint bold designs on the bottom of the paper plates. Cut tissue paper strips (1' x 9"). 12 strips for each child. Glue the tissue paper strips to the inside of one plate. Place pebbles on the plate. Glue the two plates together so the painted part of the plate is exposed and the pebbles are trapped inside.

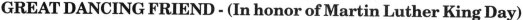

JANUARY MOVEMENT ACTIVITIES

GREAT DANCING FRIEND - (In honor of Martin Luther King Day)

In honor of Martin Luther King Day have the children play this friendship game. Begin the game by having the children pick a partner. The teacher starts the music and the partners begin dancing or skipping around the room. When the music stops – each pair of partners must team up with another pair of partners. When the music begins again, the four children hold hands and dance around in a circle. When the music stops, the children stop dancing and each pair of partners go off in search of another pair of partners.

The game continues as the teacher starts and stops the music, and the partners keep switching with new partners and circle dancing. Continue the game until all the children have had an opportunity to dance with each other.

OBSERVING SNOWFLAKES

The children will observe the effects of their blowing air on a paper snowflake. Give each child a snowflake attached to some thread or dental floss which is stapled to the end of a straw. The straw is used as a stick to hold the threaded snowflake. Have the children blow at the snowflake to make it dance, twirl, and spin.

OUTSIDE FUN

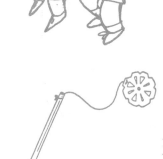

Pulling Each Other — Children love to pull one another around in the snow. Sleds with a rope handle or even cardboard boxes with handles are great fun for young children to use in the snow. One child can ride as the other child does the pulling. It is amazing how easy it is to pull something along in the snow.

Angels In The Snow — Make angels in the snow outside. Have the children lie down in the snow on their backs. Have the children flap their arms and legs back and forth as far as they can. Help the children stand up carefully and turn around and to see the "angels" they have created.

Build a Snowman — Have the whole class work together to build a snowman, complete with hat, scarf, and a carrot nose.

SNOWCONES

Borrow a snowcone machine. Crush ice in the machine to make snow. Sprinkle syrup, jello powder, or fruit juice on top. Scoop into small paper cups and let the children enjoy their unusual treat.

THROWING SNOWBALLS (inside)

Provide a basket into which the children can throw paper snowballs or white socks rolled into balls. The children will love this throwing game and it is a lot safer than throwing real snowballs.

SNOW-CAPPED LETTERS FOR JANUARY BULLETIN BOARD

JANUARY LANGUAGE ACTIVITIES

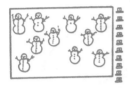

THE SNOWMAN GAME

Use a large sheet of construction paper or a file folder for the game board. Glue cut-outs of snowmen onto the board and keep cut-out hats in an envelope attached to the outside of the game board. Children match the numbers on the hats to the number of buttons on each snowman.

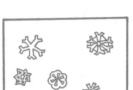

SNOWFLAKES

Cut out a variety of snowflakes and then trace the patterns onto a large sheet of paper. The children match the snowflake to its proper pattern on the paper.

THE MITTEN GAME

Place brightly colored mitten cut-outs on a game board and label them from 1 to 10. Have small white circles (snowballs) available for the children to place on the mittens according to the numeral printed on the mitten.

NUMERAL PENGUINS

Use the penguin pattern at the bottom of the page. Make 10 penguins for this math activity. Children place the penguins on a sheet of paper (skating rink) in numerical order.

Penguin Pattern

MARTIN LUTHER KING, JR. DAY

Tell the children about Martin Luther King, Jr. Discuss with them the following facts:

• Martin Luther King studied hard in school and decided to become a minister.

• He wanted to help people get along better with each other.

• He gave speeches around the country and worked hard to change laws so that all people would be treated the same.

• He was the leader of the "March on Washington" in 1963 when he gave his famous speech "I Have A Dream."

• He dreamed of the day when "freedom would ring for all people" and all people would join hands in brotherhood.

• He believed that changes could be made without violence.

Write "I Have A Dream" on the blackboard and ask the children to talk about some of their dreams. Discuss with the children how we can solve conflicts by talking with each other.

PLATE PEOPLE

Use paper plates to make a variety of people and animal puppets. Use Chinet plates. They are made of strong cardboard. Cut out eye holes and color the faces. Attach the paper plates to tongue depressors or paint stir sticks (available often "free-of-charge" at many hardware stores). The children can hold the puppet faces in front of their own faces.

THE SNOWY DAY (by Ezra Jack Keats)

The Snowy Day is about a little boy who goes out to play in the snow alone. He makes footprints, trails by dragging his feet, and angels in the snow. That night he puts a snowball in his pocket to keep for tomorrow. He wakes up to a surprise!

• Discuss the collage illustrations in the book. Glue small scraps of materials to paper to make a collage.

• Pretend that you are Peter. Pantomime the story as the teacher reads it. Do all the actions that Peter does.

• Make two snowballs. Put one outside and place one in a pocket of an old pair of pants (place in the classroom sink!) Have the children predict which snowball will melt first.

GREAT BOOKS FOR JANUARY

The Mitten by Jan Brett
White Snow, Bright Snow by Alvin Tresselt
Katy and the Big Snow by Virginia Lee Burton
Winter by Fern Hollow
In Winter by Jane Belk Moncure

MY WINTER PICTURE   NAME

Draw a picture of what you like to do in the snow.
If you do not live where there is snow, pretend that you are playing in the snow!

JANUARY FINGER PLAYS/POETRY

THE SNOWBALL

Once I had a snowball   (make circle with hands)
And it grew and grew and grew   (make circle enlarge)
Then I made a snowman   (form circle in upright)
To smile at you and you and you!   (point at children)

SNOW

The snow falls on the housetop   (stand, touch head)
Snow falls on the ground   (bend and touch floor)
The snow falls on the mountains   (stand up)
Snow falls all around   (turn around)
The snow falls on the fountain   (make water drops)
Snow falls on the tree   (stand, make a tree with arms in a circle)
But not on me!   (point at self, shake head "no")

SNOWMEN

Six little snowmen,
Standing in a row.
Each with a hat,
And a big red bow.
Six little snowmen,
Now they are ready,
Where will they go?
Wait till the sun shines,
Soon they will go.
Down through the fields,
With the melting snow.

THE SNOWMAN

Roll a snowball large,   (arms make a circle)
Then one of middle size   (two pointer fingers and two thumbs make circle)

Roll a snowball small;   (one pointer finger and thumb make circle)
Use lumps of coal for eyes.   (point to eyes)
Place a carrot for a nose.   (point to nose)
An old hat on his head,   (place both hands on top of head)
And for his necktie, tie around
A ribbon of bright red.   (make motion of tying ribbon)
A corncob pipe goes in his mouth;   (point to mouth)
Some buttons on his vest,   (point to buttons down front)
And there he stands so round and fat;
Of snowmen he's the best!

make 5

FIVE LITTLE KOALAS

Five little koalas in a eucalyptus tree,
The first one said, "Hey, look at me!"
The second one said, "I'm not a bear!"
The third one said, "I don't have a care."
The fourth one said, "Australia is my home."
The fifth one said, "I'll never roam."
Five little koalas in a eucalyptus tree,
Climbing and playing and happy to be free!
*(Enlarge the pattern included on this page,
to turn this rhyme into a flannel board
presentation. Make five koalas.)*

JANUARY FINGER PLAYS/POETRY

FIVE LITTLE SNOWMEN
Five little snowmen, happy and gay.
  (Spread arms)
First one said, "What a beautiful day."
  (wipe eyes)
Second one said, "We'll never have tears."
  (arms up)
Third one said, "We'll stay for years.
  (questioning look)
Fourth one said, "But what will happen in May?"
  (wilting over)
Fifth one said, "Look, we're melting away."
  (all lying down)

SNOWFLAKES
Snowflakes look like dainty lace.
I felt three soft upon my face.
I felt two on my chin and lip
I caught one on my fingertip.
*(Ask children to try and draw a
snowflake. Look at a snowflake
under a magnifying glass.)*

ARTISTS
"I am going to work," said Mister Thumb.
"Now who will go with me?"
Said Mister Pointer, "I will go.
You need my help you see."
And so they worked together,
As happy as could be.
They made a lovely apple
In a big tall apple tree.
They made a little bluebird.
They made a sun for me.
Mister Pointer said, "I like to work."
Mister Thumb said, "I agree."

From "A CHILD'S GARDEN OF VERSES"
by Robert Louis Stevenson
In summer when I go to bed,
It isn't dark, it's light instead.
In winter when I go to bed,
It isn't light, it's dark instead.

DRAW A CIRCLE
Draw a circle, draw a circle,
Round as it can be;
  *(draw a circle in the air with
   pointer finger)*
Draw a circle, draw a circle
Just for me.

Draw a square, draw a square,
Shaped like a door;
  (draw a square in the air)
Draw a square, draw a square
With corners four.

Draw a traingle, draw a triangle,
With corners three;
  (draw a triangle in the air)
Draw a triangle, draw a triangle
Just for me.
*(This poem can be used to teach the
concept of shape. Drawing in the air
is a fine kinesthetic-tactile experience.
Flannel board materials needed are a
felt circle, square and a triangle.)*

SNOWMAN SEQUENCING CARDS

JANUARY MUSIC ACTIVITIES

ANGELS IN THE SNOW

You can make an an - gel

In the soft white snow.

Lie up on your back and swing — Your

arms up high, then low.

RHYTHM STICKS

Pass out two rhythm sticks to every member of the class. Show them the correct way to hold and strike the sticks. Select several children who seem to know how to hit their instruments and have them perform for the rest. Then select another group to try it.

Begin by having them hit the sticks together to the slow beat of 1-2. Then repeat to a fast beat of 1-2-3. When the children have developed a feeling for the beat and respond satisfactorily, go on to other combinations.

LOOBY LOO

(As the children stand in a circle and sing the verses, they perform the actions. On the chorus, the children join hands and walk in a circle as they sing.)

1. I'll put my right hand in,
   I'll put my right hand out,
   I'll give my right hand a
   shake, shake, shake,
   And turn myself about.

Chorus
Here we dance looby loo,
Here we dance looby light,
Here we dance looby loo,
All on a Saturday night.

2. I'll put my left hand in, etc.
3. I'll put my right foot in, etc.
4. I'll put my left foot in, etc.
5. I'll put my head way in, etc.
6. I'll put my whole self in, etc.

MAKING SNOWMEN

Hea - vy snows,   warm - er   sun,
Voi - ces laugh,   cheer and shout,

Mak - ing bright the   day.
"Come and roll   the   snow

Call   the   chil - dren   out   of   doors
In - to   balls   and   you   shall   see

Time   to   run   and   play.
How   the   snow - men   grow."

FROSTY THE SNOWMAN
(Sung to the tune, "Miss Polly.")
Frosty is a snowman who is fat, fat, fat!
He always wears a very fancy hat, hat, hat..
He loves nothing more than the snow,
                                        snow, snow.
And when the cold winds blow, blow, blow.
Please stay winter don't go away.
'Cause Frosty doesn't ever want to melt away!

WINTER PLAYMATE
(Sung to the tune, "Playmate,
Come Out And Play With Me.")
Playmate, come out and play with me.
And build some snowmen, three.
Oh, come and skate with me.
Slide down the hillside.
On my big brand new sled.
And forever be,
Friends you and me!

JACK FROST
(Sung to the tune, "Mary Had A Little Lamb.")

Jack Frost painted the windows,
The windows,
The windows.
Jack Frost painted the windows,
With beautiful snowflakes.

The sun came out and melted them,
Melted them,
Melted them.
The sun came out and melted them,
Jack Frost will have to paint again!

JANUARY EXPERIENTIAL ACTIVITIES

SELF-HELP SKILLS

This is a wonderful time of year to help the children with some additional activities that promote the development of self-help skills. The sooner that children are able to zip, button, snap, etc., the easier it will be on the teachers. *(Not to mention that children feel so proud of themselves when they learn how to perform these tasks.)* Here are some ideas for you:

- Have the children practice zipping and buttoning each other's coats. This is sometimes easier than zipping your own coat and the practice is excellent.
- Practice on doll clothes that are easily taken on and off.
- Bring in an extra box of clothes to "zipper and button."
- Using ply-wood, you can easily create zipping, buttoning and snapping boards that the children will love.

YOGURT POPSICLES

You will need: 2 cups yogurt, 6 oz. frozen orange juice, 1 teaspoon honey to taste, 2 teaspoons vanilla. Pour the mixture into popsicle molds, paper cups or ice cube trays. When the mixture is partially frozen add the popsicle sticks.

WINTER WEATHER

Here are some fun ideas when you are discussing winter weather and the season of winter with your class:

- Make a sorting game of clothes for each season of the year. Have the children sort the clothes that belong to each season.
- Make a sorting game of activities done in each season of the year or in each type of weather.
- Make a daily weather chart, noting temperature and sky conditions.
- Watch the weather report on television each evening to see how often the weather reporter predicts correctly.

CONTACT PAPER MATCH

The idea of this activity is to create a matching game. You can use contact paper that has pictures or objects on the paper, or you can also use wrapping paper (then cover in clear contact paper) or wallpaper. Create a large board with various cut outs from the paper of your choice. Make small shapes of the identical patterns for the children to match on the large board.

CRYSTAL GARDEN

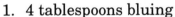

Grow a garden right in your classroom! Begin by placing five or six damp sponges in the bottom of a tin pie pan. Sprinkle the following over the sponges:

1. 4 tablespoons bluing
2. 4 tablespoons salt
3. 1 tablespoon ammonia

A crystal garden will begin to grow overnight. *(**NOTE TO TEACHER:** A garden like this is easily disturbed. Keep it in a safe place for viewing, not for touching!)*

THERMOMETERS

Place thermometers inside and outside of a classroom window. Read, record, and chart the temperatures at various times during the day all through the month of January.

MAKE YOUR OWN PLAYDOUGH

Allow the children to make their own playdough by mixing together the following ingredients:

1. 1 cup of salt
2. 2 cups of flour
3. 1 cup of water

Add food coloring to the water before mixing to create an even color throughout the playdough.

FORMS OF WATER

Examine the various forms of water. Start by placing ice cubes in a warm part of the room where they will melt quickly. Then take the water and pour it into a pan which you can heat. Use a portable burner or a real stove if necessary and observe the steam as the water boils.

FROST PICTURES

Making frost pictures is an experience that your children will really enjoy. Mix one part of epsom salt to one part boiling water. Allow time for the mixture to cool. Have the children draw pictures on colored construction paper of winter scenes; snow people, snowflakes, trees covered with snow, snow on the ground. Have the children paint their drawings with the epsom salt mixture. When the picture is dry you will see tiny crystals on the pictures.

DESIGN YOUR OWN SNOW PEOPLE

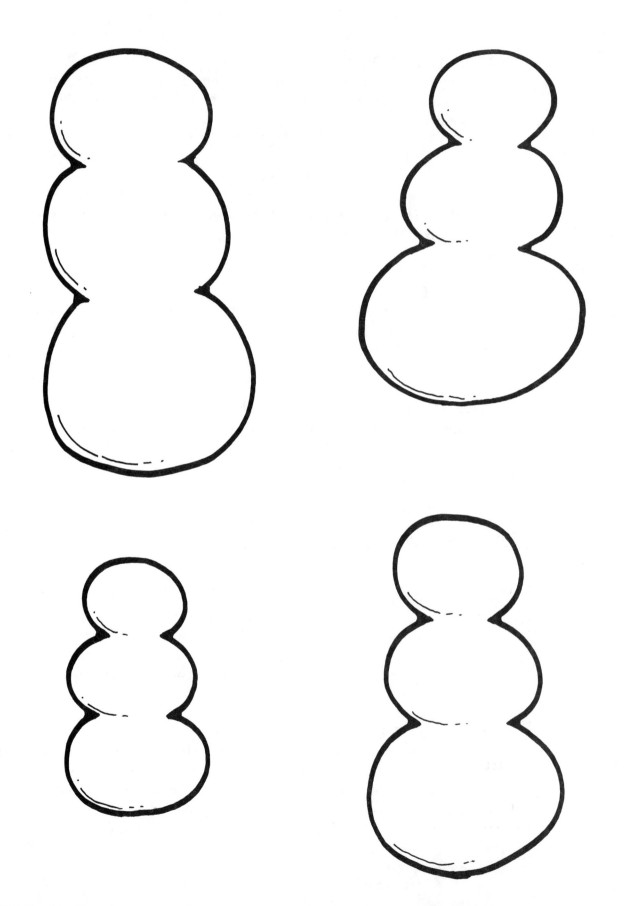

February

MY SHADOW

I have a little shadow that goes in and out with me,
And what can be the use of him is more than I can see.
He is very, very like me from the heels up to my head;
And I see him jump before me, when I jump into my bed.

The funniest thing about him is the way he likes to grow.
Not at all like proper children, which is always very slow;
For he sometimes shoots up taller like an India-rubber
    ball,
And he sometimes gets so little that there's none of him
    at all.

He hasn't got a notion of how children ought to play,
And can only make a fool of me in every sort of way.
He sticks so close beside me, he's a coward you can see;
I'd think shame to stick to big sister as that shadow sticks
    to me!

One morning, very early, before the sun came up,
I rose and found the shining dew on every buttercup;
But my lazy little shadow, like an arrant sleepyhead,
Had stayed at home behind me and was fast asleep in
    bed.

(Measure the shadows in the early morning, noon, and late afternoon.)

ELAINE'S VALENTINES

(Use as a flannel board story. Patterns are found on pages 166 & 167.)

It was Valentine's Day and Cupid was dancing his way through the woods. Cupid, you know, is like a baby angel, with snowy white wings and curly hair. He always carries a little bow and some arrows.

As he came out of the woods, he met a cat. "Good day Mrs. Cat," said Cupid. "Have you sent a Valentine yet?"

"A Valentine! What is that?" said Mrs. Cat in surprise.

"It is something you send someone you love. This is Valentine's Day. Everyone in the world is sending Valentines." And then little Cupid shot an arrow into the air, and was about to run after it, but Mrs. Cat cried, "Wait a minute, pretty Cupid. Will you not help me?"

I'm sorry," smiled Cupid, "but I only put thoughts into people's hearts, and they do the rest. But I will write some verses for you and leave them by this tree." And with that he spread his wings and flew away.

"There's no one I love better than little Elaine, and she's sick," said Mrs. Cat. "I believe I can send her something." She turned to go back to the barn when she met a squirrel.

"Good day Mrs. Cat," squirrel said. "Where are you going?"

"To find a Valentine for sick little Elaine," answered Mrs. Cat.

"There's no one that I love better than little Elaine," said, the squirrel, "I will go with you." So Mrs. cat and the squirrel went along together.

"Hello," said a robin. "Where are you going?"

"Oh, we are going to find a Valentine for Elaine. She is very sick," said the squirrel and Mrs. Cat.

"Oh, may I please go with you? There is no one that I love better than little Elaine?"" said the Robin.

"Oh, yes," replied the squirrel and Mrs. Cat. So Mrs. Cat, the squirrel and the robin walked along together.

The three friends finally reached the barn. Mrs. Cat quickly ran up the stairs to loft. Tiny "meow" sounds were coming from under the hay. Mrs. Cat gently picked up a tiny gray kitten from under the hay.

"You are going to be Elaine's Valentine present," said Mrs. Cat. She will love you so much!"

"What will I give Elaine?" said the squirrel.

"You can carry the Valentine verse that Cupid will leave us on the tree," said Mrs. Cat.

"And what about me?" said the Robin. "What will I give Elaine?"

"You will sing her a song," said Mrs, Cat.

The three friends arrived at the tree, found the note that Cupid had left and walked along to Elaine's house.

Elaine opened her eyes and found the tiny gray kitten from Mrs. Cat, heard the beautiful music from the robin, and found this verse left from the squirrel:

> *"Little friend, so kind and true,*
> *These Valentines we send to you.*
> *Our very dearest love to tell.*
> *We hope that you will soon be well."*

Elaine picked up the kitten and hugged it and the kitten said "Meow."

STORY PATTERNS

Patterns for the story "Elaine's Valentine," found on page 165.

STORY PATTERNS

Patterns for the story "Elaine's Valentine," found on page 165.

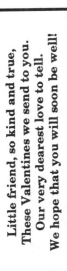

Little friend, so kind and true,
These Valentines we send to you.
Our very dearest love to tell.
We hope that you will soon be well!

WILBUR WOODCHUCK ON GROUNDHOG DAY

The children can pretend to be Wilbur Woodchuck and crawl around on hands and knees. Some can be Mother Woodchuck. It may be necessary to define "hibernation" and "woodchuck" and "groundhog" before reading the story. The children pantomime the words in bold type.

Wilbur Woodchuck was **sleeping soundly** in his large burrow. It was winter and like many animals he was hibernating.

In the compartments or rooms of the burrow the woodchuck family was waking up. Mother Woodchuck was curious about the weather outside for it was February 2, Groundhog Day.

Mother Woodchuck went into Wilbur's room and gave him a nip on the nose. Wilbur **woke up slowly** and **shook his head**. He **rubbed his eyes** and **crawled out of bed**. He **yawned**. **Squatting on his rear legs** he looked at his mother and then at his soft bed. Wilbur did not want to wake up.

Mother Woodchuck wanted Wilbur to go outside and check the weather. Wilbur did not want to go. What if it was cold and snowy? He **tried moving in all sorts of wild ways** to make his mother think he was too sick to go out. **He stood up tall** and **bent to the floor, touching it with his front paws.** Next he **squatted** and **turned all around**. That didn't work! Wilbur tried **laying down** and **swinging his legs wildly** as if he were riding a bicycle.

That did it! Mother Woodchuck nipped him on the nose and he **sat up quickly, rubbing his nose.** He wanted to rest a minute.

Mother told him it was important to check the weather. People depended on the woodchuck on February 2 to tell them about spring. If the sun was shining and the woodchuck saw his shadow, he was frightened and crawled back into his hole. That meant there would be six more weeks of winter weather. But if the day was cloudy and the woodchuck could not see his shadow, he stayed out, meaning that spring was coming soon.

Wilbur **stood up tall** and **brave**. He **marched** toward the opening of the burrow. **Slowly he crawled out with his eyes closed.** He was afraid to look. Wilbur **opened one eye, then the other. Slowly he stretched his head out, his neck, two front paws, stomach, back paws and tail. He turned in every direction . . . .**

What do you think Wilbur saw? Did the sun scare him so he ran back into his burrow? Or was it cloudy so he decided to stay outside and play? Make up your ending to the story.

ANTONIO'S SURPRISE
(A Valentine Story)

Antonio was very unhappy. Today was the day his class was to have it's Valentine party. Antonio was sick and had to stay home.

"We'll have a party here," said his mother cheerfully.

"It just won't be the same," said Antonio sadly.

That day when the children met in their classroom, they were very excited. Everyone noticed that Antonio was missing. Everyone liked Antonio and was sorry that he could not be at the party.

"What can we do to share our good time with him?" one of the boys asked.

"Let's save some of our Valentine cookies for him," suggested one friend.

"I know another thing we can do," said Sondra. "We can make him a giant card and all of us can sign it."

"Yes, let's do that," said the children.

They began to make the card. It was so big they had to make an envelope to put it in.

Everyone had such fun.

"Antonio will like that," said their teacher. "I will take the card, his Valentine box and his cookies to him this afternoon. It was sweet of all of you to think of Antonio. That is really a gift of love."

Activities:

• If anyone is sick on the day of your Valentine party, you could make that person a giant card and have everyone sign their names.

• Is there anyone else that your class would like to make a giant Valentine for?

• Discuss with the children how they would have felt if they had been Antonio? How did he feel missing the party? How did he feel when his teacher brought him the card, his Valentine box and the cookies?

LITTLE MOUSE

From the book, "Cut & Color Flannel Board Stories" by Karen Noel.
Copyright by T.S. Denison & Co., Inc.

(Put up all seven houses – hide mouse behind one house)
   Little mouse, little mouse;
   Are you in the yellow house? *(check behind the yellow house)*
(Repeat after each house)

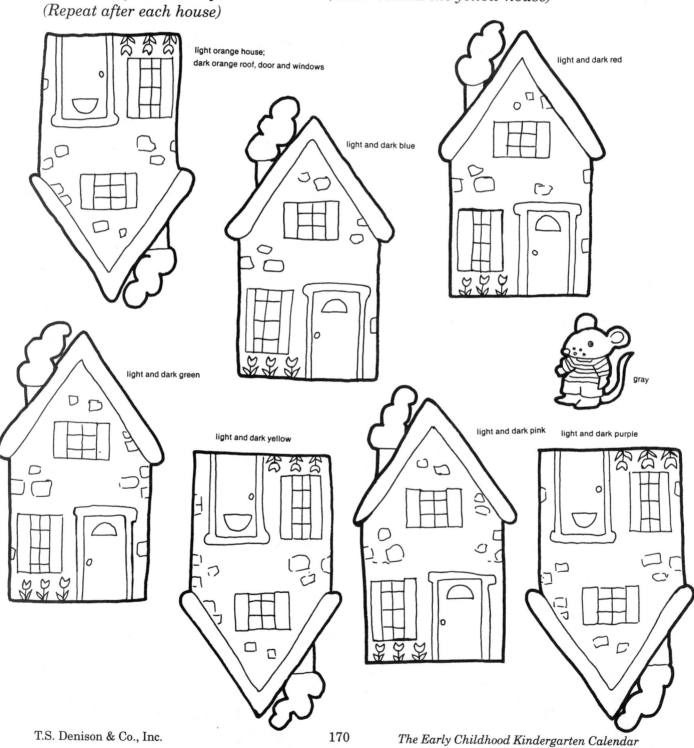

light orange house;
dark orange roof, door and windows

light and dark red

light and dark blue

light and dark green

gray

light and dark yellow

light and dark pink   light and dark purple

FEBRUARY BULLETIN BOARDS

AMERICAN FLAGS

Give each of the children a 9" x 12" sheet of white construction paper. Have the children glue on red stripes and a blue square in the corner. The children may add sticker stars. Teach the children the "Pledge of Allegiance." The children may be too little to understand all that the Pledge means, but you will be surprised with how well they will be able to recite it.

GROUNDHOG DAY

On a blue background use black letters and white clouds. The hill is white construction paper and the hole from which the groundhog appears is done in black. Brown construction paper is used for the groundhog. Write the legend of the groundhog on the space provided in the corner of the bulletin board *(found in the April chapter on page 236 under the heading "Learning About Forest Animals")*.

FEBRUARY BULLETIN BOARDS

PET SHOP

Use colored construction paper of your choice to make an awning for the window of your pet shop. Print the words "PET SHOP" across the window. Have the children make construction paper animals to display in the pet shop window.

VALENTINES

Cover the background of the bulletin board with white paper. Let the children paint hearts all over the white paper. Encourage the children to use a multitude of colors. This background can be kept up longer than the month of February. Use it as a backdrop for displaying other pieces of art.

COLOR THE HEART

LEARNING ABOUT PETS

PET "SHOW & TELL"

Plan a day (or several days over the course of a week) that the children will be allowed to bring in their pets for "show & tell." This is a very successful activity when you recruit help from the parents. All pets should be accompanied by a parent, so the parent can bring the pet home at the end of the show & tell period. (Smaller pets such as fish or hamsters could remain for an extended visit, but cats, dogs, and other animals should go home with the parent.) If parents are working or unable to assist, ask the children to bring pictures to school of their pets.

PET STORE FIELD TRIP

Plan a field trip to your local pet shop. Call ahead to arrange an appointment. Most pet store owners will enjoy helping you. Ask the store owners to describe to the children where they get their pets to sell, some of the ways the pets are cared for at the shop and some good rules about caring for a pet.

FIELD TRIP TO A VETERINARY CLINIC

Plan a field trip to your local veterinary clinic. Call ahead to arrange an appointment. Many children have taken their own pets to a veterinary clinic, but most will never have had the experience of seeing the "behind-the-scenes" activities. Ask to see where the animals are boardered, have surgery, and are kept while in the hospital. Help the children prepare a list of questions before going to the veterinary clinic.

FIELD TRIP TO AN ANIMAL SHELTER

Plan a field trip to your local animal shelter (this is often housed in association with the police department's division of animal control). Call ahead to arrange an appointment. Before the visit explain to the children what an animal shelter is and why we need people, such the people who work with animal control in our communities. The children should know that if a pet is lost, one of the first phone calls should be to animal control.

CLASSROOM PETS

Acquire a pet for the classroom. While you are teaching a unit on pets it is an excellent time to introduce a pet to the classroom. Many types of animals can be very successful in a classroom if you are willing to help the children make this a good experience (for them and especially for the animal). Fish can stay in a classroom throughout a weekend, but all other animals should go to someone's home over a weekend. Have the parents sign-up and take turns taking the animal home. The children love this, because it gives them special time with the pet. It also provides a great language experience, if you have the children report on Monday mornings the activities of the animal over the weekend stay.

LEARNING ABOUT PETS

YARN PICTURES

Provide a large piece of paper, kitten cut-outs *(pattern at the bottom of this page),* and yarn. The children can color the kitten, and then glue the kitten and yarn onto the paper. Discuss how kittens like to play and that yarn is often a favorite toy.

FROG PUPPET

Reproduce the frog pattern *(bottom of page)* for each child in your class. The children can color the frog, cut it out and tape or glue the frog to a popsicle stick or tongue depressor to create their own frog stick puppet. The frog puppet can be used when the children learn the rhyme "FROGS" found on page 190.

MATCHING THE PETS
TO THEIR HOMES

HEART NECKLACES

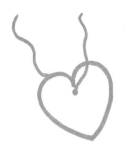

Here is a wonderful recipe for creating clay objects and projects that require no baking.

Cook over low heat 2 cups salt, plus 2/3 cup water. Heat the mixture until bubbly (this causes no change in the texture). Remove from the heat and add 1 cup cornstarch dissolved in 1/2 cup cold water. Stir quickly. Mix with hands if necessary. If too dry add a bit more water. The dough should be pliable like playdough. This playdough will become very hard. It will harden at room temperature in 36 hours and can be painted.

Use this recipe to create heart necklaces. Form hearts with the dough by hand or use a cookie cutter. Poke a hole in the top of the heart and allow to dry for 36 hours. Paint the heart. String the heart so it can be worn.

LINCOLN LOG CABINS

Using two school milk cartons you can make Lincoln's cabin. Cover the milk carton with brown construction paper. One of the cartons is the actual cabin. Draw doors and windows or paste on a construction paper door and windows. The other milk carton is the chimney. Stand it upright next to the cabin and attach with tape.

GEORGE WASHINGTON

This popular silhouette (in white) can be pasted to a sheet of blue paper and a piece of red yarn tied to the top makes a red, white, and blue picture. You may enlarge the face of Washington (found on page 192) to use as your patter for the white face. You will need to draw the face for the children, but the children will enjoy cutting it out.

The children may want to make red, white and blue pictures of their own, showing something that they have learned about either Washington or Lincoln. The children may remember Lincoln's log cabin, George Washington liked to ride horses, or they may want to illustrate the "cherry tree" story.

MARBLE PAINTING

Marble painting! Now that's exciting! Cut paper to fit in the bottom of the pie pan or other type of metal pan. Squeeze a few drops of paint onto the paper. Put one or two marbles in the pan. Hold the pan and gently roll the marbles around. The marbles will create some interesting designs with the paint.

FEBRUARY FINE MOTOR ACTIVITIES

CUTTING OUT VALENTINES

For many young children, cutting out a heart is a very difficult task. Although it can be difficult, it is sometimes surprising how many preschoolers, when given the opportunity to practice, can cut out a heart. Show the children how to fold a piece of paper in two. Draw the outline of a heart on the fold and give the children practice in cutting on the line. Once the children have successfully cut out hearts following the line that you have drawn, let them try to cut out their own hearts. Many children will be able to do this.

Make a collage with all the hearts that the children have cut out.

VALENTINE MAILBOXES

Give each of the children two pieces of red construction paper in heart shape using the full size of the paper. Punch holes all around the edges. Lace yarn through the holes leaving the top open. Use this as the container for the Valentines that each recieves to take home. The children will want to decorate the front of their Valentine containers.

VALENTINE CARDS

Use construction paper, doilies and flower pictures cut from magazines. Fold the construction paper in half. Glue the doily in the center on the front of the card. Glue the pictures of the flowers on the doily .

Let the children dictate to you what they would like to say on the inside of their Valentines. Adding a photograph on the inside of the card is an extra nice touch that parents will truly appreciate.

VALENTINE BRACELET

Make the bracelet from a strip of construction paper. Glue small hearts on the paper or use cute Valentine stickers. Staple or glue the strip to fit over the child's wrist. *(Even little boys enjoy wearing things that they have made.)*

LINCOLN'S LOG CABIN

Give each child a peice of construction paper and eight to ten popsicle sticks. Have the children glue their popsicle stick on the sheet of paper *(as illustrated)*. When the popsicle sticks are dry, the children may add construction paper windows and a door.

Show the children pictures of real log cabins. Let the children try to build a log cabin with "Lincoln Logs."

FEBRUARY FINE MOTOR ACTIVITIES

HANDY ENVELOPE

You will need: a plastic tray, fingerpaints, sponge brush, and 9" x 12" envelopes.

What you do: Put a small amount of paint in the tray. Spread the paint on the palm of the hand with the sponge. Press the hand onto the back of the envelope. Repeat the handprinting process until the back of the envelope is filled with handprints. You can use different colors for variety. Let dry. Use the envelopes to send special notes to friends or they may be used to take home valentines from you Valentine's Day party.

EDIBLE NECKLACES

You will need: Lifesaver candy, any cereal with a hole in the center, dried fruits, thread/dental floss or string, licorice, darning needle, or a children's plastic needle.

What you do: Thread the needle. Have the children make an edible necklace by threading different foods together. Continue threading until the necklace will fit over the child's head when tied. The children can wear their necklaces and later enjoy them as a snack.

MOBILE

Ask parents to donate old valentines or greeting cards. Have the children make mobiles with the discarded cards by cutting out the pictures on the cards and gluing them to colored pieces of construction paper. Attach thread or yarn to the top of the card and then string onto a hanger.

This is a fun cooperative learning project where a group of 4 or 5 children would work on the mobile together.

HEART FLOWERS

You will need: red, pink, and green construction paper, glue, scissors, tongue depressors, markers and glue.

What you do: Cut out hearts (either red or pink) for the flower. Cut out two smaller green hearts for the leaves. Glue the flower to the top of the tongue depressor and the leaves to the middle of the tongue depressor. Draw a face on the flower and give as a gift to your favorite valentine!

It is fun to collect all the hearts and place them in a vase for a centerpiece for a Valentine's Day party. When the party is over, the children may take their heart flowers home.

I LOVE YOU CARDS

Cut out the hearts. Color the "I," "heart," and "U." Turn over and decorate the back of each heart. Fold on the dotted lines. Open the heart and read the message (I LOVE YOU)!

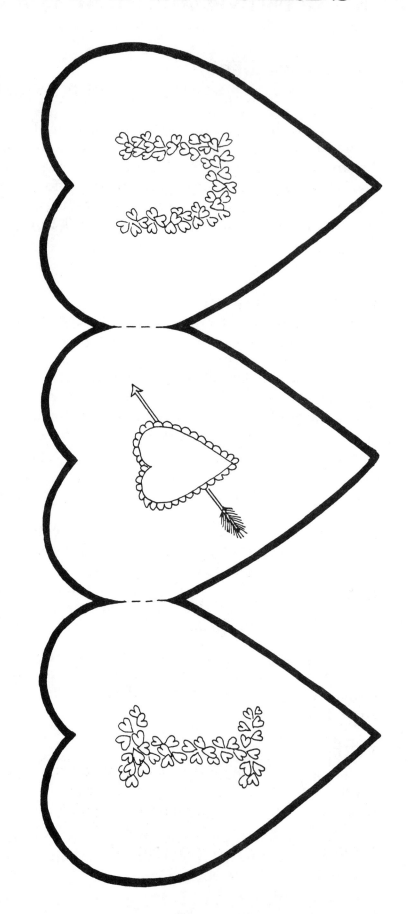

FEBRUARY MOVEMENT ACTIVITIES

TORPEDO LAUNCH

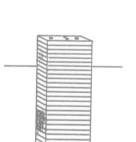

Place a paper cup on the floor in front of a player who is sitting on a chair. *(Tape the cup to the floor so it can't tip over.)*

The player holds a long cardboard tube (i.e. the center tube from a roll of wrapping paper.) With one hand the player holds the tube. With the other hand, the player places a marble in one end of the tube. The object is to allow the marble to roll down the tube and shoot out into the paper cup.

Special Note: whenever small children play with marbles there should be supervision! Even a mature 4 or 5 year old is not beyond putting something as small as a marble in their mouth. If the tube is large enough you can substitute the marble for a ping-pong ball.

DOMINO TOWERS

Dominos can provide tons of fun for small children. Ask your children to discover how many dominos they can stack before the tower falls over.

Another fun variation to simply stacking dominos is to time the children. How many dominos can they stack in thirty seconds? in one minute? in ten seconds?

BALLOON BASKETBALL

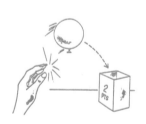

Balloon basketball is a wonderful indoor game, that is actually a "quiet" gross motor activity. Place a big box in the middle of two chairs. Each chair should be facing the box. Have the children sit on a chair. Give one child all "red" balloons. Give the other child all "blue" balloons. *(You can use any two colors for the balloons)*

Let the children bat the balloons into the basketball box. When all the balloons have been hit, have the children count and see how many of their balloons they got in the box.

BALLOON VOLLEYBALL

This is another wonderful indoor game! Set up two books on a table in the classroom. The books represent the volleyball net. Two players stand on either side of the table and bat a balloon back and forth over the "net." This game is really a big "hit!"

FLYING LIDS

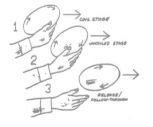

Guaranteed fun! Plastic lids are to be found everywhere: coffee cans, shortening cans, butter containers, ice cream pails, etc. and they come in all sizes. Have your children bring discarded lids from home.

These lids work as well as frisbees! *(And they don't hurt as much as a frisbee does if anyone is accidently hit!)*

VALENTINE GAME

Play a Valentine game. The children should sit in a circle. One child is selected and given a Valentine. The teacher plays some music either on a record player, tape recorder, or piano. *(Instead of playing music, you may wish to teach the children the short song listed at the end of this activity. They may sing the song as they play the game.)* While the music is playing, the child with the valentine walks around the outside of the circle, drops the valentine into the lap of a child who is sitting, and runs. The seated child grabs the Valentine, stands up quickly, chases and tries to tag the first child before he or she can sit down in the empty space.

The game continues with the second child walking around the outside of the circle while the children sing:

THE SONG — A VALENTINE GAME
(Melody: The Farmer In The Dell)
I have a Valentine
I have a Valentine
I'll take it to my friend
A "Happy Valentine."

VALENTINE MATCH

Cut out valentines and draw or paste a picture of an animal on each heart. Cut the hearts in half. Pass out the animals so that each child has one-half of the animal heart. Play music while the children walk around the room. Stop the music. Each child must look for the child who has the other half of their puzzle. Instruct the children to sit down when they have found their match and put the two pieces together. Collect the cards when all are matched and play again.

VARIATION: This game may also be played using the animal/shadow cards found on pages 183 & 184.

SHADOW FUN

Take time during the month of February to go outdoors with the children. Prepare them by reminding them about the legend of the groundhog and suggest that they try to make shadows when they are outside. If it is a sunny day, find an area where they can enjoy experimenting with their shadows.

SHADOW DANCING

The children will be working as partners. One child will be the leader, the other child will be the shadow. The teacher will play music and the leader will dance, march, skip, or move in a manner of the leader's choice. The other child must follow the leader's movements exactly. The children should switch roles at some point so that both the children have an opportunity to be the leader and the shadow.

SHADOWS – Cut out the cards and match the animal to its shadow. (2 page game)

SHADOWS – Cut out the cards and match the animal to its shadow. (2 page game)

FEBRUARY LANGUAGE ACTIVITIES

IMAGINE

The following are series of ideas that help children develop listening skills and encourages them to use their imagination. You can try all these ideas at once or you may wish to use them as separate activities. They are all very successful for providing a "calming down" or "quiet time" for the children.

Lying in the Sand - "Imagine that you are at the beach. How does the sun make you feel? Warm? Cozy? Your friend covers you with sand, letting it trickle over you slowly. How does that feel? Let the sand trickle over your body as I tiptoe once around the room."

Taking a Bath - The children imagine they are in a bathtub filled with warm water, with their arms and legs floating. They close their eyes and feel the warmth of the water. Call attention to how warm water feels to their legs, arms and body. Use potent adjectives such as luxurious, good, marvelous, soothing, warm, great or wonderful.

Can You Hear Me? - The children sit in a circle with their eyes closed. One child sits in the middle with eyes closed also, holding a toy. At a signal, one of the children creeps up stealthily and takes the toy, returning to his/her own place and putting the toy under a chair. If any child in the group hears a sound, he/she points to where the sound is coming from. Then someone else takes a turn.

Time Between Sounds - Ask children to sit quietly or to lie down, close their eyes and listen for street sounds. Say, "Listen for the time between each sound." After a short period for listening, ask, "Was it a long time between sounds? a short time? What were some of the sounds you heard? Did you hear any of them more than once?

PICTURES IN THE MAIL

This is a wonderful game for encouraging vocabulary development.

Locate a large variety of envelopes; various sizes, shapes and colors. In each envelope put one picture. These pictures can be cut from magazines, they can be photographs or commercially prepared language development cards. Place all the envelopes in a large sack or totebag (something like a mail carrier would carry). Let the children take turns being the mail carrier and passing out one envelope to each child.

Once all the children have an envelope they will take turns opening their "mail" and describing what is in their picture.

FEBRUARY LANGUAGE ACTIVITIES

MEMORY MATCH

Make a memory match game for the children to play. Spaciously paste pairs of small wallpaper hearts onto a large heart. (The matching pairs should not be placed near each other.) Provide the children with squares of poster board cut large enough to cover each heart. After all the hearts are covered with squares, a child picks up two squares to see if there are matching hearts. If the hearts match, the child keeps the two squares and continues until the two hearts do not match. The game continues with the next player and ends when all the hearts have been uncovered and matched.

THE VALENTINE BEARS by Eve Bunting

The Valentine Bears by Eve Bunting is a wonderful story to use during the month of February. On October 14th, Mr. and Mrs. Bear settle in for the winter. Four months later the alarm wakes Mrs. Bear. While Mr. Bear continues to sleep, she gathers up her hidden gifts — the honey pot, crunchy dried beetles and bugs, and two Valentine poems —and then she tries to wake Mr. Bear. Finally, she tosses a can of water on him. Mr. Bear jumps up and surprises her with a box of her favorite chocolate covered ants.

• Have the children participate in the following "bear" activities: Sing *"The Bear Went Over The Mountain;"* Recite the rhyme *"Teddy Bear, Teddy Bear;"* and make the bear mask found on page 187.

SIGN LANGUAGE

Teach the children to say "I Love You," in sign language.

"I" — make a fist with small finger straight up; fist touches chest.

"Love" — make two fists with your thumbs over the fingers. Cross arms on heart.

"You" — point to person.

VALENTINE CARDS FOR SOMEONE SPECIAL

You will need: posterboard, scissors, colored tissue paper, glue (diluted slightly with water), paint brush, envelope.

What you do: Cut small hearts from the tissue paper. Cut the posterboard twice as long as the envelopes. Fold the posterboard in half (make sure the posterboard will fit into the envelope). Cover the front surface of the posterboard card with the diluted glue. Place the tissue paper hearts all over the glue surface (overlapping hearts will give the card many, many colors). Brush over the hearts again with the glue.

When the card is dry, open it, and have the child dictate a special message.

THE VALENTINE BEARS – by Eve Bunting

This bear mask accompanies the activity for the story *The Valentine Bears*, found on page 186. Make copies of the mask for each child. Decorate and cut out the bear face mask. Cut out the eye sections. Glue the bottom part of the mask to the top of a tongue depressor. The children can hold the mask in front of their face.

FEBRUARY FINGER PLAYS/POETRY

THE VALENTINE SHOP

There is the nicest Valentine shop.
Before I pass, I try to stop.
Inside the shop, I always see
Valentines for my family -
Brothers, sisters, aunts and cousins,
Friends and classmates by the dozens -
A tiny one, a nickel buys.
A dime is for the bigger size.
A quarter for a much bigger size.
A dollar for the biggest size.
(Have a Valentine box where children
can drop in Valentines for their friends.
Children can draw smallest to largest
size for seriation purposes,)
From; Rhymes for Learning Times,
by Louise Binder Scott.

RHYTHMS FOR LINCOLN'S DAY

(Play Civil War March)
Walk with (pretend) axe over shoulder
   to woods,
Chop firewood.
Split rails.
Build a log cabin.
Make a train and take Lincoln to
   Washington.
Walk with Tad on White House lawn.
   (softly, as in grass)
March to the south like Lincoln's soldiers.
   (Battle Hymn of Republic)
Sing on the chorus.

LINCOLN

Lincoln hoed the growing corn,
   (hoe)
Chopped the family's wood,
   (chop)
Built a cabin out of logs,
   (pound)
Read all the books he could.
   (read)

I'LL SEND YOU ONE VALENTINE

I'll send you one Valentine, that's what I'll do.
I'll send you one Valentine, and maybe two!
I'll send you two Valentines, wait and see.
I'll send you two Valentines, and maybe three!
I'll send you three Valentines from the best store.
I'll send you three Valentines, and maybe more!
I'll send you four Valentines, that's what I'll do,
But on each one,
I will write, "I love you!"   *From; Rhymes for Learning Times,*
by Louise Binder Scott.

BLESSED LAND, UNITED LAND

Bless - ed land, u - nit - ed land, our hearts be - long to thee; Let your song of free - dom ring From sea to sea.

FEBRUARY FINGER PLAYS/POETRY

FIVE LITTLE VALENTINES

One little Valentine said, "I love you."   (hold up fist; extend one finger)
Tommy made another and then there were two.   (extend another finger)
Two little Valentines, one for me.
Mary made another; then there were three.   (extend another finger)
Three little Valentines said, "We need one more."
Johnny made another; then there were four.   (extend another finger)
Four little Valentines, one more to arrive;
Susan made another; then there were five.   (extend another finger)
Five little Valentines all ready to say,
"Be my Valentine on this happy day."

STARS AND STRIPES

Red, white and blue,
Red, white and blue.
Red means brave,
White means pure,
The color blue means true.

Red, white and blue,
Red, white and blue.
Fifty stars for states we know,
In our flag row by row,
Some of the stars are new.

Red, white and blue,
Red, white and blue.
Thirteen stripes of red and white
Six and seven left and right,
They make a lovely view.
*(This is a difficult rhyme for young children
to learn. Have the children say only the lines
"Red, white and blue." After you have recited
this poem several times bring in an American
flag for the children to really examine. Count
the white stripes. Count the red stripes. Count
the stars. Show the children a map of the United
States. Explain how each star represents a
different state. What is the name of your state?
Where is your state on the map? Which star on
the flag would the children like to pretend is
their state's star?)*

TO MY VALENTINE

If apples were pears
And peaches were plums
And the rose had a different name.
If tigers were bears
And fingers were thumbs
I'd love you just the same.

VALENTINE

Valentine, Valentine
Who will be my Valentine?
Valentine, Valentine,
I'll be yours, if you'll be mine?

FEBRUARY FINGER PLAYS/POETRY

KITTY
I have a little kitty,
(extend first and fourth fingers as ears)
He is as quick as he can be.
(make a quick sideways motion with hand)
He jumps upon my lap,
(cup one hand in palm of the other hand)
And purrs a song to me.
(Make a stick puppet of a kitty from the pattern found on page 175. Use the kitty puppet as you say this rhyme.)

FROG
I love dogs.
I love cats.
A silly frog,
Jumped out of my hat.
I was not frightened,
Do you see,
Because he waved my hat,
And said "hello" to me.

WIGGLING PUPPIES
One little puppy, one
Wiggled his tail and had wiggling
      fun
      (wiggle finger)
Two little puppies, two
Wiggled their bodies as puppies do.
      (wiggle whole self)
Three little puppies, three
Wiggled their noses happily.
      (move nose)
Four little puppies, four
Wiggled their shoulders and
wiggled some more.
      (move shoulders)
Five little puppies, fat and round,
Wiggled their ears when they heard
      a sound.
(This rhyme will be easy for the children to learn. Choose five children who join in a set one at a time, as the rhyme is being dramatized.)

FOR MY FRIENDS
To every little friend of mine,
I'll send a pretty Valentine.
      *(make heart shape with
      thumbs and fingers)*
This one is like a little book;
      (close palms together)
You'll find a message if you look.
      (open palms)
I'll use an envelope for this.
      (two fists together)
I'll write my name, then seal a kiss.
      *(one hand closes on fingers of
      other hand)*
What color shall I give to you?
Orange, purple, green, or blue?
Yellow or pink? White or red?
Or maybe a lacy one instead.

GOLDFISH PETS
One little goldfish lives in a bowl.
      (hold up one finger)
Two little goldfish eat their food whole.
      (hold up two fingers)
Three little goldfish swim all around.
      (hold up three fingers)
And although they move,
They don't make a sound.

Four little goldfish have swishy tails.
      (hold up four fingers)
Five little goldfish have pretty scales.
      (hold up five fingers)
1, 2, 3, 4, 5 little goldfish, tired as can be.
All can rest in their fishbowl sea.
      (close eyes, put hands on lap)
(Make five goldfish to use on the flannel board.)

FEBRUARY MUSIC ACTIVITIES

GEORGE WASHINGTON

George Wash-ing-ton was our first pres-i-dent, a long long time a-go. He dressed so diff-erently, as you can sure-ly see, His pic-tures tell us so.

He wore a wig with a bow tied in back, a three cor-ners time had his hat. His shirt had ruf-fles, his shoes sil-ver buck-les, Now would your dad dress like that?

TO HONOR LINCOLN

Let us hon-or Lin-coln, Kind and fair was he, Mak-ing our great coun-try Strong in lib-er-ty.

Let us hon-or Lin-coln, March-ing, march-ing all, Wav-ing flags and sing-ing, Walk-ing straight and tall.

ABRAHAM LINCOLN

GEORGE WASHINGTON

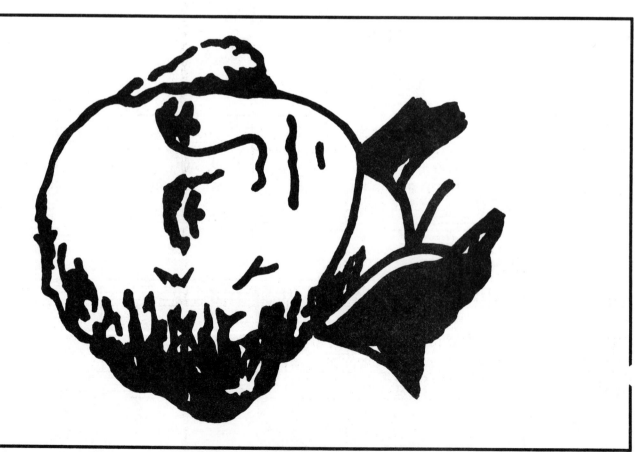

VALENTINE'S DAY ACTIVITIES

VALENTINE CARD HOLDERS

For this project you will need to purchase red plastic plates. Each child will need one full plate and 1/2 of another plate. Punch holes around the edge of the plates as illustrated. Have the children lace the plates together with yarn. Have the children decorate a white paper heart to glue or tape on the front of the Valentine card holder. Finish it by punching a hole in the top and tying a bow with the yarn.

The Valentine's Day card holders will look very nice hanging on the bulletin board. Small children also enjoy having their Valentine's Day card holders taped to the back of their chair. By putting the card holders on the back of each child's chair, the children will be more able to pass out their Valentines independently.

RED AND WHITE DAY

About two weeks before Valentine's Day, have a "red and white" day. On that day, take pictures of each child holding a large sign that says, "I Love You." Attach the pictures to a tagboard frame with glue or tape, and decorate the frames with Valentine's Day stickers. These make great gifts for parents or grandparents.

CANDY BOXES

Small wood boxes can be purchased inexpensively at your local craft store. Allow the children to paint the boxes with white paint. Sponge paint a pink heart on the top of the lid of the box. Fill the box with Valentine's Day candy or small cookies.

This project is easy and will impress the children. To be able to make something as special as a wooden box is a real thrill.

VALENTINE TREATS

For a special treat at your Valentine's Day party, make cupcakes with white cake mix. Just before baking, add a drop or two of red food coloring to the batter. Frost the cupcakes with white icing. Add red sugar sprinkles to the top of the icing.

VARIATION: If you decide that you do not want to bake cupcakes, here is another fun easy-to-make idea: Purchase plain cake donuts. Provide the children with frosting and red sugar sprinkles and let them decorate their own donut for the Valentine's Day party.

Here is another fun idea that children love! Add a drop or two of red food coloring to a carton of milk. Shake well and serve, "pink" milk with the cupcakes. "Pink milk" is always a hit and something the children will tell their parents about.

VALENTINE'S DAY HEARTS

March

THE LITTLE RAINDROP'S JOURNEY

Our story is about a little raindrop. It fell from a cloud along with many other raindrops. What do you suppose happened to them? This little raindrop could have landed in one of many places: on the roof of a house, on the street, in your hair, but it landed on the side of a hill. As soon as the little raindrop hit the ground, it lost it's round shape. It was then that the raindrop began its long journey.

The raindrop ran down the side of the hill and into a brook. The brook carried the raindrop to a river and it traveled in the river until at last the river reached the big ocean. Our raindrop traveled a great distance. Can you tell about all the places it had been before it reached the ocean? It had fallen from a cloud to the side of a hill, down the hill to a brook, along the brook to a river and at last to the ocean.

How many of you think that the big ocean was the end of the little raindrop's journey? No, it was in the ocean that the little raindrop began another part of its journey. The sun shone so brightly on the big ocean. It shone so brightly that it made the surface of the ocean very warm. As the surface of the ocean became warm some of the water turned to vapor. Have you ever seen vapor? If you had been near the ocean on that warm day you wouldn't have seen any water vapor at all. You see, water vapor is invisible. Our little raindrop was part of the surface of the ocean. It became water vapor and was soon in the air.

For many days the water vapor from our little raindrop was in the air. It stayed water vapor as long as the sun was warm. And the air was warm as long as the sun continued to shine.

But one day the sun didn't shine. The air became very cold. When the little raindrop was very warm it had turned into water vapor. Now that the water vapor was cold, what do you suppose happened to it? It changed back into tiny drops of water. The tiny drops of water joined other tiny drops of water to form a big cloud. All the tiny drops of water in the cloud came together to form larger drops of water. Soon the drops of water became too heavy to stay in the cloud. What happened to our little raindrop then? It fell to the ground once more.

Again the little raindrop could have landed anywhere. This time it did not land on the side of a hill, it landed in a flower garden. It landed in a flower garden and soaked into the ground until it reached the roots of a flower. We know that flowers need water to live. The little raindrop traveled up the roots of the flower to its stem and leaves. Again the sun shone brightly. This time it shone on the flower garden and on the leaves of the flower where the little raindrop had traveled. The sun did the same thing to the leaves of the flower that it had done to the ocean. It warmed the leaves and again the little raindrop became invisible water vapor. Again the little raindrop was part of the water vapor in the warm air.

We know what happened when the sun did not shine and the water vapor became cold. Once more the water vapor became little drops of water and came together to form a cloud. Once more the drops became so big that they began to fall from the cloud to the ground.

Where do you think the little raindrop fell this time? It could have fallen into another flower garden or in a forest or maybe in your own backyard.

(Turn into a flannel board story by using the patterns found on pages 197 & 198.)

STORY PATTERNS

Patterns for the story, "The Little Raindrop's Journey," found on page 196.

STORY PATTERNS

Patterns for the story, "The Little Raindrop's Journey," found on page 196.

ST. PATRICK'S DAY LEGENDS

There are many Irish legends. Tell the children some of the folktales that are known such as:

ST. PATRICK AND THE SNAKES

Many tales tell how St. Patrick banished snakes from Ireland. One legend states he scared the snakes by beating on a drum. Another legend, says he tricked a snake into crawling inside a box, sealed the lid shut and heaved the whole thing into the ocean.

THE FAIRY'S HARP

Old Irish legends tell us that a little fairy in Ireland plays beautiful music on a sacred harp. One day the harp is stolen by the God of Darkness. The God of Light and God of Art set off to find it. They discover that it is hanging on the wall of a cold, dark castle. They bring it back to the light of day for the little fairy to play her beautiful music which made everyone happy again. The Irish say that the fairy plays the harp for St. Patrick's Day. In fact, they say that she is the spirit of St. Patrick.

LEPRECHAUNS

Leprechauns were tiny old men who made shoes for the fairies of Ireland. They were rich and were know to hide or bury their gold. People would often try to catch the leprechaun who would promise to tell where his pot of gold was buried. People could hardly believe what the leprechaun would say because he would always trick them. One leprechaun told a man that his gold was buried under a weed. The man tied a handkerchief to the weed and ran off to get his shovel. When he came back, the leprechaun was gone and every weed had a handkerchief tied around it. He had been tricked by the leprechaun.

THE LION AND THE MOUSE

Tell the children the story of, *The Lion and The Mouse*. Have the children retell the story using the finger puppets. Reproduce the patterns and glue onto tagboard. Let the children color the patterns and cut them out. The teacher should cut out the finger holes.

Mouse

Lion

THE TORTOISE AND THE HARE

Tell the children the story of, *The Tortoise and The Hare*. Have the children retell the story using the finger puppets. Reproduce the patterns and glue onto tagboard. Let the children color the patterns and cut them out. The teacher should cut out the finger holes.

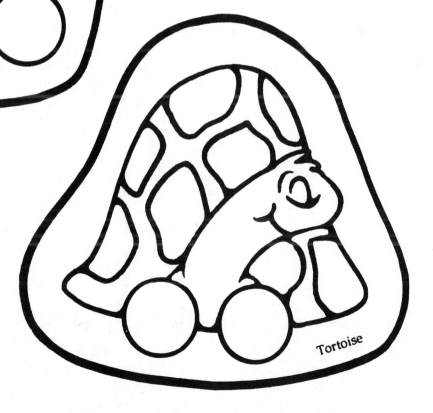

Hare

Tortoise

MARCH BULLETIN BOARDS

ABC BULLETIN BOARD

This is a wonderful bulletin board to keep up all year long. Each week display one alphabet letter. Ask the children to brings things from home that begin with the sound of that particular letter. Display the objects up on the bulletin board. Try to use more objects than pictures. The objects look adorable on the bulletin board and more concrete than pictures for the children.

EXTRA BIG WEATHER WINDOW

Cover the background of the bulletin board in light blue paper. Let the children make a mural of an outdoor scene. Encourage the children to show a multitude of weather conditions: snow, rain, hot, cold, wind, clouds, lightning, etc. The children will delight in the "silliness" of having all the weather conditions in one scene. When the children are finished, the teacher adds black window panes.

MARCH BULLETIN BOARDS

LOOKING OUT TO SPRING

Hang brightly colored streamers from a classroom window to make curtains and tie them back with bright red bows. Make flower pots full of tulips to line the window sill. You may also wish to make a bright yellow sun and some fluffy white clouds (glue cotton onto white paper).

CIRCUS TIME

Display a "Circus Time" bulletin board scene. Copy, color, and cut out the circus characters found on pages 204 -209. Create the three performance rings and allow the children to decide where each of the characters will be displayed. Encourage the children to talk about the various animals and circus people in the scene.

CIRCUS BULLETIN BOARD PATTERNS

THE WEATHER

Providing daily weather activities will:
- Increase vocabulary
- Make children more aware of the environment.
- Help children to make appropriate choices of clothing for various weather conditions.
- Teach the seasons.

WEATHER VOCABULARY: sun, sunny, cloud, cloudy, rain, rainy, hail, storm, thunder, lightning, snow, snowy, wind, windy, cool, cold, chilly, warm, hot, foggy.

WEATHER WHEEL

Using tagboard, cut out a large circle. Divide the circle into sections. In each section draw and color a picture depicting a certain weather condition; sunny, rainy, snowy, cloudy, etc. Choose the weather conditions that are the most appropriate for the climate of your region. Laminate for durability. Attach an arrow to the center of the circle with a brad, so the arrow is moveable.

The weatherperson *(child)* should move the arrow to the picture showing the days weather conditions. Encourage descriptive vocabulary.

WEATHER WINDOWS

The teacher will need to make several windows from tagboard. On the back of each window draw in the window panes. On the other side of the windows draw different weather conditions. Attach a loop to the top of each window so they can be hung on a wall or bulletin board. Hang all the windows so the plain, window pane side is showing. The weatherperson will only turn around the window that depicts that day's weather condition.

Every so often it is fun to mix-up the arrangement of the windows. This will keep the weatherperson on their toes!

WEATHER WILLIE

On a large sheet of tagboard draw the figure of "Weather Willie" *(or Weather Wendy!)* Cover the figure in clear contact paper or laminate. Use small pieces of self-stick velcro on the top of the head, shoulders, hands, feet and waist. Make clothing to fit the figure. Laminate the clothing and use the other side of the self-stick velcro to correspond with the velcro pieces on the figure.

Weather Willie or Weather Wendy is now ready for the children to dress for the appropriate daily weather conditions.

WEATHER FELT HANGING

This is a spectacular teaching aid that will last for many, many years. It is not complicated, but looks as if you have labored for many hours! It is well worth the time and expense to create this lovely teaching tool.

The "Weather Felt Hanging" provides the children with the experience of adding felt pieces to make a picture of the day's weather. The children will be able to learn about the four seasons by adding snow, flowers, leaves, etc. to the hanging. You can use this wall hanging to show the children what seasons look like in different parts of the country. *(Ex; If you live in Florida you can show the children what January looks like in Minnesota!)*

The background of the wall hanging is made from light blue felt. Glue a strip of green felt to the bottom to represent grass. Cut a piece of white felt, the same size as the grass for snow and yellow or mustard colored felt for autumn grass. Glue a brown tree trunk with branches to the background. Below are some suggestions of the felt pieces that you can create for your Weather Felt Hanging. Attach a small piece of velcro to the back of all the pieces that you will be putting on and taking off the felt hanging.

(This same teaching tool can also be made with construction paper.)

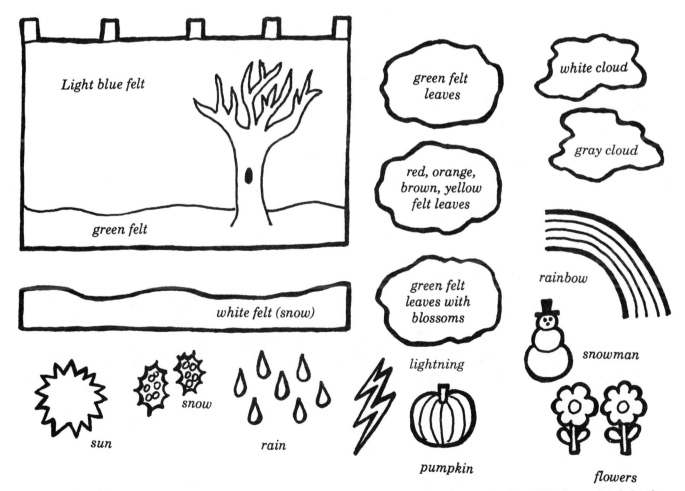

BEANIE LETTERS

You will need twenty-six 3" x 5" index cards, glue and uncooked beans (or any form of macaroni). Use the glue to "paint" one upper case letter on an index card. Let the children lay the beans on top of the glue to form the letter. It is fun to make a set of upper and lower case letters. When you have made the alphabet letters they can be used for a variety of activities:

- Use as flashcards.
- Try putting the cards in alphabetical order.
- Use both sets of cards and have the children match upper and lower case letters.

MAKING LETTERS USING CLAY

The teacher should make a set of alphabet cards. Draw one letter to a card. Give the children clay or playdough. Show the children how to roll the clay to form a long "snake." Shape the clay to form the letter on the card.

When you first introduce this activity, use the easiest of the alphabet letters; C, S, D, O, X, L, V, etc. Work up to the more difficult letters as the children become more proficient in using the clay.

FORMING LETTERS USING GLUE

Provide the children with cards that have an alphabet letter already printed on the card. Have the children "trace" the letter using white glue. Let it dry. Have the children use his/her index finger to "feel" the way the letter is made as he/she says the name of the letter aloud.

I SPY LETTER FUN

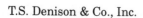

Use old phone books, magazines or directories (perferably with larger print) and a colored pen or crayon. Tear out one page from the discarded book and print one letter of the alphabet at the top (upper and lower case, depending on the type of print used.) Let the child use the crayon to color a small dot over each letter that he/she finds which is the same as the one printed at the top of the page.

ALPHABET ACTIVITIES

FISHING FOR LETTERS

You will need: a dowel rod or stick, string, magnet, construction paper, paper clips, scissors, pen or pencil.

Attach a magnet to one end of the string. Tie the other end of the string to the dowel to complete the "fishing pole." Make 30 construction paper fish. Print one alphabet letter on each of the fish. On the remaining 4 fish draw a star *(or use a star sticker.)* Attach a paper clip to each fish.

Lay the fish on the floor or on a table top with the letter or star side face down. Let the children go fishing to see how many fish they can catch by saying its correct name. The fish with stars are to be considered "free fish."

PICTURE PERFECT

This is a more difficult alphabet task. Many children may not be ready for this as yet. But for those children who are, it is a wonderful activity.

Write an alphabet letter on the child's paper. Ask the child to draw as many pictures as possible which begin with that particular sound. If possible, the teacher or parent can print the word next to each picture the child draws. This will help the child see the continuous use of that particular sound at the beginning of all the names of the pictures which are drawn.

MAGAZINE PICTURE FUN

You will need: Old magazines, catalogs, newspapers, scissors glue, paper.

Print a letter of the alphabet on the child's paper. Have the child look through the magazines and cut out those pictures which begin with the sound of that letter. Then the child can paste the pictures onto the paper. The fun is seeing how many pictures can be found for the letter.

FINDERS KEEPERS OF LETTERS

You will need: old magazines, catlogs, newspapers, scissors, glue, paper.

Print an upper and lower case letter on the child's paper. Have the children look through the magazines to locate the same individual letter in print, regardless of size or color. Cut out the letters and glue the letters onto the paper.

UPPER CASE ALPHABET

A B C D

E F G H

I J K L

M N O P

Q R S T

U V W

X Y Z

LOWER CASE ALPHABET

a b c d

e f g h

i j k l

m n o p

q r s t

u v w

x y z

MARCH FINE MOTOR ACTIVITIES

BALLOON DECORATING

During the Circus unit, decorate your classroom with balloons. Give each of the children a blown-up balloon and some stickers. Let the children place the stickers on the balloon wherever they wish. Hang from the ceiling for a festive display.

CLOWN FACES

Give each of the children a white paper plate. Let the children paint a clown face. Encourage the children to use many different colors of paint. When the paint is dry, blow up a small balloon for a nose. Poke a hole in the clown's face where the nose should be. Push the knotted end of the balloon into the hole. Tape the knot in the back to secure. The clown now has a three-dimensional nose. Glue on yarn for hair.

WIND SOCK

Have the children draw brightly colored pictures on 12" x 18" pieces of paper. Roll the paper into a tube so the picture faces out. Tape or staple together. On the inside bottom , tape brightly colored streamers to complete the wind sock.

RAINBOW YARN PICTURES

The children are going to make yarn rainbows. You will need: red, orange, yellow, green, blue and purple yarn. Dip the yarn in liquid starch or white glue. Wipe off excess liquid. Place the yarn on paper to form a rainbow.

FUN WITH THE WIND

Have the children make a fan from a 6" x 15" piece of paper. Children decorate the paper and fold the fan lengthwise. (See illustration.) The children can make wind by fanning themselves, curtains, mobiles, etc. Draw two squares of the same size on the chalkboard. Wet both. Fan one — notice it dries faster than the other one.

PAPER BAG KITES

Make paper bag kites by giving each of the children a lunch-size paper bag. Decorate the bag with markers, crayons, or stickers. Have the children paste three or four colored streamers onto the bottom of the bag. Punch a hole through the top of the bag piercing both sides. Open the bag. Cut a piece of yarn about a yard long. String through the holes and tie ends together to make a loop handle. (See illustration.)

LEPRECHAUN PATTERN

A large bean bag puppet board can be made from this pattern by using an opaque projector. Enlarge the pattern to the full size of a large sheet of posterboard. Color and paste onto the posterboard. Cut out holes for the face and hands.

MARCH MOVEMENT ACTIVITIES

PIPE CLEANER TOSS

Place a plastic bottle on the floor. Bend five pipe cleaners into circles. Let the children have fun trying to toss the circle pipe cleaners onto the top of the plastic bottle.

This game can be played in teams or the children will enjoy playing this individually.

WHERE AM I?

Ask the children to close their eyes. The children must keep their eyes closed until you tell them that they may open their eyes again. The teacher will say the name of a body part and the children will touch that body part. For example; "Touch your ears; touch your ankle; touch your wrist."

FORWARD/BACKWARD

The concepts of moving forward and moving backwards are not always easy for young children. There are many fun activities that you can do with your class to reinforce these concepts.

TOY CARS - are wonderful for demonstrating and experimenting with moving forward and backwards.

SIMON SAYS - The teacher can give the children directions to move forward and backwards, such as, "Take 2 steps forward. Take 3 steps backwards." The children love playing this game and it will teach them the concepts of forward and backward.

TRICYCLES

If your school does not own any tricycles I urge you to invest in several. If you are lucky you may find parents who are willing to donate a used tricycle. Keep your eye out for tricycles at garage sales.

Using a tricycle or a pedal car provides children with excellent gross motor practice. It also helps children with eye- hand coordination and surprisingly enough, it helps children learn how to share. If you only have a couple of tricycles, the children will quickly learn how to take turns.

THE "CLIMBING" FOLLOW-THE-LEADER GAME

One child will be the leader and climb in a specific pattern over the jungle gym or "climber." The other children will observe the leader from the ground and then duplicate his action.

MARCH MOVEMENT ACTIVITIES

MARCH

Discuss with the children that "March" is the name of the month, and that it is also an action that children can perform. Who knows how to march?

Play some music for the children that is appropriate for the movement of marching. Have a parade with classroom musical instruments.

THE CIRCUS BAND

Invite the children to be in the circus band. Provide them with rhythm sticks, drums, tambourines, jingle clogs, and tone blocks. Play a record of circus music and let them enjoy playing along.

ST. PATRICK'S DAY PARADE

Have a St. Patrick's Day parade. Play a recording of bagpipe music for the children. *(Your local library will most likely have an Irish record that you can check out.)* Ask everyone to wear "green" to school. Explain to them that a big parade is held in Ireland on St. Patrick's Day every year and everyone wears the color green. The "Wearin' of the green" is a symbol of springtime and the green grass of Ireland.

LEPRECHAUN HUNT

Invite the children to look for a leprechaun. Have pre-cut tiny shoe prints along a pathway that leads them to a treat, such as gold-foil wrapped chocolate coins or a plate of shamrock-shaped sugar cookies.

FLYING AIRPLANES

Talk about airplanes. Show the children pictures of some of the first planes and pictures of what airplanes look like today. Discuss how planes can help us.

Draw and cut out a jet plane. *(Follow the illustration when you are making your pattern.)* Reproduce this pattern for each child in your class. Have the children cut out the airplanes and draw in windows, pilot, etc. Fold the airplanes and take them outside to fly.

FREE DANCING

Children love to dance. Dancing is the most fun when children are allowed to move in any way they want.

Using various accessories when free-dancing will enhance the experience. Here are some ideas:

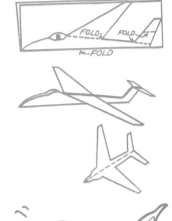

- Sheer Scarves — one per child.
- Balloons — requiring close supervision.
- Jingle Bells — sewn on elastic bands to fit child's wrist or ankle.
- Tom-Toms or Bongo Drums
- Flashlights — covered with colored cellophane and used by the teacher to spotlight dancers.

SHOWY SHAMROCKS

1. Reproduce the patterns on green construction paper.
2. Cut out the shamrock leaves and stem.
3. Arrange and paste the leaves and stem on a paper plate so the pieces form a shamrock.
4. Take a large piece of green tissue paper and cut it into 1 inch squares.
5. Put your pencil eraser in the middle of a small tissue square. Bring up the edges around your pencil.
6. Put a dot of glue on the bottom of the tissue.
7. Place the tissue on the shamrock.
8. Continue to put the tissue pieces on the shamrock until it is filled.

MARCH LANGUAGE ACTIVITIES

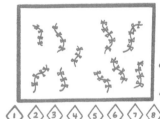

THE KITE GAME

In a file folder or on a large piece of drawing paper, draw 10 kite tails, each having 1 to 10 bows. *(Follow the illustration.)* Cut small kites from construction paper and label with numerals from 1 to 10. The children match the kites to the tails with the corresponding number of bows.

TALK ABOUT CLOWNS

Many preschool and kindergarten children are afraid of clowns. They do not necessarily make all children laugh.

Provide the children with books that show pictures or drawings of clowns. Collect pictures of clowns and put them in a booklet for the children's book corner.

LET'S BE CLOWNS

Bring in a variety of things that the children can use to dress up like clowns: funny hats, ties, ribbons, bows, big shoes, wild print shirts, and if you are brave enough, let the children experiment with some make-up. The children will have loads of fun!

JEREMY BEAN'S ST. PATRICK'S DAY By Alice Schertle

Before you read the story, *Jeremy Bean's St.Patrick's Day* by Alice Schertle to the children, provide them with the following activity:

Enlarge the patterns next to this activity *(bow, snake, hat, shamrock)* and make them in green construction paper. Put each picture into a box. *(You will need four boxes.)* Show the boxes to the children. Before you open each box have the children guess what might be in the box. Open the box with the shamrock last! Read the story to the children.

GILBERTO AND THE WIND by Marie Hall Ets

The story of, *Gilberto and the Wind,* is a wonderful story to read to your class when you are talking about the wind and weather. Gilberto hears the wind and goes outside to play. He watches the wind blow his balloon, the clothes drying on the line, apples falling off the tree, and breaks his umbrella. When the wind stops, he thinks it must be asleep, so he lies down and goes to sleep too.

Teach the children the poem "The Wind," by Christina Rossetti.

Who has seen the wind?
Neither you or I.
But when trees bow down their heads,
The wind is passing by.

GREAT BOOKS FOR MARCH

Spring by Fern Hollow • *Winnie the Pooh and the Blustery Day* by A.A. Milne • *Rain* by Peter Spier • *Taste the Raindrop* by Anna Grossnickle Hines

MARCH FINGER PLAYS/POETRY

THE WIND

The wind came out to play one day.
He swept the clouds out of his way.
   (make sweeping motion with arms)
He blew the leaves and away they flew.
   (make fluttering motions with fingers)
The trees bent low and their branches did too!
   (lift arms and lower them)
The wind blew the great big ships at sea.
   (repeat sweeping motions)
The wind blew my kite away from me.
   (follow direction in verse)

RAINDROPS

Some little raindrops come quietly down,
   (children tip-toeing)
They hide in the grass and do not make a sound.
   (children hiding)
But some little raindrops are scolding us,
   (shaking finger)
They splash on our windows and make such a fuss.
   (tap fingers on floor)
Come, little raindrops, so that we can see,
   (beckon)
If you are quiet little raindrops, or noisy as can be!
   *(children's own choice to go quietly and hide or noisly
   and tap on things)*

THE MARCH WIND

This March wind rattles the windows and doors.
This March wind whistles and blusters and roars!
This March wind seems angry and bends giant trees.
This March wind will scatter whatever it sees.
This March wind blows softly, a kind, gentle breeze.
Then I sleep nicely, as ever you please. *(From Rhymes for Learning Times, by Louise Binder Scott)*

ABC FINGERS

I can make letters with my fingers.
Shall I show you how?
Watch me make the alphabet.
I will do it now.
First, I will make a little *a*.
Is little *a* your name?
Next I'll make the better *b*.
In this finger game.
C is the easiest one to do.
I will make it now for you.
*(Encourage the children to use their fingers to
demonstrate other alphabet letters. This rhyme
is from the book, Rhymes for Learning Times,
by Louise Binder Scott.)*

PINWHEELS

Wh! Wh! Wh! Wh!
Watch my pinwheels go.
Wh! Wh! Wh! Wh!
All I do is blow!

Wh! Wh! Wh! Wh!
See my pinwheel run!
Do you have a pinwheel?
Pinwheels are such fun!
*(This poem could be adapted
to a choral reading. Pinwheels
could be made as a class
project also.)*

THE LITTLE SHOEMAKER

Do you hear the tiny clamor,
   The click of the leprechaun's hammer?
      Tip-tap, rip-rap,
      Tick-a-tack-too!
Scarlet leather, sewn together,
   This will make a shoe.
Left, right, pull it tight.
   Summer days are warm,
Underground in winter,

Laughing up a storm!
I caught him at work one day, myself,
   In the ditch where foxgloves grow -
A wrinkled, wizened, and bearded elf,
   Spectacles stuck on his nose,
   Silver buckles on his toes,
   Leather apron, shoe in his lap -
      Rip-rap, tip-tap,
      Tick-a-tack-too!

MARCH FINGER PLAYS/POETRY

THIS CIRCUS CLOWN

This circus clown shakes your hand.
This circus clown plays in the band.
This circus clown has enormous feet.
This circus clown dearly loves to eat.
This circus clown has a round red nose.
This circus clown has white teeth in rows.
This circus clown has very sad eyes.
He laughs, then frowns, and then he cries.
This circus clown bends way down.
What would you do if you were a clown?
*(Ask the children to draw a picture of
what they think this clown looks like.
You can also have a discussion with the
children using the last line of the rhyme
as a "discussion starter.")*

THE ELEPHANT

The elephant has a trunk for a nose,
And up and down is the way it goes;
    *(clasp hands together, extend arms,
    and raise and lower them)*
He wears such a saggy, baggy hide!
    (relax body)
Do you think two elephants would fit inside?
    (hold up two fingers)

WIGGLES THE CLOWN

I wear a funny little hat.
I have a funny nose.
Sometimes I'm thin.
Sometimes I'm fat.
My shoes have floppy toes.
I wiggle, wiggle all about.
I jiggle up and down.
I make children laugh and shout.
It's fun to be a clown.
*(Children usually go right up to the
business of making appropriate
motions for each line and seem
to laugh and giggle quite
spontaneously.)*

YELLOW DAFFODIL

Here is a yellow daffodil
That nods from left to right;
    *(raise arms and weave back
    and forth)*
Here are the leaves so soft and
    green,
That guard it through the night.
    *(hold up ten fingers, then
    bring them together and
    fold hands)*

THE CIRCUS IS COMING

The circus is coming, the circus is coming!
    Hooray! Hooray!
The circus is coming, the circus is coming!
    Today! Today!
Two chimps act so silly. Each one makes a face.
Three fine circus horses are trotting in place.
Four elephants came holding each other's tail,
Walking so slowly along like a snail.
The tigers and grizzly bears growl and they roar.
Two tigers, two bears, and of course that makes four.
The circus is coming, the circus is coming!
    Hooray! Hooray!
The circus is coming, the circus is coming!
    Today! Today!

THE FIRST BOUQUET

Boys and girls are happy when wild flowers begin to grow so they can pick them. The very first ones they look for are the pussy willows and crocus flowers, growing where ice and snow has melted away. The pussy buds and crocuses are furry little plants that do not freeze in the cold air because they wear fur coats. What color are their fur coats?

What are the crocuses telling the pussy willows?

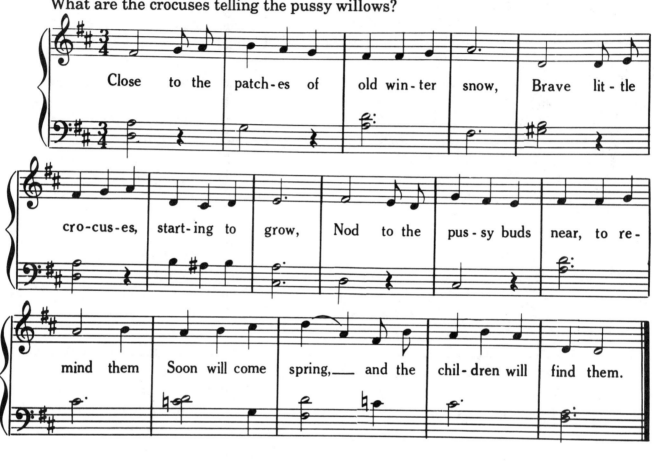

Close to the patch-es of old win-ter snow, Brave lit-tle cro-cus-es, start-ing to grow, Nod to the pus-sy buds near, to re-mind them Soon will come spring,___ and the chil-dren will find them.

1.

A B C D E F G
Z Y X W V U T

H I J K L M N
S R Q P O N M

2.

O P Q R S T U
L K J I H G F

V W X Y Z.
E D C B A

MARCH MUSIC ACTIVITIES

MAKE A RAINBOW

(Sung to the tune of: "Skip To My Lou.")

From the book, "Songs for the Flannel Board" by Connie Walters. Copyright by T.S. Denison Co., Inc.

Take some **limes** and put them in a pot
Stir them, stir them, stir them a lot!
Pour it out now; what will it be?
The prettiest GREEN - you ever did see!!

Take some **berries**; put them in a pot
Stir them, stir them, stir them a lot!
Pour it out now; what will it be?
The prettiest BLUE - you ever did see!!

Take some **grapes** and put them in a pot
Stir them, stir them, stir them a lot!
Pour it out now; what will it be?
The prettiest PURPLE - you ever did see!!

Take some **cherries**; put them in a pot
Stir them, stir them, stir them a lot!
Pour it out now; what will it be?
The prettiest RED - you ever did see!!

Take an **orange**; put it in a pot
Stir it, stir it, stir it a lot!
Pour it out now; what will it be?
The prettiest ORANGE - you ever did see!!

Take a **lemon**; put it in a pot
Stir it, stir it, stir it a lot!
Pour it out now; what will it be?
The prettiest YELLOW - you ever did see!!

Red and orange, yellow and green-
Blue **and** purple colors are seen!
Put them together; what will it be?
The prettiest **rainbow** you ever did see!!

HOP LITTLE RABBIT

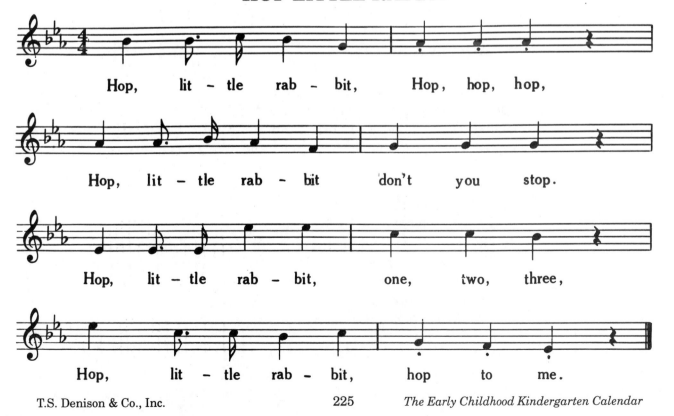

Hop, lit – tle rab – bit, Hop, hop, hop,

Hop, lit – tle rab – bit don't you stop.

Hop, lit – tle rab – bit, one, two, three,

Hop, lit – tle rab – bit, hop to me.

SHAMROCK PUDDING

The children can individually prepare their own shamrock pudding. Spoon a small amount of pistachio instant pudding mix into each cup *(1 tablespoon for 1/2 cup of milk)*. Add milk and have the children shake until an even consistency is obtained. Sprinkle with green sugar sprinkles.

PINWHEEL

Cut a paper into a 6" x 6" square. Draw a diagonal line from corner to corner. Trace a penny in the center. Cut diagonal lines to the outside edge of the circle in the center. Punch holes in pinwheel following the illustration. Punch a hole through the top of a straw. Fold, without creasing, each corner to the center and fasten together with a brad. Hold in the wind and watch your pinwheel spin!

MATCHING TEXTURES

You will need: a collection of empty thread spools, glue, scissors, and various materials such as flocked wallpaper, sandpaper, wool, chintz, velvet, dotted swiss, yarn, etc.

What to do: Material is cut to fit the spool. Pairs of spools with matching material are prepared. Spread the glue all over the spool and apply the material. The children will enjoy feeling and matching the identical spools. It is really fun to try and find the pairs with eyes closed.

TORNADO IN A BOTTLE

Fill a clear 2-liter soft drink bottle 2/3 full of water. Add five or six drops of blue food coloring and shake well. Next add 1/3 cup of vegetable oil and let settle on the top of the water. Make sure the bottle lid is screwed on tightly. Hold the bottle in one hand and rotate the top of the bottle in a quick circular motion with the other hand. Watch the tornado appear.

BIRD'S NEST SNACKS

Make Bird's Nest Snacks for a special treat!
1. Bring to a boil 1/2 cup butter, 1 cup sugar and 1 cup light corn syrup.
2. Remove from heat and add 1 cup of peanut butter and 6 cups of Cherrios cereal.
3. Shape into bird nests.
4. Add M&M 's or jelly beans for eggs.

April

THE HO-HUM STORY

From the book, Quiet Times, by Louise Binder Scott
Copyright by T.S. Denison & Co., Inc.

Teacher: Once there was a sleepy kitten,
   She said, "Ho-hum. I am sleepy now,
   So I will curl right up! Meow!"   *(Children curl up.)*
Children: And she did. Ho-hum!
   When cats are sleepy as they can be,
   They yawn and yawn, like you and me. Ho-hum!

Teacher: Once there was a panting puppy.
   He said, "Ho-hum! I chased a cat and I ran a mile,
   So now I'll have to rest a while."   *(Children sit quietly.)*
Children: And he did. Ho-hum!
   When puppies are sleepy as they can be,
   They yawn and yawn, like you and me. Ho-hum!

Teacher: Once there was a long-eared rabbit.
   He said, "Ho-hum! Rabbits play and rabbits hop, *(Children move up and down)*
   But sometimes rabbits have to stop."
Children: And he did. Ho-hum!
   When rabbits are sleepy as they can be,
   They yawn and yawn, like you and me. Ho-hum!

Teacher: Once there was a new-born calf with wobbly legs.
   She said, "Ho-hum! Because I was just born today,
   I think I'll lay down in this hay."   *(Children curl up.)*
Children: And she did. Ho-hum!
   When calves are sleepy as they can be,
   They yawn and yawn, like you and me. Ho-hum!

Teacher: Once there were some children who ran and played and they were tired. They lay quietly. They closed their eyes. Their mouths opened in big yawns and soon they were as quiet as snowflakes or flower petals.

(If children should happen to go to sleep, clap hands softly and say:
   "Wake up, wake up today,
   It is time to work or play."

DAVY CROCKETT AND THE BEAR

I'll bet you don't know how Davy Crockett learned to grin at bears. It all started back when Davy was a little boy and loved to play in the woods. Davy tried to imitate every sound he heard in the woods. He heard the green snake slide along and say, "Ssssss, sssss," and Davy played "I"m a sssss-snake. I'm a sssss-snake. Here me sssss, hear me sssss!"

He heard a frog saying, "Ccc-roak, ccc-roak," and Davy played "I'm a frog, I'm a frog. Hear me ccc-roak, hear me ccc-roak!"

He heard the black crow as he flew and said, "Caw, caw," and Davy played "I'm a crow, I'm a crow. Hear me caw, hear me caw."

He heard the woodpecker knock on the wood with his bill, "Rrrrat-tat-tat-tat, rrat-tat-tat-tat," and he said, "I'm a woodpecker, I'm a woodpecker. Hear me rrrat-tat-tat-tat, hear me rrrat-tat-tat-tat!"

He learned to make the sounds so well that when you heard a "Ssssss, sssss," you were not sure if it was Davy or a snake. And if you heard a "Ccc-roak, ccc-roak," you didn't know if it was Davy or a frog. If you heard "Caw-caw," it might be Davy or it might be a crow. And if you heard "Rrrat-tat-tat-tat, rrrat-tat-tat-tat," it probably was a woodpecker, but it might be Davy.

One day Davy was out in the woods when something brown and furry came along. Can you guess what it was? Well, it said, "Grrrr." You say, "Grrr," and see what it sounds like. "Grrrr!" You're right - it was a bear! Davy wasn't a bit afraid of that bear. He started walking toward it. Guess what the bear said, "Grrrr, grrrr." That pleased Davy, so to be polite, he answered back, "Grrrr, grrrr." This surprised the bear, but he didn't want Davy to come any closer, so he took a deep breath and growled very loudly, "Grrrr, grrrr!" Davy thought this was so funny, he growled right back, "Grrrr, grrrr!"

The bear was mad so he bared his teeth like this, and growled, "Grrrr, grrrr." Davy was so amused, he laughed out loud. He thought the bear was grinning at him, so he bared his teeth like this, just like the bear and growled, "Grrrr, grrrr." That bear was so upset by Davy grinning at him that he turned and ran away.

Davy said, "I'm a bear, I'm a bear. Hear me grrr, hear me grrr." And that's how Davy Crockett learned to grin at bears.

(Use as a flannel board story. Patterns are found on page 230.)

STORY PATTERNS

Patterns for the story "Davy Crockett and The Bear," found on page 229.

BENNY HELPS THE EASTER BUNNY

The children can pretend to be the baby bunny and pantomime the actions in the story. It might be helpful to define "quail" and "pheasant."

Benny was a tiny, teeny bunny who was only a few weeks old but already had heard of the Easter Bunny and his important job of delivering Easter eggs. Benny was **sitting** in the tall grass of a field that was his home. He **hopped** a few steps further, to **munch** some grass. All the while he was thinking, why couldn't he help the Easter Bunny as some of the other rabbits did? After all, he was a bunny too! He **stretched** and **scurried** through the weeds, **jumping** over a stick, and **stopping** quickly by a tree. Benny was trying to prove to himself how able he was for the job.

He **walked around** a tree and **sat frozen, wiggling his nose** and **turning his ears.** He **smelled** and heard a fox approaching. If he stayed frozen the fox might not find him, and his fur matched the color of the grass. The fox came closer and closer. Benny **shook** with fear. He **turned to the left, then to the right**, and **scampered** as fast as he could. He **jumped** over a fallen branch, **leaped** across a nest of pheasant eggs, **crawled under** a stick and **squatted** in some bushes. The fox had long given up the chase but Benny **sat, breathing deeply** and still **shivered.** The little rabbit **walked** over to his mother and **sat** by his own nest.

There the Easter Bunny was passing out eggs to the other bunnies who would help him deliver them. Benny wanted to help but the Easter Bunny told him he was too young. Next year he would be an adult and could help. The tiny, teeny bunny **crawled** into his soft nest in the tall grass and **curled up in a ball to sleep.**

Next morning he **woke** very early before all the other rabbits. He **stretched out his front paws, then his back paws**, and **washed his ears by licking his paw** and **rubbing it** over his ears several times. He had an itch on his back so he **rolled** in the grass to scratch it. Benny **sat**

down to think. His cottontail **wiggled**. He was hungry so he **hopped on one foot, then the other, then on both**, to the other end of the field to eat some grass. He found some tender pieces, **pulled them up** and **ate** them. He **chewed slowly** and **wiggled his nose**. As he **moved** through the grass, he noticed speckled eggs laying on the weeds. No one was around! Someone forgot to deliver these eggs. Here was Benny's chance to help the Easter Bunny.

Bending down to **pick up** the eggs, he **carefully piled them in his arms. Slowly he walked, stepping over** rocks and sticks. He **left four eggs** at Mr. Woodchuck's burrow, and **skipped** on to Mrs. Muskrat's den, where **he left four more eggs. Scampering**, he **tripped** over a stone. Luckily the eggs rolled to the ground. Benny **got up slowly, rubbing his knees and toes. Bending down** he **picked up** the remaining eggs for Mrs. Raccoon.

Benny **raced** back home to tell the Easter Bunny of his deed. When he returned home, **he sat to rest**. There was great excitement, for Mrs. Quail was screaming and crying. Someone had stolen her twelve speckled eggs from her nest by the tall grass where Benny had breakfast.

The little bunny realized that he had made a mistake. He had picked up Mrs. Quail's eggs from her nest where she was trying to hatch them. He thought they were Easter eggs. Benny had to save those eggs! He **raced** to Mrs. Raccoon's and **found the four eggs**, he **ran** to Mrs. Muskrat's den and **picked up the other four eggs**. Benny was worried that he would be too late! He **scampered** to the Woodchuck's burrow to **find only two eggs** by the opening. Benny was frantic! He **dug** and **crawled down** a tunnel of the burrow. There lay the last two eggs. They must have rolled down the hole. He **picked up the eggs** and **skipped back** to the Quail nest. He **bent down** and **put all twelve eggs back** in their place.

Hurrying, he **hopped** back to his home to announce to Mrs. Quail that her eggs were safe in their nest again. Benny sat, **resting** and **breathing deeply**. He told the Easter Bunny about his mistake. The little bunny learned that he was not old enough to help the Easter Bunny. The little bunny felt terrible about his mistake, but was glad that Mrs. Quail's eggs were safe.

BABY GOSLING

Baby Gosling was hatched out of an egg that was laid by her mother, Mrs. Goose. One day, Baby Gosling slipped away from her mother and from her brothers and sisters and she found a cool pond of water. Oh, it was such fun to glide along in the water. ***Baby Gosling swam and she swam and she swam.*** *(Children say this line with the teacher each time it is repeated in the story.)*

Baby Gosling was lonesome. She saw a squirrel on the bank of the pond. "Hello," said baby Gosling in a very soft voice, "Would you like to play with me?" But the squirrel did not answer because she was sound asleep.

So Baby Gosling swam and she swam and she swam. Soon she came to a turtle. The turtle was very still. "Hello," said Baby Gosling in a very soft voice. "Would you like to play with me?" But the turtle's head was tucked inside it's shell and it was sound asleep.

So Baby Gosling swam and she swam and she swam. Then she saw a rabbit. The rabbit was lying down with it's long ears back and it was sound asleep.

There seemed to be no use in trying to find someone to play with. ***So Baby Gosling swam and she swam and she swam.*** Soon her swimming became slower and slower and slower until she couldn't swim anymore at all.

She climbed out of the water and found a soft bed of grass and leaves, and tucked her head under her wing. Soon Baby Gosling was sound asleep like everything else by the blue sparkling pond. And that is where Mrs. Goose found baby Gosling.

(Ask, "Did Mrs. Goose awaken her baby or let her sleep? How would a baby gosling or duck sleep?" Describe a gosling.)

APRIL BULLETIN BOARDS

MATCH MOTHER ANIMALS TO BABY ANIMALS

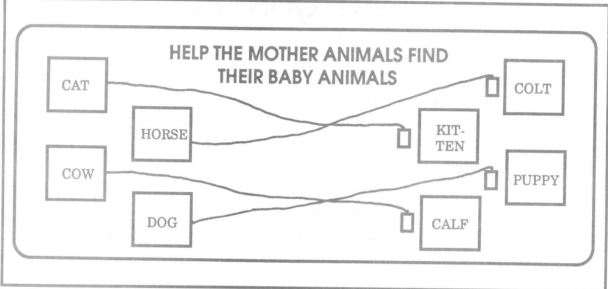

On one side of the bulletin board put up pictures of mother animals. On the other side of the bulletin board put up pictures of baby animals in a mixed-up order. Secure a piece of yarn to each mother animal that will reach the length of the bulletin board. Tape the other end of the yarn as to form a needle. Next to each baby animal place a piece of cardboard stapled to the board on the sides and bottom. The children can now match the mothers to the babies by taking the string and inserting the tape needle into the correct cardboard pocket by the correct baby.

MR. RABBIT

The teacher should cover the background of the bulletin board in a pastel color, and draw an outline of a rabbit. The children take turns, working in small groups, gluing cotton batting to the inside of the rabbit. When the rabbit is completed the children can make colorful construction paper eggs to put all around the rabbit.

APRIL BULLETIN BOARDS

FOREST SCENE

Cover the background of the bulletin board with white paper. Have the children color or paint a forest scene (no animals!) Have the children make trees, hills, and flowers. Each day when you present a new forest animal to the children, add that animal to the forest scene. *(Patterns for animals found on pages 239 & 240.)* You may need to enlarge the animal patterns. By the time you are teaching a unit on forest animals your bulletin board will be a masterpiece!

GIANT FLOWER GARDEN

Cover the bottom two-thirds of the bulletin board with green construction paper to represent grass. The upper third cover with blue paper to represent the sky. Have the children make MANY flowers. Use different art media: tissue paper flowers, construction paper flowers, egg carton flowers, wallpaper scrap flowers, etc. The possibilities are endless. This bulletin board will make you feel like "Spring."

LEARNING ABOUT FOREST ANIMALS

Patterns of forest animals are found on pages 239 & 240.

Learning More About Rabbits

A rabbit is small and has very long ears. There are wild and tame rabbits. The tame ones can make fine pets. A tame rabbit digs a burrow. The babies are born with their eyes closed and they have no fur. Rabbits have a sharp edge on their upper front teeth.

One of the most interesting rabbits is the cottontail. It has a fluffy white underside to its tail. Cottontails weigh about three pounds. They like long grass and weeds where they can hide from enemies such as coyotes, wolves and bobcats. Cottontails usually come out at night. The mother may have from two to six babies. She may have several litters a year. Cottontails have strong legs that let them leap fast and far.

Learning About Groundhog Day

The custom of Groundhog Day came from England. People believed that the weather could be forecast for the next six weeks. The groundhog or woodchuck has a long sleep until February 2. Then he sticks his head out of the ground. He looks around to see if he can see his shadow. If he can see it, he goes back into his hole. This means that there will be six more weeks of winter. That statement has not been proved.

Learning More About Raccoons

A raccoon is about 32 inches long from nose to tip of tail. It weighs about 25 pounds. It is covered with long, coarse gray hair with black tips. It has grayish-white tail with black rings. There is a black patch around each eye with a ring of white around it. Raccoons have long legs and strong claws.

They eat frogs, turtles, crayfish and other animals that live in the water. They also like berries and fruits. They wash their food before they eat it. The bad things they do are raiding chicken coops and eating eggs. The female has from three to six babies in April or May. The babies are blind at birth. When they cry, they sound like real babies.

Learning More About Porcupines

The American porcupine is about 2 feet long. The tail is thick and is about 7 inches in length. The black quills are stiff hair, which are hollow spines that stand up. Porcupines eat plants only, such as buds, twigs and leaves. They gnaw their food. They live in dens. Young porcupines are born in the Spring. Porcupines are feared because they shoot their quills when afraid or angry. Some people eat porcupine flesh which is very fat.

Learning More About Fawns

Female deer have one fawn the first time, and after that, each year she may have twins or even triplets. She licks the fawn's wet fur after it is born. When the fawn is an hour old, it can stand up. It follows its mother on its wobbly legs. She gives her baby milk. The mother licks her baby all over. Then it folds its legs under it and goes to sleep.

LEARNING ABOUT FOREST ANIMALS

Patterns of forest animals are found on pages 239 & 240.

Learning More About Deer

There are 60 kinds of deer; among them, mule, caribou, elk and moose. A deer is an animal with bones on its head. The bones are like horns with hard layers of skin. A deer runs from danger of wolves, coyotes and bears. It lives from 10 to 20 years.

Learning More About The Coyote

It is a member of the dog family. It weighs about 30 pounds and is about 36 inches long including a 12 to 15 inch tail. It can run 40 miles an hour and it hunts chipmunks, rabbits and mice. It also eats berries and prickly pear cactus. It lives about 13 years.

The coyote's parents are mates for life. They have their babies in the spring and treat their babies with love and attention. At night, they serenade with howls and whines.

Learning More About Skunks

A skunk is a black and white furry mammal. It is a member of the weasel family. It is about the size of a cat with short legs and an arched back. It has a short tail. Near its tail are two scent liquid glands that give out a terrible odor. It is there to protect the skunk from enemies. A skunk that is scared can squirt the liquid up to ten feet. If its glands are removed, it makes a friendly pet.

Skunks are night animals. They sleep during the day. They live in hollow logs or dens. Skunks kill harmful insects, rats and mice.

Learning More About Bats

Most bats live in caves, attics or dark places of shelter. There are more than 900 species. Most of them hang upside-down when resting. All bats can see, but poorly. They are harmless but they may get rabies and a bat's bite can be dangerous. Bats have sharp teeth. The hands serve as wings. They eat half their weight in insects each day.

Learning More About The Screech Owl

A screech owl has keen ears. They hide behind its soft feathers. The owl sleeps during the day. It hunts at night. It has sharp talons on its strong legs. It catches mice. When a screech owl hears a gurgling in the brook, it knows there are snails and crayfish around. If it thinks there is an enemy around, it will pull in its feathers and stretch out long. Its eyes become narrow. In this way, the owl looks like a branch of a tree. By the time a screech owl is three weeks old it can swallow a whole mouse. A grown-up owl can eat its own weight every day. Owls cannot move their eyes.

Learning More About Butterflies

A butterfly is the most beautiful insect in the world. It carries pollen to flowers and as a result we have fruit. Caterpillars hatch from its eggs and then turn into butterflies. Butterflies do no harm. They are found everywhere in the world. They fly during the day, while moths fly at night. When resting, butterflies fold their wings over their heads. They have feelers. There are many kinds of butterflies. Encyclopedias label them and show their colorful pictures.

LEARNING ABOUT FOREST ANIMALS

Patterns of forest animals are found on pages 239 & 240.

Learning More About Squirrels

Like a rat, a squirrel is a rodent. It has big front teeth that gnaw. It can run 15 miles an hour. It has a very long bushy tail. There are many kinds of squirrels. Some are tiny and some are 12 inches long. Some live on the ground, and others in trees. They can jump from limb to limb for they have flaps of skin beside their bodies. Some squirrels are black. Others are gray or brown.

A red squirrel lives in northern United States and in Canada. It is very active. It is red and its lower parts are white. A black stripe runs along its side. It lives in trees. Nuts and grain are its foods. It often eats fruit, insects or bird's eggs.

The gray squirrel is larger than most squirrels. The mother has two to four babies. They are tiny with no hair. When an enemy comes, a gray squirrel can flatten its body on the limb of a tree and appear to hide. Like red squirrels, gray squirrels chatter.

Learning More About Woodpeckers

It has a very strong bill that bores holes in trees. It bores holes to find insects. Woodpeckers have strange toes or claws that can climb up and down trees. Two toes are pointed to the front. Two toes are pointed to the back. Woodpeckers have stiff tail feathers. They have long tongues with little barbs or hooks on the tips. They can spear insects with their tongues. Their voices are loud. Their feathers are spotted black and white or brown and white. Some males have red or yellow feathers on their heads. Most encyclopedias or books on birds have pictures of woodpeckers.

Learning More About Muskrats

Muskrats have sharp front teeth. They carry plant stalks, mainly cattails and twigs to a muddy place in the middle of a marsh. They pile up the stalks beneath the "house" and dig a burrow up into the center. When Winter arrives, they pile more cattails on top and sides until the walls are a foot thick.

Learning More About Toads

There are many kinds of toads. They are related to frogs, but spend more time on the land and have rougher and drier skin. Toads lay eggs and eat flies and other small insects. Toads do not have tails.

Learning More About Mosquitoes

Female mosquitoes sting. There are about 2000 kinds of mosquitoes. A mosquito has a round head attached to its chest by a thick neck. It has feelers in front of two round eyes. There are two wings which have scales that can rub off. When a mosquito flies, it moves its wings about 300 times a second. Its legs are long. Mosquitoes hatch eggs. The humming sound is made by wings beating against the body.

FOREST ANIMAL PATTERNS

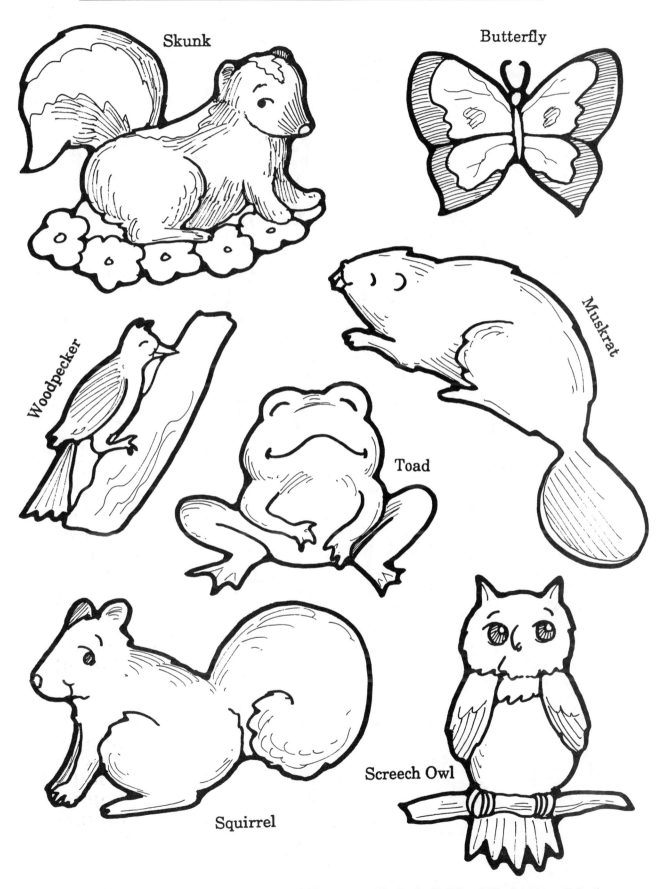

Skunk

Butterfly

Muskrat

Woodpecker

Toad

Squirrel

Screech Owl

FOREST ANIMAL PATTERNS

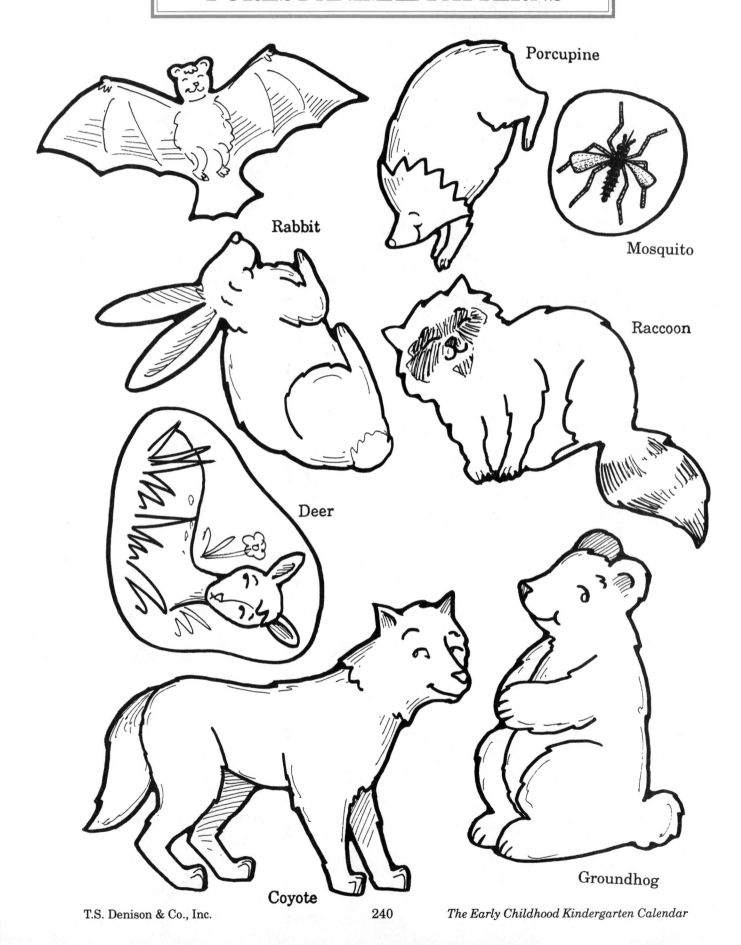

Porcupine

Mosquito

Rabbit

Raccoon

Deer

Coyote

Groundhog

APRIL FINE MOTOR ACTIVITIES

BABY CHICK

The body of the chick is 6" x 18"; the head 5" x 12"; the beak is 2" x 4"; the wings are 4" x 4 (cut 2 triangles); circle for hat is 6"; cylinder for the top of the hat is 3" x 9" , and; the feet are cut from 2 pieces of paper 2" x 4". Follow the illustration in assembling the baby chick.

A dried flower adds a nice touch for the top of the chick's hat.

COLORING REAL EGGS

Coloring real eggs is always a favorite activity of young children. Use cold-water dyes in the classroom. Use a color crayon to print each child's name on an egg. The name will show through the dye once it is colored. The children will all want to eat the eggs they personally colored!

CANDY CUP

You will need: Construction paper, scissors, glue, small plastic cups, plastic sandwich bags, candy, permanent markers, pencil.

What you do: Cut two identical construction paper daisy-type flowers between five and seven inches in diameter. Roll up the petals of the top flower using a pencil. Glue the flowers together in the middle alternating petals. Glue the cup to the center of the flower. Write the child's name on the cup using a permanent marker. Fill the plastic bag with candy and put in it in the cup. Use as a party favor, or place marker at your spring or Easter party.

RAIN FIGURES

The rain figures hat is cut from a 6" square; the coat is cut from a 12" square; the arm is cut from 6" x 2" paper; the girl's legs are 2" x 6"; the boy's pants are 3.5" x 6", and; the shoes are cut from 4" x 2" paper. Use the illustration to guide you through the assembly of the rain characters.

Creating a large umbrella on a wall and displaying the rain figures under the umbrella makes a very decorative room display.

EYE DROPPER ART

Fill an ice cube tray with water. Add food coloring to the water in the ice cube tray. Give the children paper towels as their art paper. Using eye droppers the children can create some beautiful designs by dropping the colors onto the paper towels. When the paper towels are dry, they can be framed with construction paper and put on display in the classroom.

APRIL FINE MOTOR ACTIVITIES

PEANUT PACKING BUNNIES

You will need: styrofoam "peanuts," black construction paper and glue.

What you do: The child is given a sheet of 9" x 12" black construction paper. The styrofoam peanuts and glue are placed on the work table. The child applies the glue to a peanut and then presses it on the construction paper.

There are several methods for using glue that work well:
- Using fingers to apply the glue from bowls.
- Using glue in plastic squeeze bottles.
- Using cotton swabs to apply the glue from bowls.

EASTER EGG COOKIES

Use an egg shape cookie cutter and make Easter egg cookies from already-prepared sugar cookie dough. Roll out the dough and cut the shapes with the cookie cutter.

Add food coloring to egg yolks. Children can "paint" the mixture on the cookies. Use "new" paint brushes or cotton swabs. It will dry to a glossy finish and is completely edible.

AN EASTER BREAKFAST

Give each child a white paper plate. Have the children look through magazines and cut out pictures of food that they would enjoy for breakfast. Ask the children to create a meal and glue the pictures on the plate.

THE EGG TREE

The teacher should find a small branch for each child in the room. (If the weather is nice, the children could go on a walk and find their own branches.) Fill small containers with plaster and insert the tree branch. Allow plaster to dry overnight.

Supervise the children closely, as you let them spray paint the tree branch. When the paint is still wet sprinkle with glitter. The glitter will adhere to the branch and remain "sparkly."

The children can make paper eggs that are decorated with glitter, sequins, markers, paint, etc. Punch a hole in the top of the egg and tie a string through the hole. Hang these beautiful eggs on the tree.

The parents will love these trees when they are brought home. They can be decorated for any season of the year.

APRIL FINE MOTOR ACTIVITIES

EASTER BASKET

Small milk cartons such as the kind that children use daily make good baskets. Open, clean, dry, and push up straight the four sides at the top of the carton. Trim away two of these sides and curve the remaining two.

Mix tempera paint with a small amount of soap flakes (not detergent) and a little liquid paste or glitter glue, so that the paint will stick to the waxed carton. Colors such as purple will need two coats unless the tempera is very thick.

When dry, attach a handle to the two curved sides. (Pipe cleaners work well.) Fill the basket with Easter grass. Put in real colored Easter eggs for the children to take home.

EASTER BASKET VARIATION

You can also make Easter baskets by attaching pipe cleaners to green plastic strawberry baskets. *(Ask parents to collect these for you!)* Add Easter grass and fill with jelly beans, small boxes of raisins, Easter eggs that you have dyed at school, stickers, or any other small treats.

SPRINGTIME CHICKS

Following the example given in the illustration, provide your children with the shapes necessary for creating this "springtime chick." Discuss the circle and triangle shapes.

This project is extra fun if you use felt fabric instead of construction paper. Glue the yellow and orange chick pieces onto green felt. Movable eyes are also a fun addition!

COFFEE FILTER RAINBOWS

Put some water in an ice cube tray. Add food coloring to the water. Provide eye droppers and coffee filters (flattened) and let the children make designs with the colors.

The color will spread and run into the other colors on the coffee filters which creates an interesting effect for the children. It is also a fun way to demonstrate to the children how two colors mixed together can make a new color.

WE DO AS THE ANIMALS DO

The classroom will be divided into two sections; half the class will be adult animals and the other half of the class will be baby animals. The object of the game is for the baby animals and the adults animals to find each other. The teacher will secretly assign an animal to each child. The teacher must make sure that there are pairs of animals; one adult cat and one kitten; one adult cow and one calf, etc. On the teacher's signal the children move around the room in the same manner as the animal they have been assigned. After all the baby animals have found either their mother or father, repeat the game assigning the children a new animal.

EASTER EGG HUNT

Ask the parents to help you by saving L'eggs containers. (There are good for many different types of activities!) Make sure you have one container for each child in your class. Put a sticker or some type of small surprise in each of the containers and hide them in your classroom. Let the children go on an Easter Egg Hunt. Tell the children they can only find one egg. Once they have found an egg they should go and sit down.

ANIMAL PICTIONARY

You will be surprised at how well preschoolers and kindergarteners can play this game. Have all the children sit on the floor in front of a large chalkboard. Have one child come up to the chalk board. Whisper the name of an animal in the child's ear. The child must try and draw the animal and the other children must guess the name of the animal that the child has drawn.

Make sure that all the children have a turn drawing on the board.

CALL YOUR LOCAL PET STORE/
ANIMAL SHELTER/ZOO/ HUMANE SOCIETY

It is surprising what you can receive for your classroom when you ask. Many pet stores, your local zoo, animal shelters or the Humane Society will bring a variety of animals to visit your classroom. Call any of the above listed places to see who would be willing to come to your classroom and share some information and the experience of animals with your children.

APRIL MOVEMENT ACTIVITIES

FLOWER MIX-UP

Invite the children to play flower mix-up. Provide each of the children with a colored flower to wear around their neck. To make the flower necklaces, cut out flower shapes from colored construction paper. Punch a hole at the top of each flower and string a long piece of yarn through the hole. Laminate for durability (and so you can save this game for years to come!) Divide the flower colors as equally as possible among the children. The children will sit in a circle wearing their flower necklace. The teacher calls out, "yellow flowers, mix-up." The children wearing yellow flowers change places with each other. Continue calling flower colors until all the children have had a chance to mix-up. The game ends when the teacher calls, All flowers mix-up!"

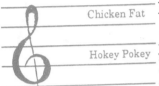

EXERCISE TO MUSIC

There are many excellent children's records available to encourage young children to exercise. Many of you will remember the record, "Chicken Fat," and "The Hokey Pokey." Children delight in music and the rewards from daily exercise are wonderful.

FITNESS CENTER

To encourage your young children to exercise, set up a creative play exercise center. Include tumbling mats, ankle or wrist weights, towels, tape recorder with a "work-out" tape, water and paper cups. Be sure to supervise and discuss safety in this creative play area.

SWEATBANDS

All serious athletes enjoy wearing sweatbands while they work out. The children will love being able to "work-out" and look the part with their fancy sweatbands.

Stretch headbands can be purchased inexpensively at your local drug store or department store. Allow the children to use fabric paints to personalize their own sweatband.

BALLOON CATCH

You will need: Inflated balloons and funnels. If you do not have funnels, roll tagboard into a funnel shape and tape it onto a tongue depressor.

What you do: Place the balloon on the funnel. Push the funnel up to toss the balloon into the air. As the balloon comes down, try to catch it! The children will have fun with this activity and it is very good for eye-hand coordination and muscular control. As the children become more adept, the class can count out loud each successful catch.

PROFESSOR BERT BUNNY

Color the pieces and cut them out. Cut out the four strips on the following page to make accordion arms and legs. (The legs should be longer than the arms.) Glue all the pieces together to form Professor Bert Bunny as seen in the example.

example

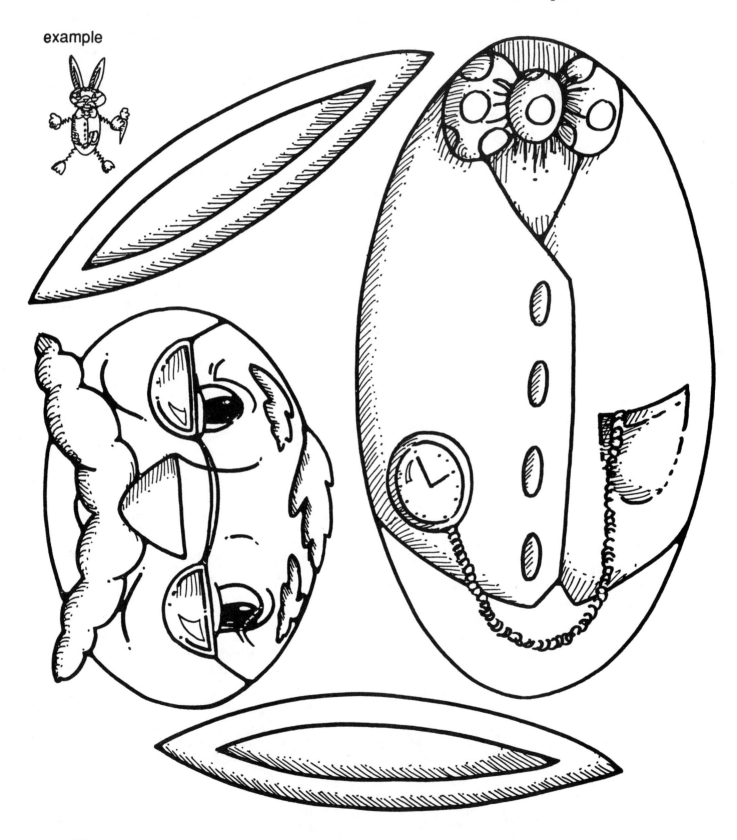

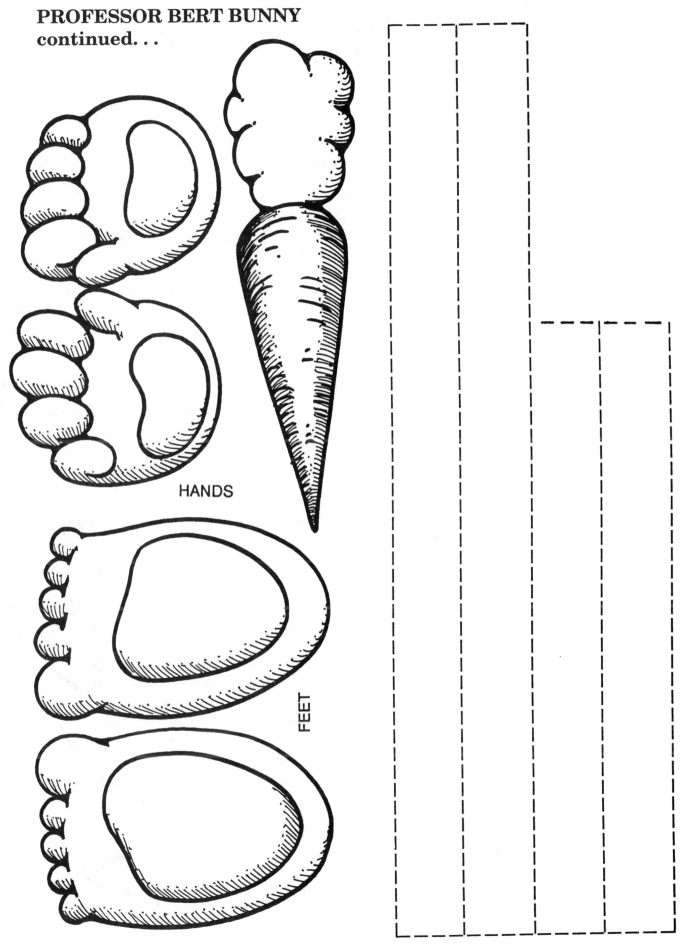

PROFESSOR BERT BUNNY
continued. . .

HANDS

FEET

APRIL LANGUAGE ACTIVITIES

PETER RABBIT

The *Tales of Peter Rabbit* by Beatrix Potter are wonderful stories to share with young children during this time of year. Not only will the children enjoy the stories but there are many fun activities that you can do in your classroom to enrich the stories:

• Let the children take turns dramatizing the story as you read it.
• Have the children illustrate a picture of their favorite character from the story; Peter, Flopsy, Mopsy or Cottontail.
• Make a picture of a rabbit using cotton.
• Have the children make up a new story about Peter, Flopsy, Mopsy and Cottontail.

ANIMAL GUESS

Let each of the children, one at a time, think of an animal that the rest of the class has to guess. The child who is thinking of the animal should give the class three to five clues. Ex; My animal lives on a farm. My animal likes to eat carrots. My animal has a fluffy tail. (Yes, you are right! The animal is a rabbit.) For those children who have a difficult time thinking up the clues, the teacher can carefully guide them through the process. Ex: What does your animal like to eat? Where does your animal like to sleep? Does your animal have fur or feathers?

BIG BOOK OF BABY ANIMALS

This is a wonderful class project. Have each of the children draw a variety of baby animals and cut out pictures of baby animals from old coloring books or magazines. The teacher will mount these pictures on large pieces of tagboard or poster board. Be sure to put all the same animals on a page(All the cats on one page. All the horses on another page, etc.) Print the name of the animal on the top of the page. Cover each of the large posterboard pages with clear contact paper.

When the pages are complete the teacher can prepare a cover, punch three holes in the left hand side of the pages and tie together with heavy string or yarn.

Your class has created an excellent "Big Book of Baby Animals." You will be able to use this book while teaching and the children will have hours of enjoyment "reading" their published work!

APRIL LANGUAGE ACTIVITIES

APRIL FOOL'S FUN

Collect a number of silly or outrageous pictures from magazines. Laminate for durability. Display the pictures for the children to look at and discuss. In a group, ask the children to make up a silly story about what is happening in the picture.

EASTER PARADE by Mary Chalmers

You will be sharing the story, *Easter Parade,* by Mary Chalmers. Before you read the story to the children, prepare the following activities:

• Show the children pictures of parades. Talk about what a parade is and ask if any of the children have ever been to a parade, or been in a parade?

• Place a toy chicken, rabbit, and duck and several other animals in a paper bag. Have the children take turns picking out an animal from the bag and identifying it. After each child takes out an animal, ask, "Is this an Easter animal?" Set the chicken, rabbit, and duck on a table in front of the children when you read the story.

MUSHROOM IN THE RAIN by Mirra Ginsburg.

Read the story, *Mushroom in the Rain,* by Mirra Ginsburg. This story is about an ant who gets caught in the rain and hides under a mushroom. A butterfly, a mouse, a bird, and a rabbit all take refuge under the same mushroom. How is there room for all — mushrooms grow and grow in the rain.

• *Pre-Reading Activity* — Give the children edible mushrooms. Dip them in salad dressing to make them taste better. (Tell the children they should only eat mushrooms that are bought at the store.)

Post-Reading Activity — Retell the story sitting under an umbrella that is only partially open. Divide the class equally into the animal groups from the story. When you come to a certain animal in the story, those children assigned that animal come and join you under the umbrella. As each group joins you open the umbrella a little more.

RAIN, RAIN, GO AWAY

Make an umbrella and raindrops from felt to be used on the flannel board. Place the umbrella on the flannel board. Have the children place the raindrops, OVER, ON, UNDER, and BELOW the umbrella.

Recite the nursery rhyme, *Rain, Rain, Go Away.*

TOILET PAPER TUBE BUNNIES

Materials needed: White construction paper, empty toilet paper tubes, pink tempera paint, brushes, scissors, glue, and cotton balls.

Method of preparation: A bunny face is cut out of white construction paper for each child. (See pattern below.)

Procedure: Bowls of pink paint and brushes are placed on the work table. Each child is given a toilet paper tube to paint. When the paint is dry the child glues a bunny face on one side of the toilet paper tube and a cotton ball on the reverse side. (The bunny face may be reinforced with a stapler.) Children may draw bunny paws on the tube with a felt-tipped marker.

bunny face pattern

empty toilet
paper tube

staple

cotton ball
(glued on back)

bunny paws drawn on
with a marker

APRIL FINGER PLAYS/POETRY

KITTEN IS HIDING

A kitten is hiding under a chair,   *(hide one thumb in other hand)*
I looked and looked for her everywhere.   *(peer about hand on forehead)*
Under the table and under the bed,   *(pretend to look)*
I looked in the corner and then I said,
"Come kitty, come kitty, I have milk for you."   *(cup hands to make dish and extend)*
Kitty came running and calling "Mew, mew."   *(run fingers up arm)*

THINGS I SAW

I heard a bee go buzzing by.   *(move hand swiftly in front of body)*
I saw two butterflies in the sky.   *(hold up 2 fingers)*
I watched three bunnies hop down the lane.   *(hold up 3 fingers)*
They jumped in a hole before the rain.   *(bring thumbs and pointer fingers together to form a hole)*

MOTHER ROBIN RED

Here is Mother Robin Red.   *(point to thumb)*
Here is the apple tree.   *(point to first finger)*
Where she kept her children
There were one, two, three.   *(count other three fingers)*

THE RABBIT

He has two long ears and a fluffy tail,   *(hold hands above head for ears)*
And he likes to wiggle his nose.   *(wiggle nose)*
Carrots are his favorite food,   *(pretend to eat carrot)*
And he hops wherever he goes.   *(hop around)*

SPRING

Spring must be here,
It must be so.
I picked a pussy willow.
That is how I know.
(Pretend to be picking pussy willows and dance around.)

EASTER EGGS

Five pretty Easter Eggs laying on the floor,
(Child's name) picked one up and then there were four.
Four pretty Easter Eggs underneath a tree.
(Child's name) picked one up and then there were three.
Three pretty Easter Eggs in a basket by you,
(Child's name) picked one up and then there were two.
Two pretty Easter Eggs left out in the sun,
(Child's name) picked up one and then there was one.
One pretty Easter Egg left all alone,
(Child's name) picked one up and now they're all gone.
(The children sit in a circle to repeat rhyme. The teacher selects the first child and the child says his name at the appropriate time and then selects the next child and this is repeated to the end of the game. Practice with name recognition can be part of this activity with the teacher holding name cards to be read. Number cards can also be used for number recognition.)

(Betty Ruth Baker - Waco, TX)

APRIL FINGER PLAYS/POETRY

STRIPED CHIPMUNK

A little striped chipmunk
Sat up in a tree,   *(make a fist and protrude thumb)*
Counting all his chestnuts,
One, two and three.   *(point to three fingers)*
When little Betty Boston went out to play,
The chipmunk flipped his tail,
And ran far, far away!   *(hide hand behind back)*

SQUIRREL IN A TREE

This is a squirrel that lives in a tree;   *(make fist; hold two fingers erect)*
This is the tree which he climbs;   *(motion fingers climbing up opposite arm)*
This is the nut that he takes from me;   *(make small circle)*
As I sit very still sometimes.   *(fold hands)*
*(You can turn this rhyme into a flannel
board activity. Make a felt squirrel,
tree and nut.)*

RAIN ELF

Rain, rain, rain, rain!
Pouring on our roof -
Sounds like racing horses,
Thundering on the hoof!

Roar, roar, rumble, roar!
The clatter it does make!
I really fear the thunderclouds
Are playing pat-a-cake.

TURTLES

One little turtle feeling so blue;
   (hold up one finger)
Along came another. Now there are two.
   (hold up two fingers)
Two little turtles on their way to tea;
Along came another. Now there are three.
   (hold up three fingers)
Three little turtles going to the store.
Along came another. Now there are four.
   (hold up four fingers)
Four little turtles going for a drive;
Along came another. Now there are five.
   (hold up five fingers)

Rain, rain, rain, rain!
Down my window pane -
Run, run, run, run,
Down the water drain.

Do you suppose that some one -
(A water elf no doubt!)
Has pulled the stopper in the clouds
And let the water out?
*(This is a fun poem for the children to
try to illustrate. What do they think
the elf looks likes? What is that elf
doing in the clouds? Do you think you
can pull a stopper out of the clouds
to release the rain?)*

THE CAREFUL BUNNY

When I think about the Easter Bunny, I always picture a big, white rabbit that is old and gentle and wise. His eyes are pink and his ears are pink inside. His nose is pink too and it wiggles like all bunny noses. His whiskers are long and white and his eyes twinkle with kindness. He has strong and nimble legs. He is just as busy as Santa Claus. There is so much to plan and do for Easter Day.

Close your eyes and tell me what you see when I sing this song.

Suggestion: Sing the song lightly and carefully hold a beautiful Easter Egg in your "paws."

BUNNY FINGER PLAY

(put one hand behind back to be the puppy)
A little bunny rabbit,
With his ears up straight,
(put up two fingers for bunny's ears and touch finger tips of other three fingers for bunny's nose)
Hopped into the garden patch,
(make bunny hop)
Through the gate.

A puppy saw him nibbling,
(slowly bring other hand round to front)
In a row of peas.
Up jumped the puppy, "Go.
(make "puppy" jump)
Away, if you please."

APRIL MUSIC ACTIVITIES

JUST HATCHED
(Melody: I'm A Little Teapot)
I'm a little chick inside an egg
I'm often sleeping — curled on my legs
Soon you'll hear a pecking, pecking sound
The egg will crack and I'll come out.
      (cheep, cheep)

I'm a little duck inside an egg
I'm often sleeping — curled on my legs
Soon you'll hear a pecking, pecking sound
The egg will crack and I'll come out.
      (quack, quack)
*(Have the children curl up in a ball on
the floor and pantomime this song.)*

RAINDROPS
(Melody: Are You Sleeping)
Pitter patter, pitter patter
Hear that sound; hear that sound.
Watch the little raindrops
Watch the little raindrops
Touch the ground — touch the ground.

IN THE EGG
(Melody: Eency, Weency Spider)
In this little egg
A tiny baby sleeps
He lies so still
He doesn't make a peep
One day very soon
A pecking sound you'll hear
And before your very eyes
A baby chick appears

In this little egg
A tiny baby sleeps
He lies so still
He doesn't make a peep
One day very soon
A pecking sound you'll hear
And before your very eyes
A baby duck appears
*(Make a chick and duck stick
puppet. Hide the puppets behind
a paper cut-out of an egg. Pop out
the appropriate puppet on the last
line of each verse of the song.)*

NEW-BORN LAMB
(Melody: I'm a Little Teapot)
(Boys sing)
I'm a little baby lamb just born today
I want to run around and play
I am very hungry — I must eat
I'll grow big like daddy sheep.

(Girls sing)
I'm a little baby lamb just born today
I want to run around and play
I am very hungry — I must eat
I'll grow big like mommy sheep.

EASTER BUNNY HOP
(Melody: Shortin' Bread)
Look over here and look over there
Little candy Easter eggs are ev'rywhere
Who's the one who hides them there?
Little Easter bunny hides them everywhere
Little Easter bunny goes hopping, hopping
Little Easter bunny goes hop, hop, hop
Little Easter bunny goes hopping, hopping
Little Easter bunny goes hop, hop, hop

Songs from, Sing-A-Song All Year Long, by Connie Walters
Copyright by T.S. Denison & Co., Inc.

T.S. Denison & Co., Inc.   254   *The Early Childhood Kindergarten Calendar*

RABBIT PUZZLE

Color, cut out, and paste on a piece of construction paper.

EGG MATCHING

Cut an egg shape from heavy cardboard. Glue on pretty wallpaper on the cardboard and cut in half. *(To decorate the egg, you can also paint or color the tagboard egg shape.)* Cut the egg in half. Make several of these eggs. The task for the children will be to match the two corresponding halves to form the whole egg.

You can also use a variety of other shapes for this activity; circles, squares, rectangles, etc. Wallpaper stores are a wonderful source for obtaining "free" wallpaper samples. Most wallpaper stores enjoy donating their outdated wallpaper sample books to school programs.

(Mrs. J. Miller - Kannapolis, NC)

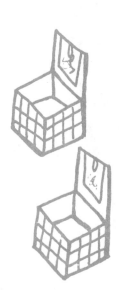

EGG BOX SORT

An egg carton is super for sorting activities. Here is a simple idea: Glue one button into each section of the egg carton, using buttons none of which are identical. Then have the child sort the buttons by putting all the identical buttons in the same section of the egg carton.

VARIATIONS: 1) Child sorts buttons by like colors.
2) Child sorts buttons by like number of sewing holes.
3) Child sorts buttons by like size.
4) Glue different kinds of beans in the egg carton sections. Child sorts beans by putting all identical beans in same section.
5) Cut a piece of posterboard 11" x 2". Cut five inverted V-shaped slots along the bottom edge so posterboard can be seated into the rear sections of the egg carton. Mark a different number of dots in each section of the posterboard. The child places as many small objects, such as buttons, discs, beans, in appropriate section of the egg carton, as indicated by the posterboard. For the older child, put numeral signs on the posterboard.

CLASSIFICATION BOXES

This is an excellent tool for providing children with the experience in classifying according to categories. You will need three one-half gallon milk cartons. Cut the sloped top off each milk carton. Cut off THREE sides of each carton to within 3" from the bottom. Cover the outside of the cartons with patterned contact paper. Now, select pictures from old catalogs or magazines that can be divided into three categories, such as clothing, animals, food, etc. Glue the pictures on 2" x 2" postercards. Cover each card with clear contact paper. Attach a paper clip on the tall side of each milk carton and clip a different category card to each.

Give the child the stack of picture cards. The child will then sort the cards by categories, putting each picture in the carton bearing the card for that particular category.

BACKWARD APRIL FOOL'S DAY

Invite the children to wear their clothes backwards or inside out to school on April Fool's Day. Introduce this silly day and encourage the children to talk about how much fun it is to be silly sometimes. Adults should also enjoy this foolish day by wearing their clothes inside out and backwards too!

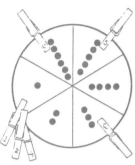

MATCHING NUMBERS TO OBJECTS

Six or eight sections are drawn on a cardboard circle with a felt-tipped marker. In each section one to six or one to eight objects are drawn. The objects in each section may be a different color. Numerals are written on wooden clothespins to match the number of objects in each section of the wheel.

Children will enjoy manipulating the clothespins as they match the numeral to the correct set of objects.

JELLY BEAN GUESS

Bring in a jar of jelly beans. Allow the children to guess (estimate) how many jelly beans are in the jar. After everyone has guessed, count the jelly beans with the children. When the counting is done, divide the jelly beans up equally among the children.

You can increase this activity by using baby food jars. Prepare several baby food jars and help the children make guesses. After guessing the number of jelly beans in the first jar, tell the children that the second jar has either "more" or "less than" the previous jar.

FILE FOLDER EGGS

You will need: a file folder or large piece of construction paper, various pieces of scrap wallpaper or wrapping paper cut into matching pairs of ovals and a small plastic bag.

What you do: One egg from each of the pairs is glued on the file folder and the remaining eggs are placed in the small plastic bag. The children take the eggs out of the bag and match them to the corresponding egg on the file folder.

WHAT COMES OUT OF AN EGG?

Make a large chart with the children, of all the different types of animals that come out of an egg. *(Chickens, ducks, ostriches, lizards, alligators, turtles, etc.)* The children will be amazed!

May

SIGNS OF SPRING

From the book, "Telling Stories Together," by Linda Haver
Copyright by T.S. Denison & Co., Inc.

In this story the children will be acting out signs of spring. When you come to . . . pause then allow the children to act out the **bold, *italicized*** phrases. After the story you might want to let the children think of other signs of spring that Jimmy and Kimmy could learn about on their next trip out of the barnyard.

Mother Sheep gently nudged her twin baby lambs, Jimmy and Kimmy. "Wake up," whispered Mother Sheep, "This is your first spring. It is time to get up and see the world. Today you may go out on your own to see all the wonderful signs of spring. I will be here in the barnyard if you need me."

Jimmy and Kimmy were so excited they began to prance all around the barnyard. "Let's go," squealed Kimmy, "I cannot wait to see spring."

As they walked toward the meadow, Jimmy suddenly became very sad. "Kimmy," said Jimmy, "We have never seen spring, how will we know what to look for while we are exploring?"

Kimmy thought for a moment then replied, "I know, let's ask some of the other animals in our neighborhood if they have seen spring. Maybe they can tell us how it looks."

Just then Freddy Frog came hopping up from the pond. Jimmy and Kimmy hurried to see Freddy and asked him if he could tell them a sign of spring.

"Sure I can tell you a sign of spring," said Freddy, "Spring is when . . . ***the warm sun shines down and all the the frogs and turtles crawl out from the mud after their long winter nap.***"

"Thank you , Freddy," said Jimmy. "Come on Kimmy we will see what else we can discover about spring."

The lamb twins had gone just a short distance when they met Samantha Skunk. "Samantha," yelled Kimmy, "How do you tell when it's spring?"

"That is easy," answered Samantha. "I can always tell it is spring when . . . ***the warm rain comes down and the flowers in the meadow burst into bloom.***"

After thanking Samatha for the help, the twins got back to exploring. Soon they came to a bee hive where a swarm of busy bees were at work.

"Hello, bees," shouted Jimmy, "Can you tell us a sign of spring?"

"Certainly," replied Bobby Bee, "A sure sign of spring is when you see . . . ***the bees flying in and out of the flowers gathering nectar and pollen."***

"Thank you for your help Bobby," said Jimmy.

"All this exploring is making me tired," sighed Kimmy. "How about if we find one more sign of spring, then go back for our nap?"

As they walked back toward the barnyard they met Harriet Hen. The two lamb twins ran right up to Harriet and asked, "Can you tell us a sign of spring?"

"Why, of course," answered Hariet. "I can always tell it is spring when . . . ***my bird friends fly back from the south and spend their time building nests."***

"You have been a big help," the lambs told Hariett, "Thank you very much."

Mother Sheep spotted her babies and went over to ask them if they had found any signs of spring.

Excitedly, Jimmy and Kimmy told their mother all about their adventure into the world. "We learned that in spring . . . ***the warm sun shines down and all the frogs and turtles crawl out from the mud after their long winter nap***. We also found out that . . . ***the warm rain comes down and the flowers in the meadow burst into bloom***. Another sign of spring is . . . ***the bees flying in and out of the flowers gathering nectar and pollen***. Also you can tell it is spring when . . . ***my bird friends fly back from the south and spend their time building nests***."

"That is wonderful," said Mother Sheep, "You have learned so much. Now it is time for your nap. Tomorrow you can go exploring for more signs of spring."

Turn into a flannel board story with the patterns found on page 261.

STORY PATTERNS

Patterns for the story "Signs of Spring," found on pages 259 & 260.
Enlarge patterns.

Jimmy

Kimmy

Barn

Sun

Flowers

Mother Sheep

Freddy Frog

Harriet Hen

Bobby Bee

Swarm Of Bees

Cloud
With Raindrops

Nest

Small Birds

Nest

Samantha Skunk

FARMER IN THE DELL

From the book, "Finger Puppets for Story Telling," by Gwenn Jones-Rives
Copyright by T.S. Denison & Co., Inc.

Sing with the children the story of, *The Farmer in the Dell*. Have the children retell the story using the finger puppets. Reproduce the patterns and glue onto tagboard. Let the children color the patterns and cut them out. The teacher should cut out the finger holes.

Rat

Child

Cat

Cheese

"The Famer in the Dell" continued.

Farmer

Dog

Wife

Nurse

MAY BULLETIN BOARDS

A FELT BOARD GARDEN

Cover part of your bulletin board with a large piece of felt or flannel. Provide the children with felt shape cut-outs. You can either make the shapes yourself or purchase commercially made felt shapes. Let the children arrange the felt shapes into flowers for the bulletin board. Be prepared for daily garden changes.

BUMBLE BEES LOVES PLANTS

Cover the bulletin board with white paper. Let the children color in the grass, flowers and sky with crayons. When the background is finished, have the children make construction paper bumble bees. Display the bumble bees on the flowers.

MAY BULLETIN BOARDS

GOOD BEHAVIOR BUTTERFLIES

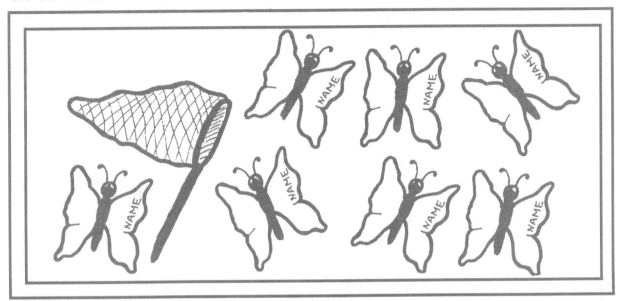

This is a fun bulletin board that encourages good behavior and builds self-esteem. Each of the children should make a construction paper butterfly. *(Pattern found on page 266.)* Facial features may be added but nothing else. Each time you "catch" the children doing something good, the children can put a sticker on the wing of his/her butterfly.

SPRING GARDEN

Cover a bulletin board or wall with light blue paper for the sky and green paper for the grass. Let the children make tissue paper flowers to line the bottom of the bulletin board. Cotton batting clouds are a nice extra touch.

BUTTERFLY PATTERN

BULLETIN BOARD PATTERN: This pattern may be used for the bulletin board on page 265. Reproduce on colored construction paper.

ART PROJECT: You might also wish to use this pattern for an art project. Reproduce the pattern on white paper. Decorate the wings of the butterfly by using cotton swabs. Dip the end of the swab into paint and dab dots of paint on the butterfly's wings. Be sure to have several swabs available for each paint container.

MAY FINE MOTOR ACTIVITIES

SCARECROW

Enlarge and reproduce the pattern next to this activity for each child. The children color the scarecrows, cut them out and attach them to a popsicle stick to make a scarecrow puppet.

For an extra fun classroom activity have the children "help" make a real scarecrow. Ask the parents to donate old clothing and straw.

FOODS GROWN ON A FARM

Give each child a large piece of paper and a stack of magazines. Have the children cut out pictures of foods that are grown on farms as well as products created from those foods. Before doing this project, make sure that you have spent time with the children discussing all the various products that come from the foods grown on a farm.

VEGETABLE AND FRUIT PAINTING

Bring in a number of raw fruits and vegetables. Cut them into various shapes. Mix up paints in shallow containers. Have the children dip the fruits and vegetables into the paints and press onto paper. Encourage the children to try and make a face with the food shapes such as the one in the illustration.

A PAPER PLATE MEAL

Give each of the children a white paper plate and cut-outs of food. Ask the children to create a meal which includes foods from each of the four food groups. When the children have finished their meals, have each of the children take a turn explaining to the class what foods are on their plate.

GROWING A CARROT

Make an outline of a carrot for each child. *(You can enlarge the illustration next to this activity.)* Have the children color their carrots. Cut a slit five inches long across the center of a sheet of paper. Below the slit draw a seed with roots. Place the carrot into the slit behind the paper. Sing the song *"Plant A Seed"* found on page 12. As you sing the song, watch the carrot grow as you slowly push it up. "Pull" the carrot from the ground.

MAY FINE MOTOR ACTIVITIES

BOOK OF KISSES

The children can make a "Book of Kisses" to give to their mothers on Mother's Day. Make booklets by cutting paper into 4 inch squares and stapling ten sheets together in one booklet for each child. Write "Book of Kisses" on the top page and invite the children to decorate the page that is the cover of the booklet.

In small groups, color the children's lips with lipstick and have them kiss each page of the book. Send it home with a note explaining that the mothers can redeem each page for a real kiss. The mom's will love this gift!

BUTTERFLY MAGNET

You will need: tissue paper, scissors, miniature clothespins, glue, self-adhesive magnetic tape, pipe cleaners.

What you do: Cut three pieces of tissue paper approximately 3 inches square. Take a piece of tissue, gather it in the middle and clip the clothespin around it. Put several drops of glue between the prongs of the clothespin to hold the tissue paper in place. Repeat the process for the other two pieces of tissue paper.

Cut a piece of magnetic tape to attach to the back of the butterfly. Use pipe cleaners around the top of the clothespin to form the antennae.

VARIATION: Instead of using magnetic tape on the back of the butterfly, you can also glue a large safety pin. The butterfly pins make a lovely gift for Mother's Day.

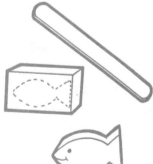

SOAP CARVING

Allow your children to try their hand at carving by experimenting with a bar of soap and a tongue depressor or wooden popsicle stick. *(Use Ivory soap bars – Ivory is a very soft soap.)*

The TEACHER will need to draw the shape on the soap for each child by scratching a line with a knife or scissors. The children then carve the soap around the shape with the popsicle stick.

Note: This project can get very messy! If it is a nice day this is a fun project to do outside!

ROCK PAPERWEIGHTS

Make paperweights out of rocks! Begin by having each child bring a rock to school. Scrub the rock clean with soap and water. Decorate the rock by painting a picture on it. This is a great project to make for either Mother's Day or Father's Day.

MAY FINE MOTOR ACTIVITIES

SHAKE-ON PAINT

You will need: White glue, construction paper, dry tempera paint, table salt, and a salt or spice shaker.

What you do: Put equal parts dry tempera paint and salt in a shaker bottle. Let the children draw a design with the white glue. Shake the tempera/salt mixture over the wet glue. Let dry. Shake off excess tempera mixture to be reused.

MIXING COLORS

You will need: One cup of Ivory soap flakes, mixing bowl, water, self sealing plastic bags and food coloring.

What you do: Soap flakes are placed in the mixing bowl. Water is added slowly, while stirring. The substance should remain thick. The children take turns stirring. The mixture is divided into two bowls and a different color is added to each. Spoon a small amount of each color in a plastic bag and seal. Each child is given a bag. Gently rubbing the soapy mixture together, the child observes the two colors blending into a third color.

MOTHER'S DAY CARD

You will need: construction paper, tempera paint, pie pan, scissors, and a pencil.

What you do: Fold the construction paper in half to form a card. Pour enough tempera paint in the pie pan to cover the bottom. Have the child lay the palm of the hand in the paint. Take the hand out of the paint and press the hand on the front of the card, ***with the small finger along the folded edge***. Let dry.

Leaving the card folded, cut out the handprint so the card is now in the shape of the handprint. Open the card and write a message.

CREEPY CRAWLER CATCHER

You will need: An oatmeal box for each child, screen or netting, heavy tape, scissors, and string.

What you do: Cut out windows in the box. Securely tape the screen or netting to the inside of the box. Punch a hole on each side and attach a string for a handle.

Take the children on an exploratory adventure and let them try and catch some "creatures" for their creepy crawler catcher.

FLOWER POTS

Name _____

Flowers have petals, stems, and leaves.
Draw all the stems. Draw leaves on the stems. Color all the flowers.

 *"These are my numbers."* (Laura, age 3)

Although activities directly related to numeral writing shouldn't be started until a child is four years old or until the child asks for help, the materials that he/she will use should be made available sooner. Sand, salt trays, chalkboards, finger paint, clay, and play-dough should be used in daily classroom activities so children can freely explore them before they are encouraged to use them for writing numerals.

Numerals should be presented according to their level of difficulty to write. The following progression works well: 1, 7, 9, 6, 2, 3, 4, 5, 8, 10.

Make 9" x 12" cards illustrating each numeral, and place them around the room so children can see how each is formed. When writing the numerals on cards, make the first strokes in blue and the second strokes in orange. (In the illustrations below, the solid line would be blue and the dotted line would be orange.)

"Numeral Cards"

Concepts

1. Numerals are composed of straight and/or curved lines.
2. Numerals are made using one or two strokes.
3. Numerals have a certain shape and direction in which they must face.
4. Numerals are formed by starting at the top of the paper.

Goals

1. Children will be able to correctly write the numerals from 1 to 10.

Activities

1. Cut numerals out of easel paper and put them on the easel for children to paint.
2. Encourage children to begin numeral writing by tracing numerals in the air with the index finger of their writing hand while facing the numeral card.
3. Make sandpaper numerals and encourage children to trace around them with their fingers.

I HAVE LEARNED
MY NUMBERS
1 to 10

1 2 3 4 5
6 7 8 9 10

I can write numbers.
I can count.
I can match numbers.

_____
Name

_____
Date

THE MONKEY AND THE BANANAS GAME

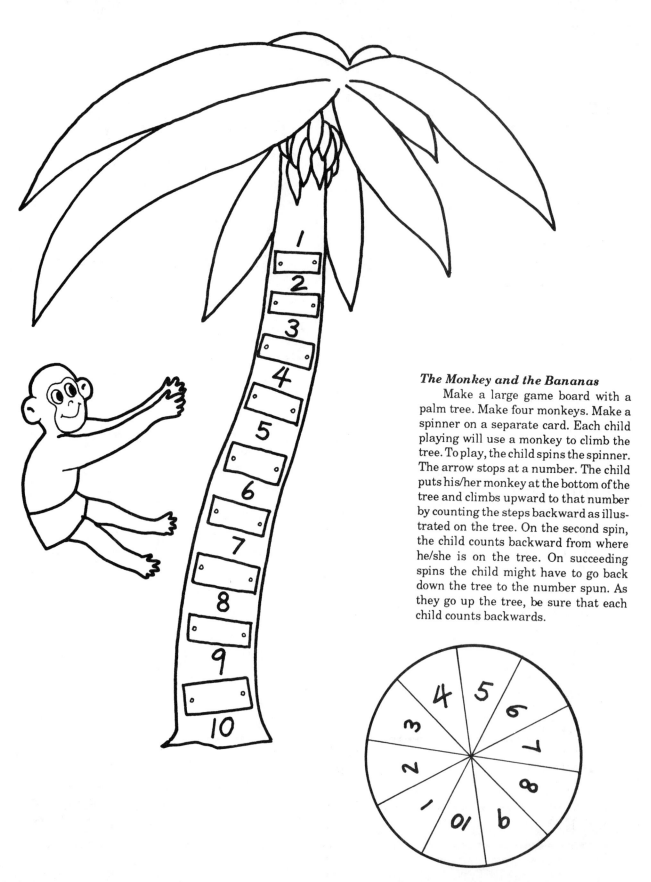

The Monkey and the Bananas

Make a large game board with a palm tree. Make four monkeys. Make a spinner on a separate card. Each child playing will use a monkey to climb the tree. To play, the child spins the spinner. The arrow stops at a number. The child puts his/her monkey at the bottom of the tree and climbs upward to that number by counting the steps backward as illustrated on the tree. On the second spin, the child counts backward from where he/she is on the tree. On succeeding spins the child might have to go back down the tree to the number spun. As they go up the tree, be sure that each child counts backwards.

COOKING AND USING NUMBERS

Here are a variety of fun recipes that help young children learn the importance of using numbers meaningfully in everyday life.

PEANUT BUTTER

You will need: 1 bag raw peanuts and 1 2/3 tablespoons cooking oil.

What you do: Roast peanuts in shell on a baking sheet for 30 minutes at 350°. Let cool. Shell enough roasted peanuts to make 1 cup. Put peanuts and oil in a blender. Start at low speed and increase to high speed. Stop when peanut butter reaches the proper consistency.

ICE CREAM

You will need: 3 eggs; 1 cup honey; 4 1/2 cups Half 'n Half; 3 teaspoons vanilla.

What you do: Beat eggs. Mix in other ingredients. Make individual ice cream freezers from a cut-off half-gallon milk carton and small juice can. Place can inside milk carton; pack layers of ice and salt around can. Fill about 1/2 full with ice cream and stir, being careful not to get salt into the mixture. Mixture will freeze in about 20-25 minutes. (mixture does not have to be stirred continuously.)

MOO SHAKE

You will need: 1 cup milk and 1 tablespoon jelly.

What you do: Pour milk into pint jar. Add jelly. Close tightly and shake until jelly is mixed well. Serve.

HONEY FUNNIES

You will need: 1 cup peanut butter; 1 cup honey; 1 1/2 cups powdered milk.

What you do: Mix peanut butter and honey together in a bowl. Add powdered milk and stir. Roll into balls. If mixture sticks to hands, lightly dust with confectioner's sugar or add more powdered milk.

SHAKE 'EM UP ORANGE BARS

You will need: 2 eggs; 1/2 cup oil; 1/2 cup sugar; 1/2 cup orange juice; 1 cup flour; 1 1/2 teaspoons baking powder; 1/2 teaspoon salt; 1 drop orange extract.

What you do: Shake ingredients in a one-quart jar. Pour into 8" x 8" cake pan. Bake 20-25 minutes at 375°.

PIZZA

You will need: 1 slice bread; 2 tablespoons catsup; 2 tablespoons shredded mozzarella cheese; pinch of oregano; pinch of garlic salt.

What you do: Cut a circle out of the slice of bread using a biscuit cutter. Spread catsup over the bread circle. Sprinkle oregano, garlic salt and cheese on top. Bake in a 325° oven until cheese is melted and the bread is golden brown.

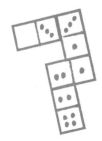

PRIMARY DOMINOES

You will need: Large dominoes, commercially manufactured or made by the teacher by painting or pasting dots on oblong blocks, plywood or cardboard. If these are very large they may be used on the floor. Use every combination up to and perhaps including five and of course, zero or blank.

How to play: Pass five dominoes to each player, place the other face down at the side as a "bank." The first child puts any domino in the center, the next player matches one end of this, if he can; if not, he may take one from the bank but must keep it if it does not match. The first child to get rid of all his dominoes wins.

TURN IT OVER

You will need: Large cardboards (perhaps 10" x 10") marked with colored squares corresponding to a set of two-inch wooden blocks. On one card, no squares, on the next, one square, etc., with corresponding numerals printed below; on the back of each card just the numeral. Start with cards up to and perhaps including five - later add others as skill builds up.

How to play: The children are called on to: 1) place the cards in order, left to right. 2) Tell how many are on each card. Then place proper blocks on it if they are correct, covering the squares. 3) "Turn it over" and build a tower of blocks on the back where only the numeral is visible.

CALL THE NUMBERS

You will need: A cardboard box, square, decorated like one of a pair of dice. Six inches is a good size. A set of numeral cards for indicating correspondences.

How to play: One child is "it" and gets to toss the "Number Box," then calls on some other child to "call the number." If this child calls the number correctly he will be the next child to throw the "number box." *A fun variation is:* After calling the number, a child may be permitted to select from rack of cards the numeral used to indicate it; or to match it with some numeral found on the room calendar, clock or charts.

UP AND DOWN

You will need: A pocket chart like a ladder, with pockets arranged perpendicularly. Numeral cards which show the numeral when in the pocket.

How to play: Have the children arrange the numerals in order, "climbing up and down." Then have the children close their eyes while one child removes a card and conceals it. Children look up and guess which numeral is missing. Increase the size of the ladder as skill increases. You can then play by removing two cards or mixing up the cards and have the children reorder them.

COVER UP

You will need: Individual cards, as in bingo, but containing only places for nine numerals each. These may be prepared in sets of six, differentiated by color of mounting, so that a class may play in separate groups. Allow advanced children to help others at each table, competition then being by tables (or colors). Many small one-inch blocks can be used for covering the numerals on the cards.

How to play: One child is asked to select a numeral, which he calls out. Those who have that numeral on their cards cover it. Another selection is made, and so on. The first child or group to cover all the numerals shouts "cover up!" *NOTE:* By keeping a record of numerals on the cards, the teacher knows which color should win.

NUMBER ACTIVITIES

SETS AND NUMERALS

You will need: Series of sets on display. These may be on the flannel board, magnetic board, on flash cards or real objects on a table. A series of numeral cards with large numerals.

How to play: The children match numerals to corresponding sets. Or the teacher may pass out numeral cards, one to each child, and let them go one by one to place the cards at the proper sets. *VARIATION:* The reverse procedure may be fun too. Lay out a number line on the floor, have the children place towers of increasing height on numerals on the line.

HOPSCOTCH

You will need: A hopscotch court marked on the floor or ground. Many playgrounds have these courts. If your school does not have a painted hopscotch court it is well worth your time to have one added to your playground.

How to play: This is essentially an individual game. Each child may use a small stone or even a small bean bag. The first player throws her marker on the section numbered "1" then hops into that section bends down and picks up the marker, then hops back to the starting zone. The child then throws the marker onto section 2, hops on section one and then two and picks up the marker and hops back. The game is continued until the marker has been thrown on each numbered section.

BEADS ON A STRING

You will need: A set of cards about 8" x 10". Numerals printed on the left side of the card, out of sequence, with a corresponding number of colored dots or squares following, and each numeral followed by a different color. Small wooden kindergarten beads may be used at first; later use macaroni beads. *(Salad macaroni, one-quater inch, dyed various colors with food coloring: place macaroni, food coloring and rubbing alcohol in a jar, shake vigorously, spread on newspapers to dry.)* Punch a hole in the top of each card, string through and tie the shoestring.

How to play: This can be done individually or it may be done in pairs, with children checking each other's finished cards. If the top row shows a numeral 3, followed by 3 red dots, the child should first string 3 red beads. Then if the second row shows the numeral 4 and 4 yellow dots, the child should string 4 yellow beads, and so on until the card is completed.

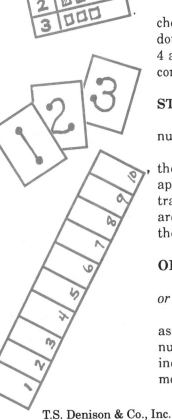

STOP AND GO CARDS

You will need: Numeral cards about 8" x 10" with green dots indicated "where the numeral begins," and red dots showing "where the numeral ends."

How to play: This activity may be introduced simultaneously with a safety lesson on the meaning of the red or "stop" color and the green or "go" color. The concept may be applied to the numeral cards. The child will point to the green dot and say "go" and then trace the numeral to the "red" stop dot is. The cards may also be laminated. When the cards are laminated the children will be able to trace the numeral with crayon and then erase their tracing with tissue.

OFF TO THE RACES

You will need: A large number line *(you can make a large number line from cardboard or a discarded window shade)*; toy cars; a "number box" or spinner.

How to play: Divide the children into teams (or simply a pair of children may play) and assign each team a different car. Let one team member spin the spinner or throw the number box. The car is then moved how ever many spaces on the number line that was indicated by the spinner. All onlookers can help by counting the spaces as the cars are moved ahead on the number line.

NUMBER CUT AND PASTE

Trace the numbers

Color the 'happy faces.'
Cut them all out.
Paste the correct number
of "happy faces" in each
box. For example next to
the 3 you should paste 3
happy faces.

MAY MOVEMENT ACTIVITIES

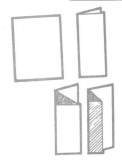

PAPER AIRPLANES

Make paper airplanes to fly outdoors. Begin with a rectangular piece of paper. Fold it in half lengthwise. Then fold one corner back so the top of the page is on the fold. Fold again so that this fold is on the lengthwise fold. Do the same with the other half of the paper. Bring the airplanes outside to fly.

LEAP FROG

While saying the rhyme "Frogs," found on page 283, allow the entire class to jump around like frogs do. When you are finished with the rhyme, teach the children how to play "leap frog."

MONKEY SEE, MONKEY DO

Choose one child to be the leader and encourage the rest of the class to imitate the leader's actions.

It is also fun to turn this "follow the leader" game into a "follow the insect game." How many different ways can the children think of to crawl?

M & M RACE

You will need: 1 to 2 pounds of M & M's, large ladle, large bowl, and self-sealing bags.

What you do: Pour the M & M's in a large bowl. Each child will take turns scooping up M & M's with the ladle and walking a short distance without spilling the M & M's. At the end of the short walk, have a plastic bag ready for the child to fill with his "unspilled" M & M's. Let the children take home their bag of M & M's.

BURIED TREASURE

You will need: Pennies or rocks that have been spray painted gold.

What you do: Hide the pennies or rocks in the sandbox. The children will have great fun digging for the buried treasure. (This activity is NOT advised for children who may still be putting things in their mouths!)

MIRROR IMAGE

The only materials needed for this activity are you and the children. Sit facing the children. Tell the children to pretend that they are mirrors. Start with simple movements and then go on to more complex motions. Let the children take turns being the one who is looking in the mirror and initiating the movements.

PLANTING AND GROWING ACTIVITIES

WHAT IS INSIDE A SEED?

You will need: a variety of seeds; lima beans, corn, sunflower, peas, magnifying glasses and bowls of water.

What you do: Soak the seeds overnight. Look for the scar on the side of the seed. (This is the spot where the seed was attached to the plant.) Slip the seed coat off the bean and split the bean into two parts. Attached to half of the bean is a very tiny plant. Use the magnifying glass to find where the roots, stem, and leaves might grow from this plant.

GROWING NEW PLANTS FROM SEEDS

You will need: Avocado seed, glass jar, toothpicks, water, pot, and potting soil.

What you do: Insert three toothpicks spaced evenly around the sides of the avocado seed; place the seed supported by the toothpicks on the mouth of the jar. The pointed end of the seed should face upward. Fill the jar with water only to the bottom of the seed. Put the seed and jar in a dark place for several weeks. Move to a sunny window when it splits at the top and the stem and leaves appear. It may be planted in a pot for further growth.

GROWING NEW PLANTS FROM ROOTS

You will need: Carrots, beets, turnips, shallow bowl of pebbles, water.

What you do: Cut off the root tip leaving about two to three inches. Set the plant in a shallow bowl of pebbles and keep it watered

GROWING NEW PLANTS FROM BULBS

You will need: Narcissus bulb, pot and potting soil, water.

What you do: Plant the bulb in rich soil in a pot. Water it daily and watch for stems to appear through the soil. Another favorite approach is to "force" bulbs in a bowl filled with enough pebbles to hold the bulb in place. Add just enough water to cover the base of the bulbs. Set bulbs in cool (but not freezing) dark place until roots form. Then bring them to room temperature.

GROWING NEW PLANTS FROM LEAVES

You will need: Bryophyllum cutting, pot and potting soil, glass.

What you do: Plant the tip of a bryophllum leaf (point where it attaches to the stem) in the soil. Keep moist. Invert the glass over the leaf so that it will serve as a minature greenhouse until the new tiny plants arrive.

You will need: Juice glass, water wax paper, violet cutting, pot and potting soil.

What you do: Partially fill a juice glass with water. Put a wax paper cover over it. Punch a hole in the wax paper and insert the short stem of a leaf cut from a violet plant. Be sure the end of the stem is immersed in the water.

MAY LANGUAGE ACTIVITIES

CLOWN PICTURES

Make a large picture of a clown on heavy poster board. *(See illustration.)* Paint the clown face with bright colors. Make a hole in the face large enough for a child's face to fit through. Have the children take turns standing behind the clown with their face making up the face of the clown. Use make-up if desired. Take a Polaroid picture.

Let the children share their picture with the rest of the class.

INSECT STUDY

Insects always fascinate young children. Check out books from your library. Read them to the class and discuss. Have the books available for the children to examine at the science table.

DRY APPLES

Dried apples are a healthy snack for the children. Cut an apple into eight equal sections. Remove the seeds and string the pieces from the ceiling for two or three days (or until dry). If possible, borrow a dehydrator and dry a variety of fruits for snacks.

LISTS OF BUGS

Have the children brainstorm and make a list of as many different types of insects as they can name. You will be surprised with how many names most children are able to come up with. List the insect names on a chart and then find pictures of those insects to put next to their name. Using the Creepy Crawler Catcher (found on page 269). let the children go on an adventure to collect insects. How many insects did they find that are on the chart? Did you find any insects that were not on the chart?

THE MOTHER'S DAY MICE by Eve Bunting

Read *The Mother's Day Mice,* by Eve Bunting. Biggest mouse, middle mouse, and little mouse live at the edge of the strawberry patch. Early one morning the three mice set out to find surprise gifts for their mother. Biggest mouse and middle mouse find their surprises. Little mouse wanted honeysuckle that grew only at Honeysuckle Cottage, but there was a big cat sitting on the porch. Then something inside the cottage gives him an idea. The little mouse runs home. Little mouse is last to give his Mother's Day surprise — he claps his hands and begins to sing a Mother's Day song and everyone joins in.

Use the patterns on page 282 to retell the story.

GREAT BOOKS FOR MAY

• *Make Way for Ducklings* by Robert McClosky • *Night in the Country* by Cynthia Rylant • *The Little Tiny Rooster* by Will & Nicolas • *Wake Up, Farm* by Alvin Tresselt • *I Know A Farm* by Ethel Collier

MICE PATTERNS

Patterns are to be used with the "Mother's Day Mice" activity, found on page 281.

MAY FINGER PLAYS/POETRY

FROGS

This little froggy broke his toe.
This little froggy said, "Oh, oh, oh!"
This little froggy laughed and was glad,
This little froggy cried and was sad.
This little froggy did just what he should
He ran for the doctor as fast as he could.
(Turn this rhyme into a flannel board
presentation. Make five frogs. Pattern
found on page 285.)

ANTS

Ant, ant, under a plant.
How many legs have you?
One, two, three, four, five, and six.
    (count fingers)
I thought you always knew.
You have two feet.
You have two legs.
    (hold up two fingers)
I have four more than you.
    (hold up four fingers)

CREEPY CRAWLY

Creepy crawly, creepy crawly
Goes old pussy cat;
    (make fingers creep
    along opposite arm)
Froggie with a speckled coat
Jumps like that!
    (make leap with arm)

FIVE POLLIWOGS

Five polliwogs swam near the shore.
The first one said, "I have been this way before."
The second one said, "I have a funny tail."
The third one said, "And a tail can help me sail."
The fourth one said, "My legs are getting strong."
The fifth one said, "It will not be very long."
The five polliwogs deep in the bog
Gave three croaks and each one became a frog.
(Discuss how a polliwog turns into a frog.
Show the children pictures of the stages of
development.)

THE LADYBUGS

Tick-tack-tick-tack! See them go!
Four little ladybugs are marching in a row.   *(hold up four fingers)*
The first one is yellow and trimmed with specks of black   *(point to one finger at a*
    time)

The second one is orange with a round and shiny back.
The third one is bright red with teeny, weeny dots
The fourth one is fancy with different kinds of spots.
Ladybugs help ranchers.
Lady bugs have use.
They eat up all the orange tree pests.
So we can have orange juice!

MAY FINGER PLAYS/POETRY

MY SPRING GARDEN

Here is my little garden,   (make bowl shape with hands)
Some seeds I am going to sow.   (motion of scattering seeds)
Here is my rake to rake the ground. (scratch with fingers)
Here is my handy hoe.   (arms outstretched in front of body, bend
                                      fingers downward.)

Here is the big, round, yellow sun, (make circle with arms)
The sun warms everything.
Here are the rain clouds in the sky. (point to sky)
The birds will start to sing.   (move forefinger and thumb several times)
Little plants will wake up soon,   (stoop slowly and then rise)
And lift their sleepy heads.   (raise arms)
Little plants will grow and grow,
From their warm earth beds.

FLY LITTLE BIRD

Fly, little bird. Go back to your tree.
    (motion of flying)
That's where your baby birds ought to be.
The tree branches sway from side to side.
    (sway body back and forth)
But your dear baby birds are safe inside.
    (close fists)
Their nest is as snug as snug can be.
    (cup hands)
Away up in a tall apple tree.
    (point upward)

IN MY LITTLE GARDEN

In my little garden with a lovely view.
Sunflowers are smiling, one and two.
In my little garden by the apple tree,
Daffodils are dancing, one, two, three.
In my little garden by the kitchen door,
Roses are blooming, one, two, three, four.
In my little garden by the winding drive,
Violets are growing, one, two, three, four, five!
(Children hold up a required number of fingers
each time. Show the children pictures of the
different flowers that are mentioned in the
 rhyme.)

SEVEN PLUMP ROBINS

Seven plump robins were hopping all around.
Picking up bread crumbs off the ground.
Two saw a yellow cat up in a tree.
Four flew away, then there were three!
One heard a black cat say, "mew, mew,"
He flew away, then there were two.
One saw a striped cat sitting in the sun.
One saw a white cat and they began to run.
Now there are no robins hopping all around
Picking up the bread crumbs off the ground.
(Turn into a flannel board rhyme by making
seven robins and the four cats.)

MAY BASKET

Up the steps,
One, two, three, four,
I will ring the bell on your front door.
I'll leave a May basket just for fun,
I'll turn around and run, run, run!
(Most preschools and kindergartens
have stairs which the children can climb
as they act out this rhyme.)

FROG CHARACTER PROP/PUPPET

MAY MUSIC ACTIVITIES

PLANT A SEED
(Sung to the tune of "Here We Go Around The Mulberry Bush.")

This is the way we plant our seeds.
Plant our seeds, plant our seeds.
This is the way we plant our seeds.
On a beautiful afternoon.

Other verses:
This is the way we water our seeds.
This is the way the sun shines on our seeds.
This is the way our carrot seeds grow.
(Use this song with the art activitiy found on page 5.)

NODDING TULIPS

Red and yel-low tu-lips,

Stand-ing in a row,_____

Nod to all who look at them.

It is spring, you know.

MY WISH

Once I took a lit-tle walk

And I made a wish.

There I found some vi-o-lets

For my moth-er's dish.

MAY MUSIC ACTIVITIES

SONGS WITH HULA HOOPS

RING AROUND THE ROSIE

Ring around the rosie
A pocketfull of posies
Ashes, ashes
We all fall down.

Four or five children and the teacher stand around a hula hoop and while holding on, sing and walk in a cirle. They all fall down together when indicated.

ROW, ROW, ROW YOUR BOAT

Row, row, row your boat.
Gently down the stream.
Merrily, merrily, merrily, merrily
Life is but a dream.

All sit. Two or three children sit inside the hula hoop. They are in the boat. The others sit around the hula hoop and while holding on, sing and sway back and forth.

HERE WE GO 'ROUND THE MULBERRY BUSH

Here we go 'round the mulberry bush,
The mulberry bush, the mulberry bush
Here we go 'round the mulberry bush
So early in the morning.

Here we jump 'round the mulberry bush
The mulberry bush, the mulberry bush
Here we jump 'round the mulberry bush
So early in the morning.

Here we tip-toe 'round the mulberry bush
The mulberry bush, the mulberry bush
Here we tip-toe 'round the mulberry bush
So early in the morning.

Four or five children and the teacher stand around a hula hoop and hold onto it. While singing the first verse they walk. While singing the second verse, they jump, and while singing the third verse, they tip-toe.

RHYTHMIC CLAPPING

The adults begin a rhythmic pattern, then assists the children in learning how to copy it. Rhythmic patterns may include hand-clapping, thigh-clapping, or foot-stamping. After the children learn one pattern, the next pattern can gradually become more complicated. The following are patterns that can be repeated over and over.

1. Clap, clap, pause
   Clap, clap, pause
2. Clap, clap, clap
   Clap, clap, clap
3. Clap, clap, pause
   Clap, clap, clap
   Clap, clap, pause
   Clap, clap, clap
4. Clap, slap (thighs)
   Clap, slap
   Clap, clap, clap
5. Clap, slap, tap, tap
   Clap, slap, tap, tap
   Clap, slap, tap, tap
   Clap, clap, clap

FROG IN THE CLASSROOM

Ask parents or other adults to collect polliwogs or tadpoles from a pond. Put them in a small bowl with the original pond water and let the children watch them grow into frogs. The bowl should be emptied every day and replaced with fresh pond water. This will provide natural food for the tadpoles.

Supplement with tiny amounts of goldfish food if needed. If you are unable to provide good living conditions for the tadpoles return them to their natural environment.

TALENT SHOW

Have an "End of the Year" talent show. Help each child prepare one special thing to do for the show. For young children there are many special acts that can be performed, such as counting to 10, singing the abc's, or saying a nursery rhyme.

Be sensitive to children who may be shy. Some children may be unwilling to perform alone, but would be willing to perform with another child. Parents will love watching the many "talents" of their children.

ANTS IN THE CLASSROOM

Bring in an ant hill with all the little ants. Place them between two pieces of glass. Cover the other surfaces with pieces of wood. Watch the ants reconstruct their homes. Be sure to give a few drops of water each day. *(You can also purchase a commercially made ant house through educational toy stores or school supply stores.)*

FROZEN BANANAS

You will need: Ripe bananas, 1/2 cup lemon juice, 1/2 cup water, popsicle sticks, toppings such as chopped nuts, melted chocolate, sesame seeds, or a mixture of finely grated nuts, wheat germ and cinnamon.

What you do: Stick a popsicle stick into a peeled banana. Mix lemon juice and water. Dip the banana in liquid to prevent discoloring. Roll bananas in any of the toppings and place on wax paper. Freeze for at least an hour.

COFFEE CAN ICE CREAM

You will need: 1 cup whipping cream, 1 cup milk, 1/2 cup sugar, flavoring.

What you do: Mix all the ingredients together with a mixer. Pour the mixture into a 1 pound coffee can. Put on the lid. Put the filled 1 pound coffee can into a 3 pound coffee can. Add ice cubes and rock salt. Put on the lid. Wrap in a dish towel and shake for 15 minutes.

Summer

SOUNDS OF THE FARM

From the book, "Telling Stories Together," by Linda Haver
Copyright by T.S. Denison & Co., Inc.

This story gives the children the opportunity to imitate sounds of a farm. Divide the children into five groups. Each group is assigned to make one of the sounds: cock-a-doodle-doo, moo, oink-oink, baaa, and putt, putt, putt.

Have each of the groups practice their sounds several times. Emphasize to the children that they are to say their sound when you point to their groups. In the middle of the story the sounds get mixed-up so they must watch you carefully to see when it is their turn.

Farmer Beck was happy being a farmer. He liked the barns, the fences, the fields, the tractor and the plow, but most of all he loved the sounds of the farm.

Every morning Farmer Beck would wake when he heard the rooster crowing, . . . ***cock-a-doodle-doo***. Then Farmer Beck would go out to the barn and milk the cows. Every morning the cows would greet him with a loud . . . ***moo***. After the cows were milked and fed, Farmer Beck would take food to the pigpen. The hungry pigs would call . . . ***oink-oink*** when they saw him coming.

Farmer Beck's next visit was the sheep pen. He would pat the sheep and listen to them say . . . ***baaa*** while they ate.

After breakfast Farmer Beck would go out and get on his tractor. He would start the tractor and hear the engine go . . . ***putt, putt, putt***. Living on a farm is wonderful, thought Farmer Beck as he plowed the fields. I get to hear my favorite sounds all the time. I can hear the rooster crow . . . ***cock-a-doodle-doo***, the cows saying . . . ***moo***, the pigs grunting . . . ***oink-oink***, and my sheep calling . . . ***baaa***. Then when I am working in the field I get to hear my tractor going . . . ***putt, putt, putt***.

At lunchtime Farmer Beck stopped working and went into the house to eat. After lunch he felt very tired so he took a short nap before he went back to plowing.

While he was sleeping, Farmer Beck had a very strange dream. He dreamed that it was the next morning and something weird was happening. Everything was extremely quiet. Farmer Beck looked out his window and saw the rooster sitting on the fence. "What is the matter?" Farmer Beck yelled to the rooster, "Aren't you going to crow . . . *cock-a-doodle-doo* this morning?" The rooster shook his head, opened his mouth and out came a loud . . . *moo*.

Something is wrong thought Farmer Beck as he walked toward the barn. "Good morning cows," said farmer Beck as he got out the milking machine. "I sure hope you remember how to say . . . *moo*." The cows looked at him and said . . . *putt, putt, putt*.

Farmer Beck hurried to the pigpen. I hope I hear the sound . . . *oink-oink*, he thought to himself. When the pigs saw Farmer Beck coming they grunted . . . *cock-a-doodle-doo*.

The next stop for Farmer Beck was the sheep pen. "Please sheep let me hear you say . . . *baaa*," he pleaded. The sheep looked at him and said," . . . *oink-oink*."

My favorite sounds are all mixed-up, Farmer Beck thought sadly. I guess I will do some plowing while I try to figure out how to fix things. He got on the tractor and started it. Instead of hearing . . . *putt, putt, putt*, the tractor went . . . *baaa*. "Oh no, even my tractor is mixed- up," cried Farmer Beck, "What am I going to do?"

Just then Farmer Beck woke up. Thank goodness that was just a dream, he thought. I guess I will get back to my plowing.

On the way to the field Farmer Beck saw his rooster sitting on the fence. The rooster greeted him with a . . . *cock-a-doodle-doo*. Farmer Beck smiled and then walked to the barn. The cows noticed him coming forward and said . . . *moo*. The pigs were laying in the mud and farmer Beck heard them grunting . . . *oink-oink*. He stopped to pat the sheep and was happy when he heard them say . . . *baaa*. He climbed on the tractor and started the engine. When he heard the engine go . . . *putt, putt, putt* he laughed out loud. This is wonderful, thought farmer Beck, all my favorite farm sounds are right where they belong.

Turn into a flannel board story with the pattern on pages 292 & 293.

STORY PATTERNS

Patterns for the story, "Sounds of the Farm," found on pages 290 & 291.

Sheep

Rooster

Tractor

STORY PATTERNS

Patterns for the story, "Sounds of the Farm," found on pages 290 & 291.

Pig

Cow

Farmer Beck

SUMMER LITERATURE RESOURCES

LITERATURE RESOURCES FOR THE THEMES OF THE FARM AND FARM ANIMALS

Brandenberg, Franz. ***Cock-A-Doodle-Doo.*** Greenwillow Books. Copyright © 1986. *Summary:* The animal and human inhabitants of a farm, quack, neigh, say "Shoo! Shoo!" and otherwise communicate in their own fashion.

Brown, Margaret Wise. ***Big Red Barn.*** Harper & Row, Copyright © 1989. *Summary:* Rhymed text and illustrations introduce the many different animals that live in the Big Red Barn.

Carle, Eric. ***The Very Busy Spider.*** Philomel Books. Copyright © 1984. *Summary:* The farm animals try to divert a busy little spider from spinning her web, but she persists and produces a thing of both beauty and usefulness.

Forrester, Victoria. ***The Magnificent Moo.*** Atheneum Books. Copyright © 1983. *Summary:* When a cow trades her moo for a cat's meow because she thinks it too loud, the moo gets traded in turn to several other animals until it finally returns to a more satisfied cow.

Gammel, Steven. ***Once Upon McDonald's Farm.*** Four Winds Press. Copyright © 1981. *Summary:* McDonald tries farming with exotic farm circus animals, but has better luck with his neighbor's cow, horse and chicken.

Galdone, Paul. ***The Cat Goes Fiddle-i-Fee.*** Clarion Books. Copyright © 1985. *Summary:* An old English rhyme names all the animals a boy feeds on his daily rounds.

Griffth, Helen. ***Grandaddy's Place.*** Greenwillow Books. Copyright © 1987. *Summary:* At first Janetta does not like her Grandaddy, his farm, or his animals - but they like her and as she gets used to them, she likes them too.

Provensen, Alice. ***A Horse and a Hound, A Goat and a Gander.*** Atheneum. Copyright © 1979. *Summary:* Four farm animals each with a distinct and highly idiosyncratic personality liven up the days at Maple Hill Farm.

SUMMER BULLETIN BOARDS

UNDER THE SEA

Cover the bulletin board with light blue paper. Using the sea creatures patterns that are found on pages 296 - 300, create an "Under the Sea" display. Reproduce the patterns. Let the children color or paint, and cut out the patterns. Sponge paint seaweed and coral on the background. Add the finished sea creatures.

CARNIVAL FUN

The teacher will need to prepare a large ferris wheel for the bulletin board. Follow the example in the illustration to create a simple ferris wheel. Have the children draw pictures of themselves. These pictures can be added to the seats of the ferris wheel.

SEA CREATURE BULLETIN BOARD PATTERNS

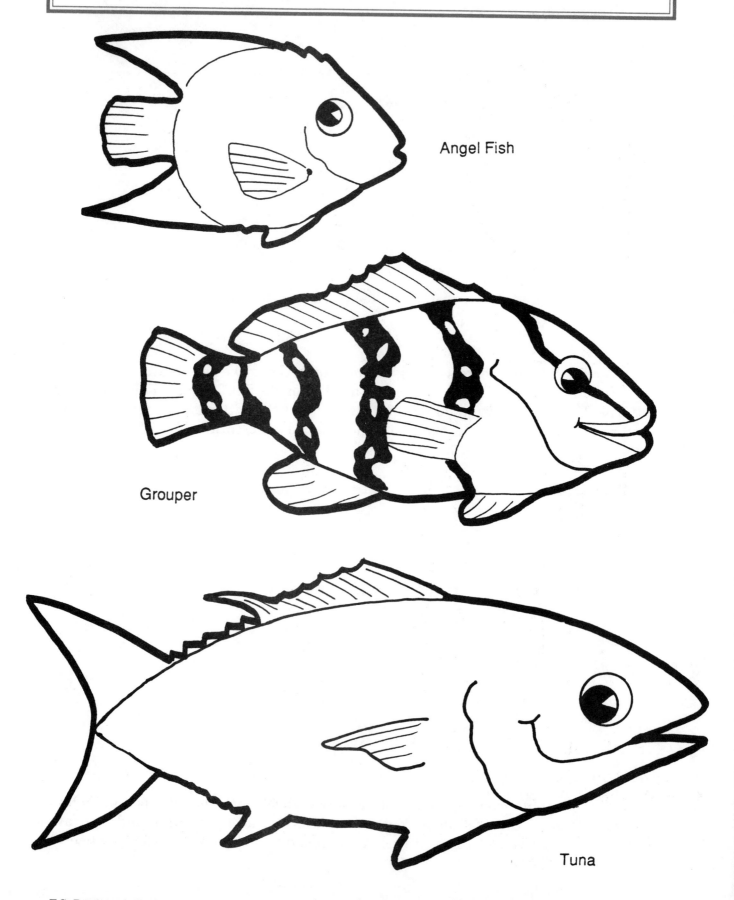

Angel Fish

Grouper

Tuna

SEA CREATURE BULLETIN BOARD PATTERNS

Squid

Blue Shark

Penguin

Coral Reef

SEA CREATURE BULLETIN BOARD PATTERNS

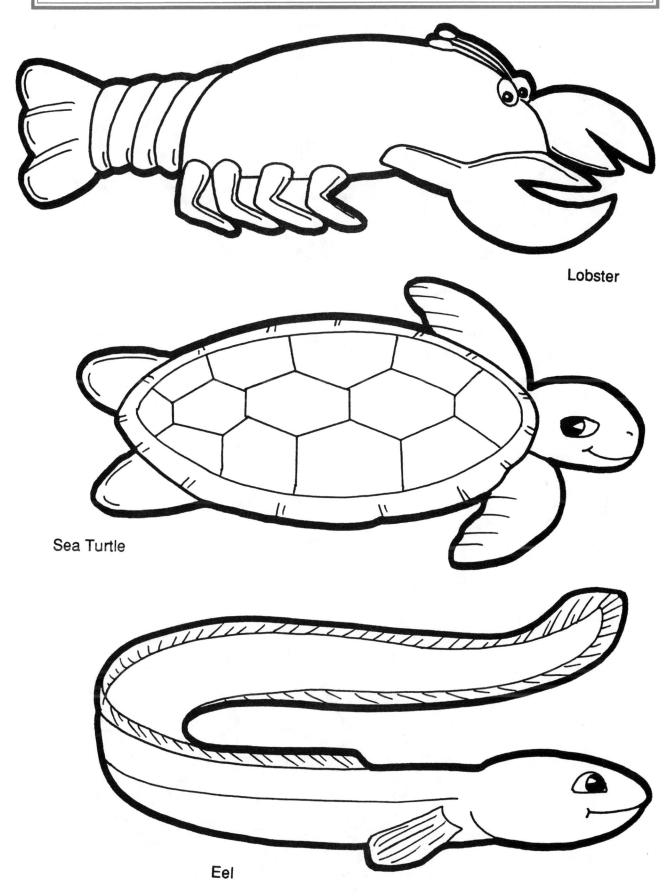

Lobster

Sea Turtle

Eel

SEA CREATURE BULLETIN BOARD PATTERNS

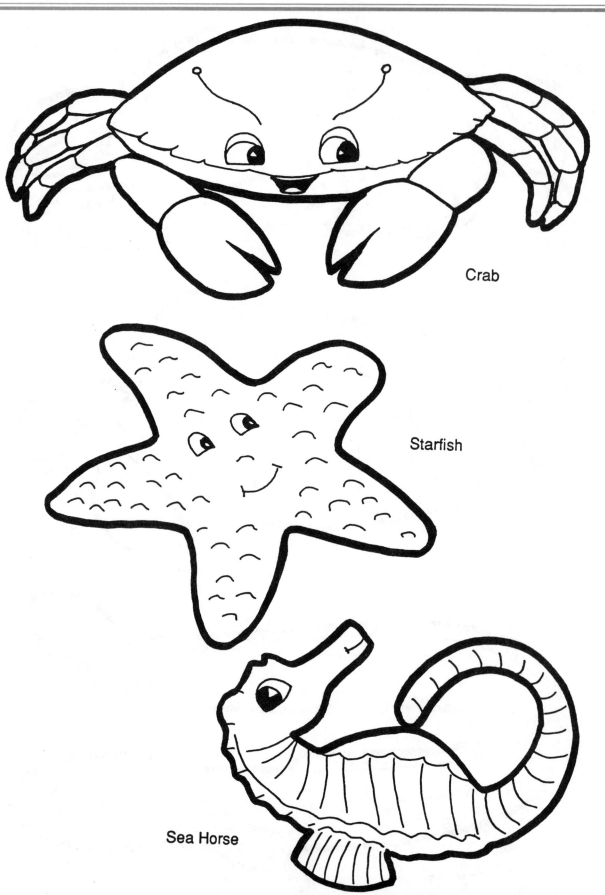

Crab

Starfish

Sea Horse

FOREST SCENE

Paint brown trees on your window or use construction paper to make the trees. Cut large green leaves out of construction paper and allow the children to tape the leaves to the branches of the trees to give the appearance of being in the woods. The children might also wish to add animals.

ROCK COLLECTING

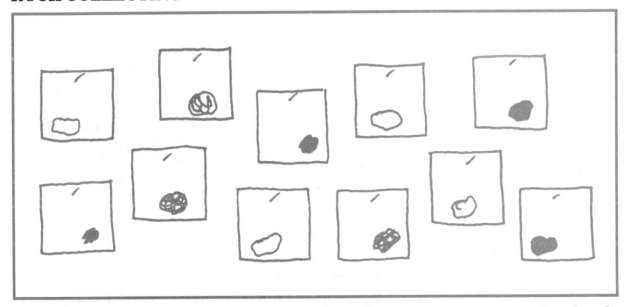

Rock collecting has always been a favorite activity of young children. Display the rock collecting accomplishments of the children on the bulletin board. Sort the rocks and place them in clear plastic bags. The children can keep adding rocks to the appropriate bags as long as the bulletin board is up. Label with names of the rocks.

SUMMER FINE MOTOR ACTIVITIES

SAILBOATS

Enlarge the pattern next to this activity to make sailboats. The children can glue wooden popsicle sticks to the back of each sail and then glue them to the back of the boat.

Hang some of the boats on your windows. Let the children pretend that they are looking out onto a lake when they look through the window and see their sailboats.

WHALES

Young children are fascinated by whales. Enlarge this pattern and make a copy of it for each child in your class. Allow the children to paint, color or decorate their whales as they please. Punch a hole in the top of the whale and tie a string. Hang the whales from the ceiling.

PUFF-PAINT SHIRTS

Ask your children to bring in a T-shirt from home that does not have any printing or pictures on it; a plain T-shirt. Purchase puff-paints at a craft store and allow the children to create their own designs for their shirts. Let the paints dry overnight before the children try them on.

Let the children have a style show with their "fancy" new shirts.

COLORED SAND JARS

Purchase a number of colors of sand at a craft store. Parents with babies will probably be able to supply you with enough small baby food jars.

Each child will pour alternating colors of sand into their jars to create interesting designs.

SUMMER FINE MOTOR ACTIVITIES

FABRIC CRAYON FATHER'S DAY SHIRTS

This is a wonderful Father's Day gift that the children can make themselves. Ask the moms to send a white t-shirt of dad's to school. Using fabric crayons have the children draw a picture on a plain white piece of paper. Be sure that they press firmly. Follow the instructions on the crayon box and iron the picture on the shirt.

CLOWNS

Enlarge and reproduce a copy of this pattern on heavy paper for each child. (Use an opaque projector to enlarge the pattern.) Allow the children to color their clown with bright markers. Attach to a popsicle stick to turn into a stick puppet.

SUN BLEACHED PAPER

This art project is just like magic for young children. Write each child's name on a piece of colored construction paper. Set the paper outside on a sunny day with a number of objects on each paper. The children will be excited to find the picture that results when the sun bleaches the areas around the objects but not the areas under the objects.

CLOUD PICTURES

Have the children make their own cloud pictures. Give each child a piece of light blue construction paper. Have them spoon on some extra thin white paint onto the center of the paper. The children then blow the paint across the paper using a straw. Encourage the children to blow the paint in all different directions. Label the pictures with the name of the object the children think the "cloud" resembles.

FATHER'S DAY TIE

You will need: Scissors, construction paper, crayons.

What you do: Cut the paper in the shape of a man's tie. Let each child decorate the tie. The children can give the tie as a Father's Day gift. The tie can be attached to dad's shirt with tape.

FATHER'S DAY CARD

You will need: Light colored construction paper, crayons or markers.

What you do: Fold the paper in half to form a greeting card. Have the child draw a portrait of dad on the front of the card. Write the following poem on the inside of the card.

Daddy is my special friend,
The two of us are buddies.
I always like the things we do,
I'm thankful for my daddy.

SUMMER MOVEMENT ACTIVITIES

RING TOSS

Children love to play carnival games. Here is a game that is not only fun but also helps to develop eye-hand coordination. You can purchase a ring toss game, or even better, make your own. Place four wooden dowel rods into an X-shaped piece of styrofoam. The rings can be made from coffee can plastic lids. Try setting a kitchen timer for two minutes and count how many rings land around a rod before the bell rings.

BINOCULARS

Make a summer hike even more fun by letting the children take binoculars with them. Each child will need 2 toilet paper tube rolls, yarn, and gem clips. Clip the toilet paper rolls together with the gem clips. Attach yarn so the binoculars can hang around the neck. Encourage the children to explore as you go on your nature hike.

MONSTER BUBBLES

You will need: 1 metal coat hanger, bottle of bubbles, 1 pizza pan.

What you do: Pour the bubbles into the pizza pan. Bend the coat hanger out into a circle and use the "hook" as a handle. Dip your monster bubble wand into the bubbles and watch the biggest bubbles in the world appear.

BUBBLE RECIPE: If you wish to make your own bubbles, here is a good recipe: 1 gallon cold water, 1 cup liquid detergent. (Allow this to sit overnight in a cool place.) Add 2 tablespoons liquid glycerin. (Glycerin is available at the pharmacy.)

ADDITIONAL WAND IDEAS: Use the plastic rings from a six-pack of soda pop, rings from canning jars, and plastic rings cut from various sized plastic lids (margarine lids, coffee lids). Let the children experiment with blowing bubbles from different sized rings.

SQUIRT GUN FUN

You will need: Squirt guns, drawing paper, markers or crayons, clothespins.

What you do: Draw a large circle with two or three smaller circles inside the larger one to form a target. Color the target. Using a clothespin, secure the target to a fence or clothesline. Have the children take turns standing behind a line and try to hit the bull's eye with water from the squirt gun. (Note: Stress the importance that even squirt guns should never be pointed at people.)

OUTSIDE OBSTACLE COURSE

Create your obstacle course by using everyday objects such as tables, chairs, trees, swing sets, hula hoops, etc. Have the children go around, over, under, through, etc. Have the children try the course backwards once they have mastered completing it going forwards.

SUMMER OUTSIDE GAMES

HOT POTATO

With one child in the center of a circle of players, a large ball is passed around. When the player in the center calls out "Hot Potato," the player with the ball in his hands will leave the circle. If a ball is dropped or a bad pass is made, the player responsible is then moved to the center. The game should be played long enough so each child has the opportunity to be in the center.

CIRCLE TAG

You will need a circle four to five feet in diameter. This can be on asphalt or cement. The child who is "it" guards the circle against the outside players who try to enter with both feet without being tagged. The first child caught in the circle by being tagged is "it."

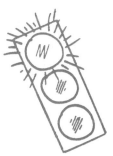

RED LIGHT

The player who is "it" stands at a goal line. The other players stand at a starting line. Facing the goal line with his back to the other players, the person who is "it" begins counting up to ten. At any point he may stop and call out "Red Light!" When he calls out, the person who is "it" turns around and anyone he catches moving must return to the starting line. The first person to cross the goal line is the winner. This can be varied by having the children jump, hop, etc.

PAPER RELAY

The first child in line has two newspapers, one which he stands on at the start. The other newspaper is placed in front of him as a stepping stone. He steps on the one in front of him, turns and picks up the paper behind him, turns and continues the same process throughout the course. Each succeeding student on the team goes through the same procedure.

ZOO PARADE

This game is played in the same manner as charades. A player pretends he is some animal and walks or hops like it. Other students must guess the name of the animal or imitate it.

SUMMER OUTSIDE GAMES

CHICKEN HOP

Facing a partner, each child crosses his arms on his chest and stands on one foot. They then hop toward each other, attempting to bump the other person off his feet. They must bump with their shoulders and keep their arms folded and hop on one foot. *(Remember to stress the word "gentle" with the children.)*

POTATO RACE

Use relay teams. Have the children walk holding a spoon with a potato in it. If the potato falls out, the child must pick it up and continue the race. *(If you are very brave, and have sprinklers ready to clean up the kids, you can also play this game using eggs!)*

ANIMAL CRACKERS

This is a fun game for increasing imaginations. Have the children pretend they are in the jungle. They stalk over the sidewalk. They cannot step on any cracks, because the cracks are traps set by the hunters. You can also use kitchen tiles or patterns on the schoolroom floor. Children are eliminated when they forget and are trapped by the cracks.

CALL BALL

The players stand in a circle with one child in the center. The child in the center tosses the ball high above the head while he calls the name of a child in the circle. The child whose name has been called tries to catch the ball before it hits the ground, or else it can be allowed to bounce once or twice before being caught. The child who catches the ball then becomes the next child to be in the center and throw the ball up in the air and call another child's name.

TEACHER BALL

Use six or eight players. One child is the "teacher" and the players line up about six feet from the "teacher" in a straight line. *(For younger children you will want to shorten the distance to under six feet.)* The "teacher" throws the ball underhanded to each child in turn. If a player misses, he goes to the end of the line and the child at the head becomes the "teacher."

SUMMER LANGUAGE ACTIVITIES

HOW DO FROGS GROW?

Talk to the children about the stages of development in the life of a frog. Find photographs of these stages to show the children. Make up a sequencing game for the children to play. The pattern for this game can be found on page 308. Copy, color, laminate, and cut apart the polliwog-to-frog sequence illustrations. Back them with felt, sandpaper, or self-stick velcro for the flannel board. You can also use self-stick magnetic tape for a magnetic board.

This page may also be reproduced for each child in the class. The children can color their own pictures, cut them apart, and take them home to share with their parents.

SCAVENGER HUNT

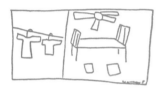

You will need: Paper, felt-tipped pens, and treasures such as gum, stickers, etc.

What you do: This game can be played outdoors. Draw six distinctive objects in your home or school. These pictures will be used as clues. On the first object, tape a picture of the first clue and so on until you have all six clues. Plant a special treasure at the last clue.

JUST ME AND MY DAD by Mercer Mayer

Read the story, *Just Me and My Dad,* by Mercer Mayer. Discuss what the children enjoy doing with their own dads. Make a display with the children. On a large sheet of paper write the words, "Dads Can Do Anything." Ask the children what their father's do at work and at home.

List the children's responses on the paper trying to get as much variety as possible. Invite the children to illustrate the activities. Hang the paper on the wall and place the children's pictures around it.

PICTIONARY GAME

You will need: Drawing paper, crayons, index cards and markers.

What you do: Draw 20 to 30 simple pictures on index cards. (Circles, trees, house, cat, letters, boat, ladder, chair, bow, sun, rainbow, table, fork, hat, bear, etc.) Each child picks a card. One child at a time then draws that picture by him/herself on a sheet of paper in front of the group of children. The child who guesses what the picture is will be the next child to draw.

Be sure that all the children have a turn at being the "artist."

DEVELOPMENT OF A FROG SEQUENCING GAME

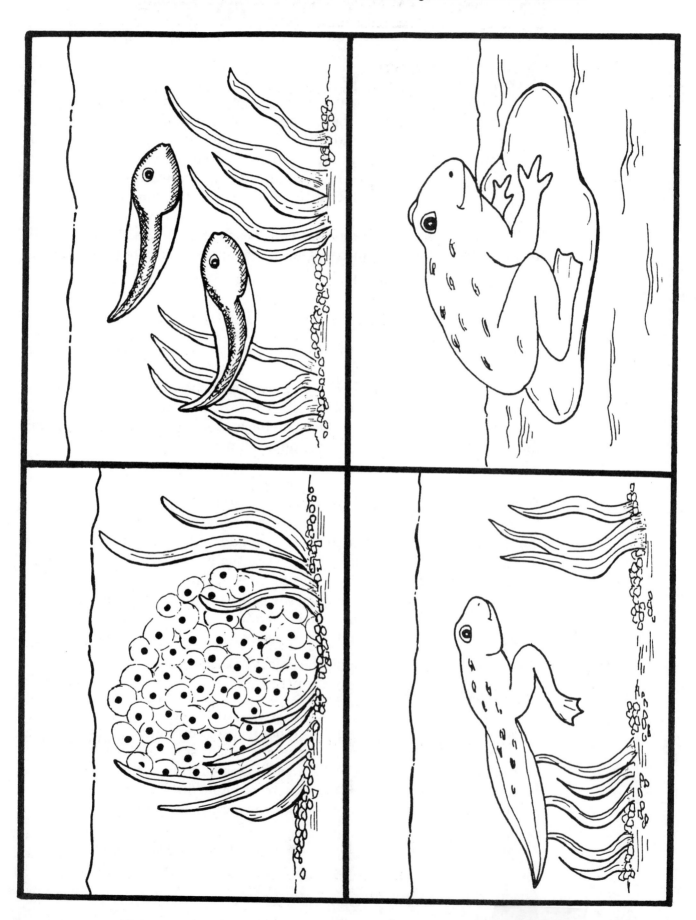

SUMMER LANGUAGE ACTIVITIES

MEASURING SAND

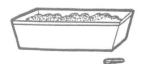

Put a large pan of sand on your math table during the summer months. (If possible, acquire a sand table to keep in your classroom.) Have a number of spoons and measuring cups available for the children to experiment with.

Help the children chart various experiments: How many spoonfuls of sand do you need to full 1 cup? How many cups of sand are needed to fill a jar?

LISTENING SKILLS PLAYHOUSE

A listening skills playhouse is a terrific addition to any classroom and it is well worth your time to construct one.

Locate a large appliance box. Often large appliance stores will be happy to accommodate you. Cut a door and two windows out of the box. Decorate the cardboard box so it looks like a playhouse. Pillows are placed inside the box.

Explain to the children that this is a quiet playhouse. It is a place where children can talk to each other, read stories and play quiet games. The children will delight in having this special house in their classroom.

GAME: Have one or two children go in the house. The teacher whispers things to the child through the windows. The child then opens the windows and whispers things back to you.

SINK OR FLOAT

Have a sink or float center set up in your classroom this summer. You will need a basin of water and a box full of things such as paper clips, bottle caps, corks, pieces of fabric, styrofoam, wood, etc. Whatever else you can find.

The children determine whether the object will sink or float and then test their decision by placing the object in the water.

Have two empty plastic boxes sitting on this table. Label one box "SINK" and the other box "FLOAT." You might wish to label these boxes with pictures of the words meaning rather than the just word. After the children experiment with an object, they can then place it in the appropriate box.

GREAT BOOKS FOR SUMMER

• *Camping Adventure* by William R. Gray • *The Berenstain Bears Go To Camp* by Stan & Jan Berenstain • *Camping Out* by Betsy & Guilio Maestro • *Beast Goes Camping* by Sheila Sanders • *The Berenstain Bears Shoot the Rapids* by Stan & Jan Berenstain • *Gordon Goes Camping* by Julie Brinckloe • *A Day In The Woods* by Ronald M. Fisher.

PEOPLE AND SPACE

STARS

Discussion:
- The sun is a star.
- There are many other stars, some larger, some smaller than the sun.
- They all look like the sun, but since they are farther away they look smaller and not so bright to us.
- Most stars are round like the sun, but they are so far away they look as though they have points.

Why Do Stars Twinkle?

Simple demonstration of the flickering of a burning candle in a darkened room will readily show why stars appear to twinkle.

ROCKETS

1. Blow up a long balloon, release, and watch it travel. This shows how rocket push into space.
2. Other examples may be found among children's own toys; for example, space guns, rocket ships, jet planes, etc.

PEOPLE AND SPACE

A Growing Display

Materials: A large simplified drawing of a globe Designate atmosphere surrounding the earth, and outer space.

Procedure:
1. Children draw, cut out and place objects in proper areas:

Land: People, plants, buildings, launching pads.
Water: Boats, fish, ships, etc.
Air: Birds, planes, clouds, insects, kites, seeds, rain.
Space: Sun, stars, moon, rockets, space ships.

Follow-up Suggestions:

1. If interest is keen enough, other planets such as Mars, Venus, Jupiter, Saturn, Mercury, etc., might be added.
2. Pursue study of rocket ships, space ships, space shuttles, space suits, and space travel.
3. Set up a current events area. Urge children to bring in newspaper and magazine cutouts showing events in space exploration.

OUTER SPACE

Help each rocket find it's planet.
Draw a line between each rocket and planet.
Stay on the course so the rockets don't crash!

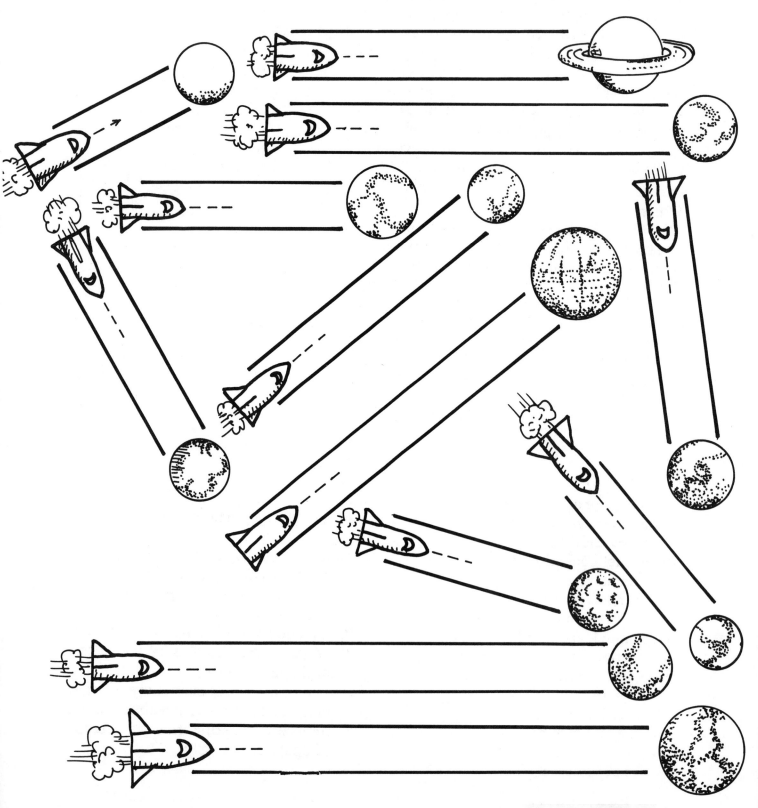

SUMMER FINGER PLAYS/POETRY

TEN LITTLE TUGBOATS

Ten little tugboats are out on the sea,
And that is where little tugboats should be.
Ten little tugboats got along fine,
Till one drifted far away, and then there were _____.
Nine little tugboats said, We can't wait!"
One went out too far, and now there were _____.
Eight little tugboats were lined up quiet even.
One couldn't keep the pace, and then there were _____.
Seven little tugboats, before you can say "ticks,"
One got lost in the fog and then there were _____.
Six little tugboats had a lot of drive.
But one tooted out to sea, and then there were _____.
Five little tugboats said, "Let's move to shore,"
But one backed up from the rest, and then there were _____.
Four little tugboats were sailing evenly.
One hit a large barge, and then there were _____.
Three Little tugboats said, "We'll carry through."
But one lost it's engine, and then there were _____.
Two Little tugboats said, "We'll make the run."
But one lost its smokestack, and then there was _____.
One little tugboat pulled up to shore.
That tugboat was successful, and now there are no more.
(Ask: "What is a tugboat supposed to do? What does it mean to be successful? The children supply the remaining number each time.)

WHAT CAN I DO

I can spin like a top.
Look at me! Look at me!
I have feet and I can hop.
Look at me! Look at me!
I have hands and I can clap.
Look at me! Look at me!
I can lay them in my lap.
Look at me! Look at me!
(The children act out this rhyme.
Ask: "What else can your feet do?
Encourage individuals to make up
their own rhymes about their
accomplishments with hands and feet.
Write down their words and make
a booklet of them.)

TEN WHITE SEAGULLS

Ten white seagulls
Just see them fly.
Over the mountain,
And up to the sky.
Ten white seagulls
Crying aloud.
Spread out their wings,
And fly over a cloud.
Ten white seagulls
On a bright day.
Pretty white seagulls
Fly, fly away!

JUMPING JACKS

I am a little jumping jack.
I jump right out of my box
   and then I jump right back.
I jump up high, I bend down low,
For that is the way that I must go.
I jump to the left,
   I jump to the right,
I jump in my box and
   I hide out of sight.
I jump up and down and
   I turn all around,
And I jump right out and
   land on the ground.
(Secure a large empty box that will
hold a child comfortably. The children
say the rhyme with you and take turns
at being the jumping jack.)

SUMMER FINGER PLAYS/POETRY

A SEASHELL

One day, a little shell washed up   *(hold shell)*
Out of the waves at sea.
I held the shell up to my ear,   *(hold shell to ear)*
And I heard it sing to me.
Sh - - - Sh - - - Sh - - - Sh!   *(children repeat)*
A little shell washed up one day,
And lay upon the sand.   *(hold shell in one hand)*
As I held it in my hand.
Sh - - - Sh - - - Sh - - - Sh!   *(children repeat)*
(This is excellent practice for the "Sh" speech sound. Bring in a conch shell and let the children one at a time hold it to their ear and hear the sound of the sea.)

HERE IS A STARFISH

Here is a starfish;   *(place one hand on table, fingers spread wide apart)*
Here is a shell.   *(show palm, hand slightly cupped)*
Here is an octopus;   *(place two palms together, fingers extended)*
Here is a bell.   *(lock fingers with one another; point down)*
Here is a fishnet;   *(interlock fingers)*
Here is a fish.   *(make swimming motions)*
Here is a birdbath;   *(two hands cupped)*
And here is a dish.   *(one hand cupped)*

DIVE LITTLE GOLDFISH

Dive, little goldfish one.
   (hold up one finger)
Dive, little goldfish two.
   (hold up two fingers)
Dive, little goldfish three.
   (hold up three fingers)
Dive, little goldfish four.
   (hold up four fingers)
Dive, little goldfish five.
   (hold up five fingers)
Dive, little goldfish six.
   (hold up six fingers)
I like your funny tricks!

LICKS

Here is a round, sweet lollipop.
I bought it today at a candy shop.
One lick, mmm, it tastes so good.
Two licks, oh, I knew it would.
Three licks, yes, I like the taste.
Four licks, now I will not waste.
Five licks keep on and on.
Six licks, Oh! It's nearly gone.
Seven licks, it's getting small.
Eight licks, and still not all.
Nine licks, my tongue goes fast.
Ten licks, and that's the last!
(The children can make construction paper lollipops. Attach to a popsicle stick or tongue depressor. Choose children to act out the rhyme. Warn them not to really lick the paper, but just pretend.)

ROARING ROCKET PUZZLE

Cut out all the pieces and arrange them on a sheet of paper.

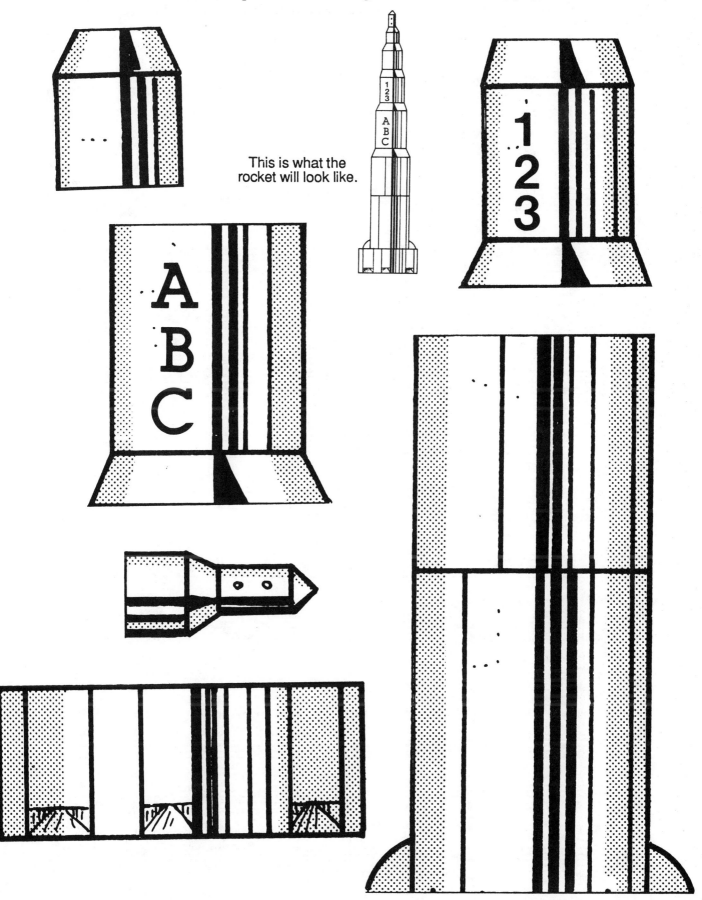

This is what the rocket will look like.

WE'LL LAND ON THE MOON

SUMMER MUSIC ACTIVITIES

FATHER'S DAY SONG
(Melody: You Are My Sunshine)

I love you daddy
My dearest daddy
You make me happy
When I am sad
I want to tell you
I really love you!
When I'm with you
I am so glad.

FOURTH OF JULY
(Melody: When the Saints Go Marching In)

Oh we will march
And sing this song
Oh, we will march
And sing this song
Everyone, please come along
As we march and sing this song.

Oh, we will clap
And sing this song
Oh, we will clap
And sing this song
Everyone, please come along
As we clap and sing this song.

We;re glad to be
Where we are free
Oh, we are glad
That we are free
Everyone come march with me
'Cause we're glad that we are free.

We're proud to be
In this country
Oh, we're so proud
Of this country
Everyone come march with me
'Cause we're proud of our country.

From the book, Sing-A-Song All Year Long,
by Connie Walters
Copyright by T.S. Denison & Co., Inc.

IN THE SEA
(Melody: Have You Ever Seen A Lassie?)

Have you ever seen a sea horse?
A sea horse, a sea horse
Have you ever seen a sea horse?
It lives in the sea.

It swims in the ocean
It plays on the reef.
Have you ever seen a sea horse?
It lives in the sea.

Have you ever seen a squid?
A squid, a squid
Have you ever seen a squid?
It lives in the sea.

It swims in the ocean
It plays on the reef.
Have you ever seen a squid?
It lives in the sea.

Have you ever seen a shark?
A shark, a shark
Have you ever seen a shark?
It lives in the sea.

It swims in the ocean
It plays on the reef.
Have you ever seen a shark?
It lives in the sea.

Have you ever seen an eel?
An eel, an eel
Have you ever seen an eel?
It lives in the sea.

It swims in the ocean
It plays on the reef.
Have you ever seen an eel?
It lives in the sea.

(Use on the flannel board. Patterns found on pages 296-300. Continue song with other sea creatures.)

SUMMER MUSIC ACTIVITIES

MARCHING BAND
(Listening)

Materials Needed

Homemade band instruments are easy and inexpensive to make. The following materials may be collected from home:

1. Two small blocks that are hit together.

2. Cymbals may consist of two lids from aluminum fry-pans with knob handles.

3. Tom-tom drums can be made from large, empty coffee cans with both ends cut out and plastic lids attached to each end.

4. Tambourines can be made from empty pie tins. Five holes are punched around the edge and using string, ribbon, or twist ties; jingle bells are secured to each hole.

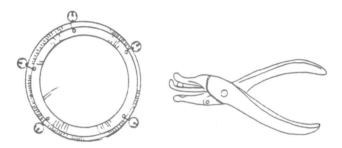

5. Rattles can be made from empty tennis ball cans with plastic lids in place. Jelly beans or M & M's are placed inside. (Food, rather than nonedible "rattlers," is safer in the event that the top falls off.)

6. Sandpaper blocks are made by gluing sandpaper to two small blocks. A scratching rhythm can be created when they are rubbed together.

Procedure

Each child is given an instrument and, accompaniment by a record or cassette, the "band" marches around the room.